TEACHING
High School Science
Through Inquiry

DOUGLAS LLEWELLYN

TEACHING
High School Science
Through Inquiry

A CASE STUDY APPROACH

A JOINT PUBLICATION

CORWIN PRESS
A Sage Publications Company
Thousand Oaks, California

NATIONAL SCIENCE TEACHERS ASSOCIATION

For information:

 Corwin Press
A Sage Publications Company
2455 Teller Road
Thousand Oaks, California 91320
E-mail: order@corwinpress.com

Sage Publications Ltd.
1 Oliver's Yard
55 City Road
London EC1Y 1SP
United Kingdom

Sage Publications India Pvt. Ltd.
B-42, Panchsheel Enclave
Post Box 4109
New Delhi 110-017 India

Printed in the United States of America

Library of Congress Cataloging-in-Publication Data

Llewellyn, Douglas.
Teaching high school science through inquiry / Douglas Llewellyn.
    p. cm.
Includes bibliographical references and index.
ISBN 978-0-7619-3937-5 (cloth) — ISBN 978-0-7619-3938-2 (pbk.)
   1. Science—Study and teaching (Secondary) 2. Inquiry (Theory of knowledge) I. Title.
Q181.L75 2005
507'.1'2—dc22

                                       2004011124

This book is printed on acid-free paper.

     09   10   9   8   7   6

Acquisitions Editor:	Kylee Liegl
Editorial Assistant:	Jaime Cuvier
Production Editor:	Tracy Alpern
Copy Editor:	A. J. Sobczak
Proofreader:	Andrea Martin
Typesetter:	C&M Digitals (P) Ltd.
Indexer:	Naomi Linzer
Cover Designer:	Tracy E. Miller
Graphic Designer:	Anthony Paular

Contents

Preface   ix
    A Call for Instructional Reform   ix
    Who Should Read This Book?   x
    Contents   xii
    Acknowledgments   xiv

About the Author   xvii

1. **Constructing an Understanding of Scientific Inquiry**   1
    A Culture of Inquiry   1
    What Science Educators Say About Inquiry   3
    What the *National Science Education Standards* Say About Inquiry   4
    What the American Association for the
        Advancement of Science Says About Inquiry   6
    Ten Questions About Inquiry-Based Learning   7
    Looking Beyond   10

2. **Learning About Inquiry Through Case Studies**   13
    Scientific Inquiry: A Case Study Approach   13
    A Case Study: Inquiring About Isopods   14
    Resources for Isopods   20
    Questions for Reflection   20
    The Inquiry Cycle   21
    Brainstorming   22
    A Definition of Inquiry   24

3. **Developing a Philosophy for Inquiry**   27
    What Is Constructivism?   28
    Traditional Versus Constructivist Classrooms   28
    Historical Perspectives of Constructivism   32
    Constructivism Today   38
    Metacognition   39
    How Adolescents Learn   40
    The 5E Learning Cycle   46
    Challenges to Creating a Constructivist Classroom Culture   51

4. **Comparing Traditional and Inquiry-Based Science Classrooms**   55
    A Traditional Classroom   55
    The Environment of an Inquiry-Based Classroom   56
    Students in an Inquiry-Based Classroom   57

Teachers in an Inquiry-Based Classroom 60
Becoming an Inquiry-Based Teacher 63

5. **Integrating Inquiry-Based Activities** **65**
Promoting Student Inquiries 65
Invitation to Inquiry 66
Demonstrations 67
Laboratory Experiences and Activities 68
Teacher-Initiated Inquiries 70
Student-Initiated Inquiries 70
Guiding Students Into Inquiry 72
Extended Inquiries: A Case Study in Bottle Ecosystem 76
An Interview With Jay Costanza 82
Questions for Reflection 87

6. **Modifying a Lab Activity Into an Inquiry Investigation** **89**
The Role of the Laboratory in Science 89
New Approaches to Traditional Labs 91
The Hydrate Lab 96

7. **Managing the Inquiry-Based Classroom** **99**
Challenges to Inquiry-Based Teaching 99
Making Time for Inquiry 100
Just Tell Me the Answer 104
Questioning Techniques 105

8. **Assessing Inquiry** **111**
The Concern About Assessment 111
Curriculum Alignment 112
Designing Assessments 113
Authentic Assessments 115

9. **Teaching Biology Through Inquiry** **129**
Investigating Yeast 129
An Interview With Dr. Dina Markowitz and Jana Penders 140
Questions for Reflection 144

10. **Teaching Earth Science Through Inquiry** **145**
Toilet Paper Timeline 145
An Interview With Dr. Tom O'Brien 151
Questions for Reflection 153

11. **Teaching Chemistry Through Inquiry** **155**
The Peanut Lab 155
An Interview With Teresa Gerchman 162
Questions for Reflection 165

12. **Teaching Physics Through Inquiry** **167**
Measuring Centripetal Force 167
An Interview With George Wolfe 174
Questions for Reflection 177

13. **Reflecting on a Teaching Career**   **179**
       The Story of Mr. Baker   180

Resource A: Inquiry Resources for High School Science Teachers   **185**
       Print Resources on Inquiry   185
       Print Resources on Inquiry Investigations   187
       Print Resources on Constructivism   188
       Print Resources on Science Standards and Science Literacy   190
       Print Resources on Demonstrations and Discrepant Events   191
       Print Resources on Assessment   192
       Print Resources on General Science Areas   193
       Multimedia Resources on Inquiry   194
       Online Resources on Inquiry   195
       Professional Organizations   197

References   **199**

Index   **205**

**CORWIN
PRESS**

The Corwin Press logo—a raven striding across an open book—represents the union of courage and learning. Corwin Press is committed to improving education for all learners by publishing books and other professional development resources for those serving the field of K–12 education. By providing practical, hands-on materials, Corwin Press continues to carry out the promise of its motto: **"Helping Educators Do Their Work Better."**

NATIONAL SCIENCE TEACHERS ASSOCIATION

The National Science Teachers Association is the largest professional organization in the world promoting excellence and innovation in science teaching and learning for all. NSTA's membership includes more than 55,000 science teachers, science supervisors, administrators, scientists, business and industry representatives, and others involved in science education.

Preface

A CALL FOR INSTRUCTIONAL REFORM

It has been more than two decades since the National Commission on Excellence in Education, a blue ribbon commission appointed by President Ronald Reagan, released *A Nation at Risk* (1983). Referring to the "rising tide of mediocrity" in American education, this disturbing report cited the state of education in the United States and called on the nation to raise its expectations for all students by developing rigorous and measurable content and performance standards and by better preparing and rewarding teachers. In *A Nation at Risk,* the commission recommended that all high school students complete 3 years of science in addition to 4 years of English, 3 years of mathematics, 3 years of social studies, and a half year of computer science.

In 1995 and again in 1999, the Third International Mathematics and Science Study (TIMSS) confirmed that our students, especially middle and high school students, were still not meeting levels of global competitiveness. Eighth-grade students were scoring near the median in science when compared to their international counterparts; however, high school students were scoring near the bottom. It has also been a decade since two nationally prominent scientific organizations, the American Association for the Advancement of Science (AAAS) (1993) and the National Research Council (NRC) (1996), have identified the benchmarks and framework for this nation to develop a scientifically literate society and compete in a global economic society. In their respective publications, *Benchmarks for Science Literacy* and the *National Science Education Standards*, each organization identified content and performance standards outlining specifically what students need to know and be able to do at grade levels K–12. The National Research Council took a further step in advocating how to meet the standards through professional and program development. In the *National Science Education Standards (NSES)* (NRC, 1996), recommendations are made to position elementary and secondary school students to be internationally competitive with their counterparts in other highly developed, industrial countries.

One common recommendation from both organizations is the infusion of inquiry-based instruction as an enduring understanding, as well as pedagogy, for teaching science. Moreover, inquiry has been identified as the preferred method of instruction within the teaching and professional development sections from the *NSES.* Therefore, the national standards suggest that elementary and secondary school science teachers develop an inquiry-based science program for their students and culture communities of learners who reflect the intellectual rigor of attitudes and social values conducive to science inquiry. In addition, the professional development of science teachers requires learning science content through the perspectives and methods of inquiry (NRC, 1996).

In January 1998, the National Science Teachers Association (NSTA) adopted its position statement, *The National Science Education Standards: A Vision for the Improvement of Science Teaching and Learning.* In that statement, the NSTA strongly supports the *NSES* by asserting the following: "Teachers, regardless of grade level, should promote inquiry-based instruction and provide classroom environments and experiences that facilitate students' learning in science . . . professional development activities should involve teachers in the learning of science and pedagogy through inquiry . . . [and] inquiry should be viewed as an instructional outcome (knowing and doing) for students to achieve in addition to its use as a pedagogical approach" (pp. 32–33).

Adding to the charge for instructional reform in science and mathematics came the report in 2000 from the National Commission on Mathematics and Science Teaching for the 21st Century, *Before It's Too Late* (NCMST, 2000). Former astronaut and Ohio senator John Glenn headed the commission, calling for an educated citizenry; the commission cited the process of inquiry as the kind of science instruction that can justifiably be called "high-quality teaching."

Last, on January 8, 2002, President George Bush signed into law the No Child Left Behind Act. This landmark piece of legislation was designed to ensure that no child in America is left behind, through educational reforms based on accountability and additional funding for states and school districts from the federal level.

Given the 20 years of blue ribbon commissions and committees, the overwhelming emphasis for science education suggests that high school science teachers should follow a standards-based curriculum and develop teaching competencies and strategies that provide engaging, inquiry-based investigations for students. This book focuses on raising a teacher's capacity to teach science through an inquiry-based process, as stated by the national standards and science education experts.

Unfortunately, the quantity of books and resources for preservice and practicing high school science teachers does not match the need. There appears to be an abundant supply of inquiry-based resources for elementary and middle school teachers, but far too few for high school teachers. *Teaching High School Science Through Inquiry: A Case Study Approach* was written to fill that gap. *Teaching High School Science Through Inquiry* is a companion book to *Inquire Within: Implementing Inquiry-Based Science Standards* (Llewellyn, 2002). Whereas *Inquire Within* focuses primarily on elementary and middle school grades, *Teaching High School Science Through Inquiry* specifically addresses the needs of science teachers in grades 9–12. Both resources are similar in format. Because of the commonalities of inquiry-based learning at the elementary and secondary school levels, some similar or repeated wording and diagrams can be found in both books. In the end, both books were written to raise the instructional capacity of all science teachers interested in becoming exemplary teachers of science and taking incremental steps toward meeting national standards.

WHO SHOULD READ THIS BOOK?

As a high school science teacher, you might feel you are already a good hands-on teacher, but you want to take the next step in becoming an inquiry-based teacher. You may have read about inquiry in your undergraduate-level courses in preparation for becoming a secondary-level science teacher, or you may have read or studied about scientific inquiry at the graduate school level. Maybe you have read articles about inquiry in *The Science Teacher* or *The American Biology Teacher* and wondered, "Am I an inquiry teacher?"

This book is predicated on the question, "How can we expect our students to engage in inquiry-based activities if we, as teachers, do not have a sufficient understanding of inquiry ourselves?" *Teaching High School Science Through Inquiry* will enable you to articulate, in detail, your understandings, attitudes, and dispositions in becoming an inquiry teacher. It will also enable you to describe, practically, why this mode of teaching fits your own "chemistry" as a high school science teacher.

If you are a teacher undergoing the process of National Board Certification (NBC), this book will also provide useful examples and background information as you complete the application process and prepare for your portfolio submission for Entry #2–*Active Scientific Inquiry*. Because the science certification for Adolescents and Young Adulthood includes requirements to demonstrate active student engagement and participation, teachers seeking NBC will need to be versed in scientific inquiry. For more information about the National Board for Professional Teaching Standards and the National Board Certification, see www.NBPTS.org.

As a science supervisor, teacher/leader, curriculum specialist, or principal interested in improving science literacy in your high school, you will be provided with suggestions to help facilitate professional development on inquiry-based instruction and the mechanisms to engage faculty in meaningful dialogue about scientific inquiry and effective teaching toward improving student achievement. Science department heads or teacher/mentors may be interested in forming a professional development/collegial study group to design and share lessons on inquiry. In this case, the case studies and reflection questions provide a means to initiate a discussion on inquiry-based strategies. Furthermore, the group facilitator should research the Japanese Lesson Study as a vehicle for improving classroom teaching. For more information, see *The Teaching Gap* (1999) by James Stigler and James Hiebert. A listserv through Columbia University's Teachers College is also available for interested participants. The Lesson Study Listserv connects subscribed members to individuals across the country who are interested or engaged in lesson study. To subscribe to the Lesson Study Research Group, send a subscription request to lsrg@columbia.edu.

If you are a college or university professor concerned about providing preservice and graduate-level students with appropriate instruction in the methodology of inquiry, this book, together with *Science Teaching Reconsidered* (NRC, 1997) and *Educating Teachers of Science, Mathematics, and Technology: New Practices for a New Millennium* (NRC, 2001), will provide an introduction to scientific inquiry and instructional reform, as well as suggestions for creating a student-centered classroom.

Competency in inquiry-based instruction is not developed solely by providing inquiry lessons to high school students or by giving them opportunities to do inquiry-based labs. The process is more than that. Inquiry is a personal and professional journey that starts with developing a constructivist-based philosophy and reflecting, both individually and with others, on your instructional beliefs and practices. In *The Courage to Teach*, Parker Palmer (1998) says that "good teaching cannot be reduced to technique; good teaching comes from the identity and integrity of the teacher" (p. 10).

You may begin your journey by accepting an invitation to inquire within the pages of this book. At the completion of this journey, you should expect to gain enough confidence in inquiry-based instruction to invite your own students to begin their own journeys.

CONTENTS

Chapter 1, "Constructing an Understanding of Scientific Inquiry," explores the meaning of inquiry. You will read several statements from the *National Science Education Standards* and the *Benchmarks for Science Literacy* to construct your understanding of inquiry. Later in the chapter, several frequently asked questions about inquiry-based learning are answered to further your understanding of what inquiry is and what it is not.

Chapter 2, "Learning About Inquiry Through Case Studies," follows a class of biology students through a unit of study about isopods characterized by student-generated questions.

Chapter 3, "Developing a Philosophy for Inquiry," lays the philosophical foundation for constructivist learning strategies and shows how constructivism complements inquiry-based learning. Although constructivism has gained much support among science educators in the last 10 years, it is not a new idea. Its theoretical foundations began with the work of cognitive psychologists such as John Dewey, Jean Piaget, and Lev Vygotsky. In Chapter 3, we will also examine the way students learn science through a constructivist approach. Chapter 3 also introduces the 5E Learning Cycle and offers ways teachers can design lessons based on a five-step constructivist model.

In Chapter 4, "Comparing Traditional and Inquiry-Based Science Classrooms," traditional and inquiry-based classrooms are compared and contrasted. By looking at the similarities and differences in students, teachers, and classroom environments, you will further your understanding of the complexions and distinctions of an inquiry-based classroom.

In Chapter 5, "Integrating Inquiry-Based Activities," inquiry investigations are compared to other hands-on science activities through a grid that divides instructional strategies into four areas: demonstrations, activities/labs, teacher-initiated inquiries, and student-initiated inquiries. The grid defines the distinct levels of inquiry-based investigations and assists teachers in selecting and sequencing the learning opportunities for students.

Chapter 6, "Modifying a Lab Activity Into an Inquiry Investigation," provides ways teachers can modify their present traditional labs to make them more inquiry-based. Becoming an inquiry-based teacher does not mean you have to revamp your entire lab collection. Often, making incremental changes and "tweaking" sections are enough to provide more ownership and decision making on the part of your students.

Chapter 7, "Managing the Inquiry-Based Classroom," discusses real challenges and situations faced by nearly every teacher seeking more time within the school year to do inquiry. This chapter also suggests the importance of good classroom management and suggests strategies teachers can use when making instructional time to do inquiry.

Chapter 8, "Assessing Inquiry," addresses how to assess inquiry through authentic assessments, portfolios, rubrics, and self-evaluations.

Chapters 9–12 provide case studies from biology, earth science, chemistry, and physics. In each case study, the reader sees how three high school science teachers and one university professor implement inquiry-based investigations in their own classrooms. Chapters 9–12 include interviews with the teachers in the inquiry lesson as they share their insights and describe their experiences, their challenges, and the rewards of teaching through inquiry. Questions for reflection are provided at the end of each case study to guide the reader or discussion group through an analysis of the case.

Last, Chapter 13, "Reflecting on a Teaching Career," takes a different turn from the "how to" aspects of inquiry, moving to a personal reflection of one high school teacher as he looks back on his 30-year career as an inquiry-based teacher.

As you work your way through this book, keep in mind a word of caution: Don't expect to become an inquiry-based teacher in just 1 year. Refining your skills and strategies takes time. I often say, "You need a crock pot to cook inquiry, not a microwave!" In most cases, teachers may need 3–5 years to perfect their inquiry teaching techniques. There are no shortcuts. Be patient, and with persistence and peer coaching, you will find yourself becoming more comfortable using inquiry teaching strategies and appropriate questioning techniques to bring about instructional changes in your classroom.

As I talk with teachers new to inquiry and those who have been teaching through inquiry for many years, there appears to be a learning curve for their experience. It starts in September with a tremendous excitement for inquiry and the teacher's enthusiasm communicated to the students, raising their level of interest. During this initial phase, inquiry is a novel learning strategy and students seem to thrive on the method of learning. By November or December, some teachers say the "honeymoon" has ended as they begin to experience resistance from students, who all of a sudden discover that the focus and responsibility of learning is on *them*, not the teacher. During this phase, students often ask, "Why don't you just tell us the answer? You're the teacher. You're supposed to give us the answer." After hearing student resistance day after day, the natural temptation for teachers may be to give in and return to the traditional way of teaching. This is a critical time for new inquiry teachers because students may challenge your beliefs about teaching and learning. For those teachers who "stick with it" and tell their students that one way they can be truly be effective teachers is by placing the onus of learning, metacognitively, on the students, the ownership of inquiry soon re-escalates as students come to realize what *real* learning entails. The learning curve for inquiry can be illustrated as in the following figure:

Level of
student
acceptance
of inquiry

Time

According to the *National Science Education Standards*, "Teachers can be effective guides for students learning science only if they have the opportunity to examine their beliefs, as well as to develop an understanding of the tenets on which the Standards are based" (NRC, 1996, p. 28). This book was written and designed to serve that purpose.

ACKNOWLEDGMENTS

In 1999, I took my first (and only) sabbatical from teaching and decided to write about inquiry-based learning. During the writing of the manuscript, I reflected on 25 years of teaching and school administration to capture what I thought scientific inquiry meant. At first, it was a very personal and inward journey into what I believed exemplary science teaching was all about. Later, it became a desire to write and communicate more effectively. Soon the writing process became a balance of *meaning* and *mechanics*, constructing an understanding of inquiry and learning how to share that understanding with an audience. The writing process seemed to reflect the evolution of how students learn through inquiry—first floundering about and then later becoming more artistic and precise with expressing both the attitudinal and the technical aspects of inquiry. In the end, I became a better student of scientific inquiry *and* a better writer.

After the publication of *Inquire Within*, I had the opportunity to present numerous professional development sessions across the country on inquiry-based learning. I met many other talented and dedicated teachers who shared my passion about scientific inquiry. The conversations before and after those sessions, along with many long-distance discussions via e-mail, led me to continue the "written conversation" specifically for high school science teachers. The challenge in *Teaching High School Science Through Inquiry* was to elaborate on the initial concepts and strategies presented in *Inquire Within*, yet provide extended vignettes, in the form of case studies, that would mirror typical classrooms of inquiry. For the case studies, I had to look no further than those earlier conversations and e-mails to share the "story" of teachers who channel their energy into engaging students through inquiry.

I sincerely appreciate the contributions and support from many dedicated and gifted science educators and friends in writing this book. Some were sources of inspiration, others were colleagues also interested in inquiry, a few were participants in an inquiry support group, some were editors and writers who helped me become a better writer, and a few were those from whom I stole ideas. Heartfelt "thanks" go out to LeAnn Avery, Ronald Bailey, Jay Costanza, Teresa Gerchman, Dr. Dina Markowitz, Joann Morreale, Thomas Mueller, Joanne Niemi, Dr. Thomas O'Brien, Michael Occhino, Lynn Panton, Jana Penders, Larry Robinson, Dr. Lorri Sheck, Debbie Stack, and George Wolfe.

An additional thank you goes to the people at Cornell University for allowing me to reference the isopod lab from Cornell Institute for Biology Teachers (CIBT) and to Dr. Norman Budnitz at the Center for Inquiry-Based Learning for allowing me to quote from his Web site. Dr. Budnitz reminded me that inquiry cannot be defined in a one-sentence, simple statement. He prefers that we think that inquiry is more complex than that. Thanks as well to the Biological Sciences Curriculum Study (BSCS) in Colorado Springs, Colorado, for allowing me to use its 5E Learning Cycle description from *Biology: A Human Approach* (1997).

I also received support and guidance from the Corwin Press staff, including Robb Clouse, Jaime Cuvier, Kylee Liegl, and Rachel Livsey, and from copy editor A. J. Sobczak.

A special thank you goes out to my wife, Ann; my daughter, Janice; and my son-in-law, Dr. Robert Fortuna. I sincerely appreciate their long-standing encouragement and support.

—Douglas Llewellyn
Rochester, New York

The contributions of the following reviewers are also gratefully acknowledged:

Liza Basden
Science Teacher
Highland High School
Highland, IL

Joan Commons
Academic Coordinator, CREATE
University of California at San Diego
San Diego, CA

Laurette Cousineau
Curriculum Specialist
Williamson County Schools
Franklin, TN

Walter Glogowski, NBCT
Science and Computer Teacher
Ridgewood High School
Norridge, IL

Sarah Stevens
Science Teacher
Gilpin County Schools
Black Hawk, CO

About the Author

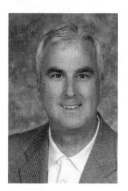 **Douglas Llewellyn** teaches science education and educational administration courses at St. John Fisher College in Rochester, New York. He is also the Project Manager for the College Board's Pre-AP science professional development programs. Additionally, he serves on the National Science Teachers Association Supervision and Coordination committee. Previously, he was the K–12 Director of Science at the Rochester City School, a junior high school principal, and a middle school science teacher. He received a graduate degree from Syracuse University and has been involved with several National Science Foundation grants on science education and systemic reform. He is a frequent presenter at state and national science conferences on inquiry-based learning and constructivist teaching strategies. His first book, *Inquire Within: Implementing Inquiry-Based Science Standards*, was also published by Corwin Press.

To contact the author, send an e-mail to dllewell@rochester.rr.com.

If (the teacher) is indeed wise he does not bid you enter the house of his wisdom, but rather leads you to the threshold of your own mind.

—From *The Prophet* by Kahlil Gibran

Constructing an
Understanding of Scientific Inquiry

The pebble that drops into a pond is like an idea that sparks inquiry. The concentric ripples represent new questions that emerge from the first germ of the idea. The ever-enlarging pattern of ripples refer to the integrated knowledge that is acquired as each question is explored, limited only by the force of the inquirer's enthusiasm for the search. The greater the interest and the more probing the questions, the more encompassing the study, the bigger the ideas that it develops, and the deeper and more meaningful the knowledge the inquirer constructs.

—From *Interdisciplinary Inquiry in Teaching and Learning* by Marian Martinello and Gillian Cook (1990)

A CULTURE OF INQUIRY

One of the most talked about topics in science education today is scientific inquiry. Whether you are discussing science literacy, standards, instructional strategies, or assessment, the phrase "scientific inquiry" likely will work its way into the conversation. Thus, for many teachers, constructing an understanding of scientific inquiry becomes a primary necessity to contributing to an articulate discussion on science education. The primary purpose of this book is to enable high school science teachers not only to develop an understanding of scientific inquiry but also to gain an appreciation of the skills, dispositions, and attitudes in creating a "culture of inquiry" within themselves as well as their classrooms. According to Reagan, Case, and Brubacher (2000):

A culture of inquiry, in short, entails not merely teachers engaged in inquiry but teachers and others collaboratively and collegially seeking to understand better and thus improve aspects of the schooling experience. For a culture of inquiry to exist and be maintained in a school, an on-going commitment to valuing curiosity, mutual respect, and support among teachers and between teachers and administration, a willingness to try new ideas and practices, and the ability to remain open to the unforeseen and unexpected are required. (p. 43)

As you journey through this book, reflect on your classroom norms and practices, share your ideas with a colleague, and keep a journal of your thoughts and progressive gains. Reflection and dialogue, especially with others who are seeking and committed to the same instructional practices as you, are important aspects of becoming an inquiry-based teacher.

Inquiry and Habits of Mind

Scientific inquiry provides an excellent means to foster the development of students' habits of mind. Marzano (1992) describes habits of mind as mental habits individuals develop to render their thinking. Habits of mind often encompass higher-order thinking skills, critical and scientific reasoning skills, problem-solving skills, communication and decision-making skills, and metacognition—being aware of your own thinking. Costa and Kallick (2001) describe habits of mind as "having dispositions toward behaving intellectually when confronted with problems, the answers to which are not immediately known" (p. 1). Although examples of habits of mind vary from author to author, the attributes usually common in science include the following:

- Commitment
- Creativity
- Curiosity
- Diligence
- Fairness
- Flexibility
- Imagination
- Innovation
- Integrity
- Openness
- Persistence
- Reflection
- Sensitivity
- Skepticism
- Thoughtfulness

As we journey further into our understanding of inquiry, we will come to see how inquiry-based classrooms promote critical thinking skills and habits of mind, as well as how these classrooms empower students to become independent, life-long learners. Hester (1994) tells us that inquiry involves critical thinking processes such as methods of diagnosis, speculation and hypothesis testing. The method of inquiry gives students the opportunity to confront problems, and generate and test ideas for themselves. . . . The emphasis is on ways of examining and explaining information (events, facts, situations, behaviors, etc.). Students when taught for the purposes embodied in inquiry are encouraged to evaluate the usefulness of their beliefs and ideas by applying them to new problem situations and inferring from them implications for future courses of action. (pp. 116–117)

The *Benchmarks for Science Literacy* (AAAS, 1993) suggests that "by the end of the 12th grade, students should know why curiosity, honesty, openness, and skepticism are so highly regarded in science and how they are incorporated into the way science is carried out; exhibit those traits in their own lives and value them in others" (p. 287). According to the AAAS (1993), "taken together, these values, attitudes, and skills can be thought of as habits of mind because they all relate directly to a person's outlook on knowledge and learning and ways of thinking and acting" (p. 281).

Why are habits of mind important to inquiry? As students engage in scientific inquiry, they demonstrate these attributes and behaviors in a collective sense as part of completing the task. According to the AAAS (1990):

It is also important for people to be aware that science is based upon everyday values even as it questions our understandings of the world and ourselves. Indeed, science is in many respects the systemic application of some highly regarded human values. . . . Scientists did not invent any of these values . . . but the broad field of science does incorporate and emphasize such values and drastically demonstrates just how important they are for advancing human knowledge and welfare. Therefore, if science is taught effectively, the results will be to reinforce such generally desirable human attributes and values—curiosity, openness to new ideas, and skepticism. (p. 185)

Wilks (1995) suggests that "the use of philosophical inquiry as a means of developing the skills of dialogue and thinking involves the teachers and their students becoming cooperative and caring co-inquirers working together in a community of inquiry" (p. 1). Wilks further comments that "a community of inquiry emerges from frequent group discussions fostered by teachers who are committed to the process of inquiry" (p. 4).

WHAT SCIENCE EDUCATORS SAY ABOUT INQUIRY

As we look toward the science educators who have devoted their professional career to studying scientific inquiry, several common themes surface. Whether the experts represent K–12 educators, higher education faculty, or the staffs of hands-on museums and national organizations, they concur that scientific inquiry focuses on the engagement of students to generate and pursue the answers to questions through careful observation and reflection.

The Center for Inquiry Based Learning (CIBL) at Duke University (www .biology.duke.edu/cibl/index.htm) provides useful definitions and information about inquiry. Hebrank (2000), a CIBL teacher, says:

> Inquiry is a way of acquiring knowledge. In inquiry-based learning, students either ask their own questions or are posed a question by the teacher. In the former case the question concerns a topic the students wish to learn about, and in the latter case the question concerns a topic the teacher wishes students to learn about. Regardless of the source of the question, inquiry-based learning requires that students play a major role in answering the question. (n.p.)

This definition, like others, stresses the role of the student as a researcher. In inquiry-based learning, the emphasis is placed on the student as an active investigator. Writing for *The Science Teacher,* Edwards (1997) says, "to have bona fide inquiry experiences, students must formulate their own questions, create hypotheses, and design investigations to test the hypotheses and answer the questions proposed" (p. 18).

Based on these thoughts, inquiry is a *means* as well as an *end* (Hackett, 1998). "In the *Standards,*" according to Hackett, "the term 'inquiry' is used in two different ways. First, inquiry refers to teaching methods and strategies. Second, the *Standards* identify scientific inquiry as content that students should understand and be able to do" (Hackett, 1998, p. 35). Similarly, in *A History of Ideas in Science Education* (DeBoer, 1991), inquiry is seen as a product as well as a process in science education.

Chiappetta (1997) also stresses the dual role of inquiry. "In contrast to teaching science *by* inquiry (general inquiry) is the notion of teaching science *as* inquiry (scientific inquiry). Teaching science as inquiry stresses active student learning and the importance of understanding a scientific topic. Here content becomes a critical aspect of the inquiry" (Chiappetta, 1997, p. 23).

Finally, for a complete and comprehensive literature review of scientific inquiry, see the Northwest Regional Educational Laboratory Program Report *Science Inquiry for the Classroom* (Hinrichsen & Jarrett, 1999), available online through www.nwrel.org/ msec/images/science/pdf/litreview.

WHAT THE *NATIONAL SCIENCE EDUCATION STANDARDS* SAY ABOUT INQUIRY

In 1996, the National Research Council (NRC) released the *National Science Education Standards* (*NSES*). In regard to the inquiry standards, the NRC states:

> Inquiry is a multifaceted activity that involves making observations; posing questions; examining books and other sources of information to see what is already known in light of experimental evidence: using tools to gather, analyze, and interpret data; proposing answers, explanations, and predictions; and communicating the results. Inquiry requires identification of assumptions, use of critical and logical thinking, and consideration of alternative explanations. (p. 23)

However, according to the *Standards*, doing inquiry involves more than just utilizing science process skills in the classroom. The *Standards* requires that high school teachers plan activities that engage students in combining process skills and critical reasoning skills to develop an appreciation for and understanding of science. According to the *Standards* (NRC, 1996), engaging high school students in inquiry helps develop

- an understanding of scientific concepts,
- an appreciation of "how we know" what we know in science,
- an understanding of the nature of science,
- skills necessary to become independent inquirers about the natural world, and
- the dispositions to use the skills, abilities, and attitudes associated with science.

The *Standards* also highlights the ability to conduct inquiry and develop an understanding about scientific inquiry:

Students in all grade levels and in every domain of science should have the opportunity to use scientific inquiry and develop the ability to think and act in ways associated with inquiry, including asking questions, planning and conducting investigations, using appropriate tools and techniques to gather data, thinking critically and logically about the relationships between evidence and explanations, constructing and analyzing alternative explanations, and communicating scientific arguments. (NRC, 1996, p. 105)

The inquiry standards set forth by the NRC (1996) are divided into three separate sets of grade levels or junctures. Each juncture identifies inquiry standards specific for that set of grade levels. These standards help science educators to define what students should know and be able to do. Reading the inquiry standards for grades 9–12 can help develop an understanding of the abilities necessary to do scientific inquiry.

At the high school level, according to the NRC, students should be able to

- identify questions and concepts that guide scientific investigations,
- design and conduct scientific investigations,
- use technology and mathematics to improve investigations and communications,
- formulate and revise scientific explanations and models using logic and evidence,
- recognize and analyze alternative explanations and models, and
- communicate and defend a scientific argument. (NRC, 2000a, p. 19)

Science teachers should become familiar with the *National Science Education Standards*. The *Standards* can be purchased in softcover, read online, or downloaded from the National Academies Press (www.nap.edu/bookstore.html). Readers may also be interested in an excellent accompanying text, *Inquiry and the National Science Education Standards: A Guide for Teaching and Learning* (2000a), that offers stories of high school teachers engaging students in inquiry (see Resource A, the "Print Resources on Inquiry" section).

WHAT THE AMERICAN ASSOCIATION FOR THE ADVANCEMENT OF SCIENCE SAYS ABOUT INQUIRY

In 1990, the AAAS published the first of two documents, *Science for All Americans*, which outlined a long-term view for instructional reform in science. It also marked the beginning of Project 2061 by the AAAS, which proposed recommendations for moving toward the goal of nationwide scientific literacy by 2061 (the year of the return of Halley's Comet). Following *Science for All Americans*, in 1993, the AAAS released *Benchmarks for Science Literacy*. It did not define curricular needs but identified specific outcomes for science education and, like the *NSES*, provided local school districts, state education agencies, and national science educational organizations with a blueprint for systemic reform.

Like the *National Science Education Standards*, Project 2061 addressed the need for integrating scientific inquiry and content. The AAAS (1993) describes scientific inquiry as being

> more complex than popular conceptions would have it. It is, for instance, a more subtle and demanding process than the naive idea of making a great many careful observations and then organizing them. It is far more flexible than the rigid sequence of steps commonly depicted in textbooks as the scientific method. It is much more than just doing experiments, and it is not confined to laboratories. If students themselves participate in scientific investigations that progressively approximate good science, then the picture they come away with will likely be reasonably accurate. But that will require recasting typical school laboratory work. The usual high school science "experiment" is unlike the real thing. The question to be investigated is decided by the teacher, not the investigators; what apparatus to use, what data to collect, and how to organize the data are also decided by the teacher (or the lab manual); time is not made available for repetitions or, when things are not working out, for revising the experiment; the results are not presented to other investigators for criticism; and, to top it off, the correct answer is known ahead of time. (p. 9)

Like the NRC (1996) *Standards*, the AAAS's (1993) *Benchmarks* is divided into separate grade levels or junctures. According to the AAAS, by the end of 12th grade, students should know the following:

- Investigations are conducted to explore new phenomena, validate previous results, test predictions, and compare theories.
- Hypotheses are used in science for guiding the interpretation of data.
- Scientists control conditions (of an experiment) in order to obtain evidence.
- Science depends upon intelligence, hard work, imagination, and even chance.
- Scientists check each other's results to prevent bias.
- New ideas often encounter criticism and are limited by the context in which they were conceived. (p. 13)

Reading the high school level inquiry statements from *Benchmarks for Science Literacy* is strongly recommended. They can be purchased through or downloaded from the AAAS Web site (www.project2061.org/tools/bsl/default.htm). You may also be interested in an accompanying AAAS text, *Inquiring Into Inquiry Learning and Teaching in Science* (see Resource A, Minstrell and Van Zee, 2000, in the section "Print Resource on Inquiry").

TEN QUESTIONS ABOUT INQUIRY-BASED LEARNING

To this point, we have been learning what scientific inquiry is. Now we want to address the questions high school science teachers often ask about inquiry-based teaching and learning.

1. I have students do many labs as part of my science course. Isn't that the same as doing inquiry?

Providing students with an opportunity to do labs, especially those that are hands-on, does not necessarily mean they are doing inquiry. Many labs and textbook activities can be very structured. Labs usually provide the students with the question to investigate, what materials to use, and most of all, how to go about solving the question by listing a sequence of step-by-step procedures of the lab. In many cases, commercially produced labs even provide a chart or table for the students to record their observations, measurements, or data. These types of labs are often referred to as "cookbook" because they provide a systematic procedure and follow a very linear path to a solution to the question. This is not to say that these kinds of lab experiences are not important, or that high school science teachers should avoid using them, but many traditional and structured labs are not real inquiry. Although most inquiry labs and activities are hands-on, not all hands-on labs and activities are inquiry oriented.

2. In my course, I start the year off by introducing students to the scientific method, and then we use it throughout the year. Is that the same as doing inquiry?

As stated in *Standards* (NRC, 1996) and *Benchmarks* (AAAS, 1993), doing inquiry does not necessarily imply following the steps of the scientific method. Inquiry incorporates the logic of problem solving that comes from the scientific method, but not necessarily the delineated, specific steps of the scientific method. The scientific method does have a role in inquiry-based labs; however, there is more to inquiry than a sequential set of procedures. According to the NRC (1996), "the standards should not be interpreted as advocating the 'scientific method.' The conceptual and procedural abilities suggest a logical progression, but they do not imply a rigid approach to scientific inquiry" (p. 144).

Many high school science teachers begin the school year by introducing the scientific method to students. The scientific method is so important to many textbook publishers that it is predominantly introduced in the first chapter of many secondary school science textbooks! In Chapter 6, we will further discuss the role of the scientific method in inquiry-based lessons.

3. When I observe a science classroom where students learn through inquiry, the lesson appears to be unstructured and open-ended. Is that good teaching?

Quite the contrary. Experienced inquiry teachers have specific goals and objectives in mind throughout their lessons. Their skills lie in empowering the students to develop their own investigations within those goals and objectives. In some high schools, a good teacher is defined as one who keeps a classroom quiet and students consumed in *seat time*. Although no one will argue that effective classroom management skills are essential for inquiry learning, an active, student-centered classroom should not be equated with chaos or unstructured instruction. Just like during any lab activity, when students do inquiry-based science we can expect the noise level to increase somewhat. To some, inquiry may appear on the surface to be unstructured and open-ended, but as student involvement increases, so does the need for the teacher to manage classroom movement and communication. When teachers use inquiry-based strategies, they may find that teaching requires more preparation and anticipation of possible student questions than traditional labs and teaching approaches do.

Bell and Gilbert (1996) report that teachers new to inquiry often feel less in control when students move about the room, make decisions about their work, and are encouraged to challenge the work of others. Although most teachers are actually in control, they perceive otherwise. To establish inquiry-centered environments, teachers need to accept changes in their role and in the atmosphere of the classroom. In Chapter 7, we will see how good classroom management and questioning skills are a prerequisite for creating a culture of inquiry. Without good classroom management, any lab, including an inquiry-based lab, will result in a chaotic situation.

4. During my class lectures and discussions, I ask students a lot of questions. Isn't that doing inquiry?

Although valuing questions is a basic commonality in all inquiry-based classroom, the misconception held by some high school science teachers is that inquiry teaching requires that the teachers ask a lot of questions. We might recall our own experiences sitting in science lectures where the teacher fired off question after question. Asking a lot of questions does not necessarily make an inquiry lesson. Again, in Chapter 7, we will see several examples of effective questioning strategies that support inquiry settings. In inquiry-centered classrooms, teachers provide open-ended experiences that lead students to raise their own questions and design investigations to answer those same questions.

5. Can all science lessons be taught through inquiry?

Although many seasoned inquiry teachers would like to believe this is true, the fact is, a good part of the content in science, especially in the high school grades, must be learned through traditional methods such as lectures, presentations, and textbooks (Hinman, 1998). Some science lessons, because of safety reasons or availability of materials, lend themselves to more structure than others and do not provide flexibility in the procedure section of the lab. As teachers, we decide which lessons are best presented through direct instruction or a teacher-led approach, and which ones can be guided through inquiry.

6. Inquiry may be appropriate for elementary and middle school students, but how can I teach through inquiry when I am expected to get students ready to

pass a final exam at the end of the course? I do not have time for inquiry in my classes.

For many high school science teachers, lecture and discussion methods are the primary means to dispense or impart knowledge to their students. These teachers see lecturing as the most effective and efficient way to transmit large amounts of content information to their students in a relatively short period. Lecturing is also the method by which many teachers learned science when they were in high school. It is also a method by which many teachers learned science when they were studying to become science teachers. Therefore, based on prior experience, we should not be surprised that so many science classes are lecture-based.

High school science teachers often talk about the time constraint they feel they are placed under. With more and more concepts being added to the curriculum, many science teachers say they are pressed to cover a great number of concepts in a school year. It is true that inquiry-based learning takes more time; however, developing higher level thinking skills and having students pose questions, plan solutions, and gather and organize data are skills that are nurtured only over time. There are no shortcuts to developing students with critical thinking skills.

I once was told the story about a physics teacher who routinely used the first 5 minutes of class to take attendance and the last 5 minutes of class to provide students an opportunity to start on their homework. If you were to multiply 10 minutes a day by 180 days per school year, you can see that this particular teacher used 1,800 minutes a year, or 36 50-minute periods, on noninstructional procedures. In addition, this same teacher taught a 5-day unit on the latent heat of vaporization that was not part of the district's physics curriculum. To find time to do inquiry or to create an inquiry-based curriculum, teachers need to utilize their time effectively and efficiently while centering on topics and concepts at the core of the curriculum.

7. How do you assess inquiry-based learning?

Inquiry-based learning can be assessed like any other concept or topic in science, but teachers need to use alternative methods of evaluation. Popular objective-type multiple-choice questions do not adequately assess inquiry-based learning. To assess students' academic progress, inquiry-based teachers often rely on using portfolios, writing journal entries, self-evaluations, and rubrics in conjunction with objective-type questions (Texley & Wild, 1998). Examples of each of these alternative assessment measures will be presented in Chapter 8.

8. I have been teaching high school science for 25 years and have seen a lot of "bandwagons" come and go in my lifetime. Isn't inquiry the latest thing for science education?

Actually, inquiry-based instruction has an enduring historical significance in science education. Those who study the history of science education know that questioning, discovery learning, and inquiry date back to the early days of the Greek scholar Socrates. Progressive education reformer John Dewey is credited as one of the first American educators to stress the importance of discovery learning and inquiry (Dewey, 1900, 1902, 1916). In his early work, Dewey proposed that learning does not start and intelligence is not engaged until the learner is confronted with a problematic situation.

Today, on the high school level, premier biology programs like the Biological Sciences Curriculum Study (BSCS, 1970, 1997) are deeply rooted in instructional methods of learning that stress the importance of inquiry-based instruction. In addition, inquiry has been and continues to be the philosophical foundation for many National Science Foundation (NSF) and National Science Teachers Association (NSTA) sponsored curriculum projects in biology, earth science, chemistry, and physics.

9. I see inquiry as "soft science" and not content-related. Is that true?

Inquiry, according to both *Standards* and *Benchmarks*, is one of the areas identified as content-related. That elevates inquiry to the same level as knowing the concepts, principles, laws, and theories about the life, earth, or physical sciences. According to the AAAS (1990), "science teaching that attempts solely to impart to students the accumulated knowledge of a field leads to very little understanding and certainly . . . science teachers should help students to acquire both scientific knowledge of the world and scientific habits of mind at the same time" (p. 203).

If students are to gain an appreciation for science and compete in the scientific and technically oriented society of the new millennium, they will need a curriculum that promotes active learning, problem solving, and ways to solve questions. Inquiry-based science is an effective means to enhance scientific literacy. Additional research has led to the conclusion that inquiry promotes critical thinking skills and positive attitudes toward science. Although inquiry is no panacea, it is one more strategy teachers can use, at the appropriate times, to engage students in investigations and satisfy their curiosity for learning (Haury, 1993).

10. I always thought inquiry is for high-achieving, college-bound science students. Can students with learning disabilities learn through inquiry?

The recommendations set forth by both the NRC (1996) and the AAAS (1993) apply to all students regardless of age, cultural or ethnic heritage, gender, physical condition, or academic ability, interest, or aspirations. The AAAS (1990) stresses that the recommendations apply in particular to those who historically have been underrepresented in the fields of science—mainly students of color, females, limited English proficiency students, and persons with disabilities. According to *Standards*, "given this diversity of student needs, experiences, and backgrounds, and the goal that all students will achieve a common set of standards, schools must support highquality, diverse, and varied opportunities to learn science" (NRC, 1996, p. 221). The ability to think creatively and critically is not solely for the high-achieving student. Inquiry-based instruction can and should be done equitably at all levels.

LOOKING BEYOND

As science teachers begin to give up some of their traditional teaching methods and attempt to implement aspects of inquiry-based teaching, it is a natural tendency to exhibit a "rearview mirror" mentality. Although looking ahead, peering out the windshield in a new direction where they are going, they also constantly check the rearview mirror and see just where they have been. For that reason, teachers new to inquiry become cognizant of the new pedagogy yet still consider their previously held models of teaching. Referring to the inquiry method, Postman and Weingartner (1969) suggest, "It works you over in entirely different ways. It activates different senses, attitudes, and perceptions: it generates a different, bolder, and more potent kind of intelligence. Thus, it will cause teachers, and their tests, and their grading systems, and their curriculums to change" (p. 27).

The great Michelangelo was said to be able to envision the image of his final sculpture in the stone block before he even started carving with a hammer and chisel. In the same light, Renoir, the French Impressionist, was able to stare at a blank canvas and see the picture he was about to paint. Like any great artist, an inquiry-based teacher needs to look beyond what the class looks like in the beginning of the school year and see the image of students working like real scientists months from now. As you look out into your classroom and see the faces of your students, what do you see?

Learning About
Inquiry Through Case Studies

SCIENTIFIC INQUIRY:
A CASE STUDY APPROACH

A case study is a description and analysis of the interaction among members in a particular situation. Cases are ideal for studying scientific inquiry because they present an opportunity for active engagement in a situation (Norton & Lester, 1998). Case studies are especially useful in science education because they emphasize that learning is founded in experience and that knowledge is constructed through problem solving (Dewey, 1938). By investigating a case study, you are actually modeling the engagement of inquiry and problem solving. Because the reader must become intellectually, emotionally, and socially involved with the incidents (Kowalski, Weaver, & Henson, 1990), the case studies in this book are based on real high school science teachers doing real investigations.

Case studies originally were used in the medical, psychology, and legal professions. Although case studies have been used at the Harvard Business School for more than 75 years, some historical records trace the origin of case studies back to ancient Greece (Norton & Lester, 1998). More recently, they have been and are being used in education, business, marketing, and human service fields as practical means to present and examine people interacting in particular situations. The purpose of the case studies in this book is to think about teachers in action and to analyze the interactions and behaviors demonstrated in the lesson.

The cases we will study convey the planning, interaction, and dialogue that can be found in a typical, inquiry-based high school science lesson. Some case studies described in this book are implicit or short-term inquiries lasting one or more classroom periods. Others represent explicit or extended inquiries lasting a month or more. As you work through a case, there are no right or wrong answers; instead of searching for "the answer," focus on developing the ability to identify underlying causal issues and phenomena found in each case study.

It is not advised to analyze a case study alone. Share your reflections with another teacher interested in inquiry or work in "support groups" in class. E-mail and discussion boards also can be viable means for a number of people to share their thoughts or reactions.

Each case study will have a similar format. The reader will be introduced to the classroom setting, the teacher and students, the subject area or grade level, and a correlation to the national science standards. All cases will be followed by questions and prompts for reflection, discussion, and analysis. In some cases, an interview with the teacher involved in the study will follow. Other times, additional readings, resources, and Web sites will be recommended for further study.

For more information on using case studies, see the National Center for Case Study Teaching in Science at http://ublib.buffalo.edu/libraries/projects/cases/case.html.

A CASE STUDY:
INQUIRING ABOUT ISOPODS

Now that we have enhanced our understanding of inquiry, let's study a class of 9th-grade biology students exploring the characteristics and behaviors of isopods. (Although the case study represents a real situation, the names of the teacher and students in this case are fictitious.) In this unit, the teacher, Mrs. Davis, is in her seventh year at Fairfield High School. Her 22 students will be exploring pillbugs (*Armadillidium vulgare*) by recording observations, raising questions to investigate, testing their ideas, collecting evidence, and communicating their discoveries about animal behavior. The pillbug lesson aligns to the *National Science Education Standards* (NRC, 1996) for grades 9–12.

Science as Inquiry Standard

Students will

- Identify questions and concepts that guide a scientific investigation. (NRC, p. 175)
- Design and conduct a scientific investigation. (p. 175)
- Formulate scientific explanations and models using logic and evidence. (p. 175)
- Communicate and defend a scientific argument. (p. 176)

Life Science Content Standard

As a result of activities, all students should develop an understanding [that]

- Multicellular animals have nervous systems that generate behavior. (NRC, p. 187)
- Sense organs detect light and sound that enable the animal to monitor what is going on in the world around it. (p. 187)
- Organisms have behavioral responses to external stimuli. (p. 187)

For practicality, consider the many advantages to using isopods versus other animals such as worms, snails, or slugs. Isopods are safe and easy for students to handle. Isopods also are ideal in states where educational law discourages or prohibits the use of vertebrates for experimentation. In addition, they do not harbor diseases that can be transmitted to humans, are practically odorless, and are easy to raise and prepare for study. Moreover, isopods, unlike fruit flies, cannot fly away and move quite slowly, making them ideal for students to observe and illustrate. Isopods also will not harm other plants and animals in the classroom. Best of all, for some teachers—they don't bite!

To introduce the lesson, Mrs. Davis assesses the students' prior knowledge and preconceptions about isopods. She poses the question, "What do you know about pillbugs? Have you ever turned over a rock or rotting log and seen these little roly-poly animals?" She has students individually record their experiences in their science journals and later has them "pair and share" what they wrote with a partner.

After several minutes of paired discussion, Mrs. Davis calls on a few students to share their responses with the entire class by stating one or more comments from their table or diagram. She places their responses on the board and organizes their thoughts into a concept map. Mrs. Davis continues by explaining that isopods are like little ecological "janitors" because they eat decaying leaves.

In the next phase of the lesson, students have an opportunity to observe and explore pillbugs in a petri dish. Before passing out the pillbugs, Mrs. Davis reminds students to wash their hands before and after handling any animal specimens. Working in groups of two, students now observe and record pillbug characteristics and behavior. At this point, Mrs. Davis also instructs the class to record questions they would like to investigate. She tells them, "As you explore your pillbugs, record your observations and questions in your science journal. We will later use this information to design and conduct our pillbug behavior investigations." She encourages them to use a two-column format for recording their observations and questions, as in Figure 2.1.

Mrs. Davis now hands out a sheet of prompting questions to initiate further explorations.

- Observe your pillbugs at first with your naked eye. Then observe the pillbugs using a magnifying lens. Later observe the pillbugs under a dissecting microscope using 4X and 10X magnification. What do you observe?
- Draw an illustration of a pillbug from a top view (dorsal side) and bottom view (ventral side).
- What is the length of a pillbug in millimeters?
- How many body sections does a pillbug have?
- How many pairs of legs does a pillbug have?
- Do all pillbugs have the same number of legs?
- How many antennae does the pillbug have?
- How many eyes does the pillbug have?
- Do the eyes appear to be simple or compound eyes?
- Describe the pillbug's outer plates or outside skeleton (exoskeleton).
- How many segments does the pillbug have?
- Do all pillbugs have the same number of segments?
- What happens when you place a pillbug on its back?
- What happens when you gently touch the pillbug? Does it roll up? If so, how long does it stay in the rolled-up position?

Figure 2.1   Two-Column Chart

Observations	Questions

Following the pillbug exploration, Mrs. Davis concludes the lesson by passing out an Isopod Fact Sheet to the students. She tells the students to read the fact sheet for homework and that tomorrow's class will start with a discussion of the anatomy, physiology, and habitat features of pillbugs.

Isopod Fact Sheet

- Pillbugs are not insects or "bugs." They belong to the order *Isopoda,* a group of crustaceans similar to lobsters, shrimp, crayfish, and crabs.
- There are more than 4,000 species of isopods.
- Pillbugs have three body parts: a head, a thorax, and an abdomen.
- Most isopods live in marine or freshwater habitats. A few species live on land.
- Pillbugs breathe through gill-like structures.
- Pillbugs have one pair of compound eyes and a pair of antenna.
- Terrestrial pillbugs are usually found under rocks or rotting logs and decaying leaves.
- Pillbugs feed on decaying leaves and other organic matter.

- Pillbugs are usually 5–15 mm in length.
- Pillbugs are wingless and have seven pairs of identical legs. Isopod means "alike legs."
- Pillbugs are gray to light brown in color.
- Pillbugs are invertebrates. Adult pillbugs are covered with an exoskeleton of armorlike plates that occasionally molt or shed (producing a new one) every 28 days to accommodate growth.
- Pillbugs, *Armadillidium vulgare,* are sometimes called "roly-polies" and resemble miniature armadillos. They use the roll-up behavior as a defense mechanism and in times of drought.
- Pillbugs differ slightly from sowbugs, *Porcellio laevis.* As shown in Figure 2.2, a sowbug has two pointed tail-like structures near its posterior and cannot roll into a ball.

Figure 2.2   Isopods

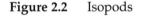

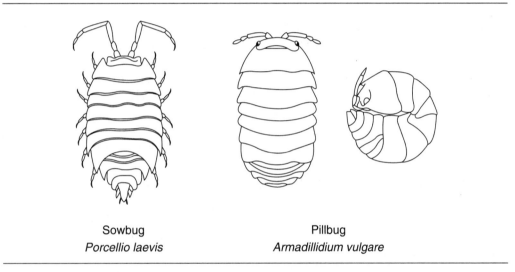

Sowbug
Porcellio laevis

Pillbug
Armadillidium vulgare

- Pillbugs most commonly mate in the spring. Female pillbugs can produce up to 200 eggs that are carried in a brood-like pouch or sac under the thorax. Young pillbugs resemble adults at birth.
- Birds and amphibians are pillbugs' natural predator.
- Most pillbugs live 2–3 years.

The next day, Mrs. Davis starts the lesson by reviewing the Isopod Fact Sheet. Students then have an opportunity to share their observations and questions from their two-column table during a class discussion. She then instructs the students to review their observations and questions and narrow down their recordings to select one important question to investigate. Students are given time to "brainstorm" their ideas, both individually and in groups. Then, one at a time, each student writes his or her one question on the board. As the students share and discuss their questions, Mrs. Davis assists in editing and rewording questions as necessary. She reminds students to write investigative questions as "cause and effect" questions and to describe how, as one factor or variable changes, that will affect another factor or variable. Students' questions include the following:

- Do pillbugs have a food or leaf preference?
- How fast do pillbugs move?
- Do pillbugs prefer a dry versus a wet environment?
- Do pillbugs prefer a cold versus a warm environment?
- Do pillbugs prefer a light versus a dark environment?
- When placed in a T-maze, do pillbugs more often take left turns or right turns?
- Do pillbugs prefer sandy soil versus loam soil?
- Are pillbugs social animals? If I place 20 pillbugs in a pile, would they prefer to stay together or spread out?
- Do pillbugs have a color preference?
- Do pillbugs prefer a rough surface or a smooth surface?
- When placed on different surfaces such as paper towels, aluminum foil, wax paper, or transparent wrap, which surface do pillbugs prefer?
- Are pillbugs attracted to magnets? Would a pillbug choose an environment with a magnetic field versus one without a magnetic field?

Each student chooses a question or teams with a partner on another question about pillbug behavior. Now, Mrs. Davis suggests that students "brainstorm" their ideas and think of a prediction based on their question. She has them write their prediction as a word statement or hypothesis in the form of an "if, then" statement. Janice and Melissa write, "If I place 20 pillbugs in a chamber where they can choose between damp and dry surfaces, the pillbugs will choose the damp surface." Rob and Mark write, "If I place 15 pillbugs in a chamber where they can choose between light and dark areas, 75% of the pillbugs will choose the dark areas."

During the design phase of the investigation, students again "brainstorm" procedures and ways to test their questions and hypotheses. They identify all the variables that could affect the outcome of the experiment and control those variables by selecting one variable, the manipulating or independent variable, to determine the outcome of the investigation. The students also select a responding or dependent variable that becomes the variable that is measured in the investigation. All other variables are controlled or stay the same. Mrs. Davis helps the students set up and design their investigation by posing the following questions:

- How will the variables in your experiment be controlled so only one factor affects the outcome?
- How will you measure whether your hypothesis is valid or not?
- Does your procedure align with the hypothesis? Does the design do what it is supposed to do?

As students are designing their investigations, Mrs. Davis provides a blank "experimental plan" (similar to Figure 2.3) where students identify and fill in the following:

- The question to be investigated
- The hypothesis to be tested (if appropriate)
- The materials needed to carry out the investigation
- The procedure of the investigation
- The data collection tables and charts

Figure 2.3   Isopod Experimental Plan

Question to be investigated

Hypothesis to be tested (if appropriate)

Materials needed to carry out the investigation

Procedure of the investigation

Data collection tables and charts

While the students are writing up their design plan, the teacher moves around the classroom, prompting each student by asking such questions as "What materials will you need to carry out your investigation?," "How many pillbugs will you use in your experiment?," "What's the manipulated variable in your experiment?," and "How will you know if your hypothesis is correct?" At the close of the period, Mrs. Davis collects each group's experimental plan and approves each one before the investigation can begin.

The next day, about half the students are ready to start their investigations; others are still revising their questions or getting materials and setting up their experiments; and others are redesigning and "tweaking" their design plans for the teacher's approval. For the next 2 days, students are immersed in collecting evidence, recording data, and drawing conclusions. The room is transformed into a virtual laboratory of experimentation! Mrs. Davis proudly watches the students share their ideas and act like real scientists.

As the investigations come to a close, students busily use the computer lab to organize their observations, data, and evidence into graphs and charts. Each group must also prepare to communicate its results through reports and presentations. In this class, students are required to complete a final written laboratory report and make a 5-minute presentation to the class on their findings. In the final report, students analyze the data and draw conclusions about the validity of the hypothesis. The report is an extension of the original design plan but now includes data organized in a table or chart and plotted on a graph. As part of the write-up, students are encouraged to use spreadsheets and graphs generated by computer to explain their results. In addition to the final report, students communicate their findings to the class by using a trifold poster board exhibit or a PowerPoint presentation.

RESOURCES FOR ISOPODS

For more information about pillbugs and isopods, see the following resources.

Burnett, R. (1999). *The pillbug project: A guide to investigation.* Arlington, VA: National Science Teachers Association. (This book is for elementary and middle school teachers but may also be helpful for high school teachers.)

Glase, J., & Palmer, J. (1993). *Isopod orientation.* Ithaca, NY: Cornell Institute for Biology Teachers, Cornell University.

Mikulka, T. (December, 2000). Isopod inquiry. *The Science Teacher, 67*(9), 20–22.

www.udel.edu/msmith/pillbugs.html

www.zoo.org/educate/fact_sheets/sowbug/sowbug.htm

QUESTIONS FOR REFLECTION

1. Why did Mrs. Davis have students "pair and share" their prior experiences?

2. Why did Mrs. Davis place students' responses on the board?

3. What are the benefits of making a concept map?

4. Why did the teacher have students explore their pillbugs before presenting and explaining the Isopod Fact Sheet?

5. How difficult is it for a teacher to monitor 8–12 investigations going on simultaneously?

6. What is the value in having students make presentations to the class? How can presentations support speaking and listening skills? Computer skills?

THE INQUIRY CYCLE

"Inquiring With Isopods" is just one example of an exploration that encourages students to raise questions. In analyzing the group's work, the *Inquiry Cycle* (see Llewellyn, 2002) represents aspects of most inquiry-based investigations (see Figure 2.4):

Figure 2.4   The Inquiry Cycle

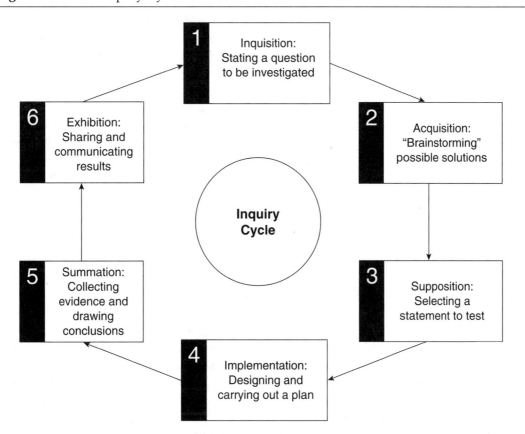

1. Inquisition—stating a "what if" or "I wonder" question to be investigated

2. Acquisition—brainstorming possible procedures

3. Supposition—identifying an "I think" or "If . . . then" statement to test

4. Implementation—designing and carrying out a plan

5. Summation—collecting evidence and drawing conclusions

6. Exhibition—sharing and communicating results

During the inquisition phase, students usually initiate their inquiry by exploring and posing a question. The question is often stated as a "What if . . ." question. The question can originate from an open-ended exploration, as with the isopods, or as a discrepant event, or a teacher-directed activity. In the "Inquiring About Isopods" investigation, the inquisition phase was initiated by the initial exploration activity.

During the acquisition phase, students rely on their prior experience to brainstorm possible ideas and solutions to the inquiry. Here students ask, "What do I already know about pillbugs to answer the question?" In the acquisition phase of the isopod exploration, students' prior conceptions about isopod behavior may have affected how they perceived the outcome of their question.

During the supposition phase, students consolidate the information under study to propose a "testable" prediction or an "I think . . ." statement. This phase generally includes stating a hypothesis to test the question being investigated.

During the implementation phase, students design a plan to address or test their prediction and carry out the plan.

During the summation phase, students record and analyze their observations to compare them to the original "What if . . ." statement.

Finally, during the exhibition phase, the students communicate their findings and new information in the form of a written laboratory report, a poster display, an oral report, or a PowerPoint presentation. In the isopod lesson, the groups were eager to share their discoveries and new knowledge about invertebrate behavior.

The inquiry cycle can serve as a general format for teachers planning inquiry-based investigations for their students. We should be reminded that the model serves as a general approach to raising and answering questions. Following the inquiry cycle, students often enter and reenter the phases at different aspects of their inquiry process. Thus, the cycle serves as a model to guide students through their inquiries and investigations.

BRAINSTORMING

As you can see, during the acquisition phase, brainstorming is an essential element of scientific inquiry. Brainstorming is not a tool for determining the best solution to a problem or issue but rather a means for generating as many ideas or solutions as possible to a question, a problem, or an issue. As high school science teachers, we often underutilize the value of brainstorming in the inquiry process. This may be due to the added amount of time the discussion process takes. Often, we are in a rush to move the inquiry process along as quickly as possible. In any event, for students to be effective problem solvers, we must teach them how to engage in a thoughtful dialogue and brainstorm ideas to become effective group members. When we take time for students to be involved in brainstorming, we foster higher-level thinking skills such as analyzing, synthesizing, and making judgments and evaluations, as well as habits of mind such as creativity, openness, and reflection. Teachers who plan for brainstorming sessions during scientific inquiry communicate to students that discourse and dialogue are integral aspects of the classroom culture.

Before beginning any effective brainstorming session, ground rules must be set. This does not mean that rules or boundaries are set so tightly that students cannot be creative. It does mean, however, that a code of conduct for person-to-person interactions has been set. It is when this code of conduct is breached that people stop being creative and the brainstorming and sharing process degenerates.

The best way to set meaningful ground rules is to have the students or teams create their own. In the beginning of the school year, and before small group discussions, allow students to create their own brainstorming ground rules. This should provide an opportunity to practice the skills necessary for an effective brainstorming session. It also allows the students or teams to take ownership of acceptable and unacceptable behaviors. Once the list of ground rules is generated, be sure to gain consensus that brainstorming sessions will be conducted according to them, then post them in a highly visible location in the room.

With procedures for setting ground rules in mind, the following are key rules that high school students often identify as useful when conducting a brainstorming session.

- There are no dumb ideas. It is okay to give a wild or wacky idea. This is a brainstorming session, not a serious discussion that requires only serious solutions.
- Don't criticize other people's ideas. This is not a debate, discussion, or forum for one person to display superiority over another.
- Build on other students' ideas. Often, an idea suggested by one student can trigger a bigger or better idea by another student.
- Strive for quantity over quality; the more creative ideas, the better. As the teacher/facilitator, make a challenge to the teams to come up with as many ideas as possible.
- There are no "put-downs" or judgments made of individual ideas or suggestions.
- All ideas are recorded. One team member may be selected as the recorder.
- Everyone in the group is encouraged to contribute.
- There are no lengthy discussions. Contributions made should be to the point. Set a time limit on the discussion/brainstorming session.

To clarify the roles and responsibilities of the individual group members, consider the following preparation questions:

- What is the desired outcome of the brainstorming session?
- Who will lead or facilitate the brainstorming session to meet the outcome?
- Who can write quickly enough to record the ideas contributed without slowing down the group process?
- Who will keep time for the discussion session?
- Who will report the findings of the brainstorming session to the entire class?

During the inquiry process, a brainstorming session usually starts with an idea or a question. The question, in turn, often leads to a divergent level of thinking toward a solution to the question. Everyone in the group is given a chance to talk or give input without comments or a debate. This is followed by a convergent level of thinking designed to build consensus in reducing all the possible solutions to a manageable few, discussion of the few that remain, and selection of an acceptable procedure to investigate.

During this process, the teacher makes periodic process checks with each of the groups and clarifies questions that are unclear or confusing. Students may need assistance from the teacher in eliminating or combining procedures to form a better investigation. Students may also need assistance in ordering individual steps of the investigation into a logical pattern or sequence. In the end, students should determine if the procedure or solution is appropriate and meets the purpose of the question. In other words, does this procedure lead us to answering the question being investigated?

Why Brainstorming Fails

Science teachers may find that during the inquiry process, brainstorming sessions sometimes fail because of the role played by the facilitator, a pivotal part of the discussion process. Thus, the teacher's selection of the student facilitator is extremely important. A good facilitator creates a trusting climate, stays neutral throughout the discussion, treats all members as equals, listens intently, remains flexible, and provides closure to the discussion. A poor facilitator, on the other hand, becomes the center of the group's activity, puts down other students' ideas, does not manage group conflict, is passive, allows a few people to dominate the process, or lets discussion ramble.

A DEFINITION OF INQUIRY

As you can see from the isopod investigation, inquiry is the scientific process of active exploration by which we use critical, logical, and creative thinking skills to raise and engage in questions of personal interest. Driven by students' curiosity and wonder about observed phenomena, inquiry investigations usually involve

- generating a question or problem to be solved,
- brainstorming possible solutions to the problem,
- stating a hypothesis to test,
- choosing a course of action and carrying out the procedures of the investigation,
- gathering and recording the data through observation and instrumentation to draw appropriate conclusions, and
- communicating their findings.

As high school students communicate and share their explanations, inquiry helps them connect their prior understandings to new experiences, modify and accommodate their previously held beliefs and conceptual models, and construct new knowledge. In constructing newly formed knowledge, students generally are cycled back into the processes and pathways of inquiry with new questions and discrepancies to investigate.

In the isopod investigation, we saw students exhibiting five essential features of classroom inquiry:

- Learners are engaged by scientifically oriented questions.
- Learners give priority to evidence, which allows them to develop and evaluate explanations that address scientifically oriented questions.
- Learners formulate explanations from evidence to address scientifically oriented questions.
- Learners evaluate their experiences in the light of alternative explanations, particularly those reflecting scientific understanding.
- Learners communicate and justify their proposed explanations. (NRC, 2000a, p. 35)

Finally, learning through inquiry empowers high school students with the knowledge, skills, and dispositions to become independent thinkers and lifelong learners. Teachers can encourage students to use communication, manipulation, and problem-solving skills to increase their awareness of and interest in science and guide them on their way to becoming scientifically literate citizens.

The inquiry approach requires a different "mind-set" and different expectations on the part of the teacher. In subsequent chapters, we will describe in more detail this mind-set and the role teachers and students play in inquiry-based classrooms.

Developing a
Philosophy for Inquiry

A prerequisite for becoming an inquiry-based teacher is embracing a philosophical mind-set founded on the ideals and principles of constructivism. Today there are as many interpretations of constructivism as there are interpretations of inquiry, yet many high school science teachers may still be unaware of the publicity that constructivism has attained in the last 20 years and its implications of constructivism for science education, instructional reform, and, specifically, inquiry-based classrooms.

Although it has implications for the classroom, constructivism is not about teaching strategies, nor is it about designing curriculum. Rather, it is one theory or philosophy about how an individual learns, one in which the student is embedded in active engagement and is constantly constructing and reconstructing knowledge through environmental interactions. Because the tenets of constructivism align closely with the practice of inquiry, it becomes essential that inquiry-based teachers have a firm foundation in the propositions of constructivism.

This chapter will (a) introduce the philosophy and historical developments of constructivism that have shaped our understanding of how students learn science, (b) discuss how one's prior knowledge and misconceptions can influence learning, and (c) present constructivist learning strategies compatible with inquiry- and learner-centered classrooms. By understanding constructivist principles, we can better envision our role as inquiry-based teachers. For that reason, it becomes crucial that science teachers interested in inquiry be able to articulate their philosophy of teaching and learning, and apply it to classroom practice. After all, our values, beliefs, and even prejudices about teaching and learning are reflected in our classroom culture. Our classrooms, in a sense, mirror and resonate what we believe is good teaching and learning.

WHAT IS CONSTRUCTIVISM?

Constructivism is a theory about how we come to know what we know. It is founded on the premise that children, adolescents, and even adults construct or make meaning about the world around them based on the context of their existing knowledge. We do this by reflecting on our prior experiences. In this way, each of us "constructs" our own mental models, or schema, as we activate our experiences to develop new conceptual structures. In a constructivist point of view, the learner is constantly filtering incoming information based on his or her existing conceptions and preconceived notions to construct and reconstruct his or her own understanding. Thus, the meaning of "knowing" is an active, adaptive, and evolutionary process.

The constructivist perspective is startlingly distinct from earlier views and theories about learning. Behaviorism, one earlier view, is built on the premise that learning is an acquisition or change in observable behavior initiated through stimuli and responses. Although behavioral psychology or operant conditioning is considered useful when applying positive and negative reinforcements, it does not account for the cognitive aspect of learning. Objectivism, occasionally paired with behaviorism, presumes that all knowledge exists externally and independently from the learner, and that learning consists of imparting that body of knowledge from one person to another. Contrary to behaviorists' and objectivists' views, constructivists do not subscribe to the supposition that students "absorb" information from the teacher; nor do constructivists believe that knowledge is imparted, acquired, or transmitted from one individual to another. Constructivists believe that learning is self-regulating and socially mediated as the student actively engages, interacts, and operates within the confines of his or her environment. Learning, to the constructivist, is focused on cognitive, not behavioral, processes. Constructivists do not view the mind as a "blank slate" or an "empty vessel," as in John Locke's famous expression *tabula rasa*; teachers cannot dispense or pour information directly into a student's head. In the constructivist approach, the student is an active participant in the learning process. Students enter our classrooms with years of prior knowledge and even misconceptions that greatly affect how they interpret and make meaningful interpretations of the phenomena being studied. According to the National Research Council (2000b), "students come into the classroom with preconceptions about how the world works. If their initial understanding is not engaged, they may fail to grasp the new concepts and information that are taught, or they may learn for the purposes of a test but revert to their preconceptions outside the classroom" (p. 14). This chapter and the accompanying case studies will focus on the attention science teachers need to place on what their high school students are thinking about as they undertake inquiry investigations.

TRADITIONAL VERSUS CONSTRUCTIVIST CLASSROOMS

To "construct" an understanding of constructivism, let's consider two classrooms: one traditional, teacher-centered, and one constructivist, student-centered. In this case study, Mrs. Hennessey, a biology teacher at Northshore High School, is presenting an introductory unit on "how the leaf carries out photosynthesis" to her general biology students. In this classroom, student desks are arranged in straight rows, with the teacher's desk in the front center of the room. Mrs. Hennessey uses a single textbook for studying biology, along with several demonstrations and labs she has mastered from use over many years. During the unit, students take notes, fill out handouts and worksheets that emphasize rote memorization, and, when time and supplies are available, perform laboratory activities that verify information that was presented on previous days. Mrs. Hennessey starts the unit by telling students that photosynthesis is the process in which green plants use light energy to make food. She goes on to explain that "photo" means "light" and "synthesis" means "to put together," and she indicates that "photosynthesis" is quite an appropriate name for the process. Students then copy the formula for photosynthesis, in both words and chemical notation, as she writes it on the board. Mrs. Hennessey continues by explaining in detail the process of photosynthesis and the role that light, carbon dioxide, and water play in making food for plants. Later in the first day's lesson, Mrs. Hennessey goes on to describe the production of sugar and oxygen as products in photosynthesis.

The following day, she teaches the importance of photosynthesis by introducing the carbon dioxide cycle and the interdependence of plants and animals in their quest to survive. The teacher presents a lab experience to view the cross section of a leaf and identify the different leaf cells. During the lab, students use the cross section and their textbooks to label the different cell layers and structures of the leaf. At the end of the lesson, students use their notes and textbook to prepare for a paper-and-pencil unit test. In the test, students are asked to define the term "photosynthesis" and state its formula. Another section includes labeling a cross section of a leaf similar to the illustration from the lab.

In this classroom, Mrs. Hennessey is the information provider and views the students as passive learners who have come to the classroom to know and master a fixed body of information. Information is divided into distinct and separate parts, with little emphasis on the students internalizing the information.

Mr. Travers is also a biology teacher at Northshore High School, and, like Mrs. Hennessey, he is presenting an introductory unit on photosynthesis to his general biology students. In Mr. Travers's classroom, student desks are sometimes arranged in straight rows, sometimes in groups of four, and sometimes in the shape of a "U." Mr. Travers allows the purpose of the lesson to determine the appropriate room setup. Mr. Travers uses several textbooks and primary sources for studying biology. He keeps a collection of *Science* and *Scientific American* magazines on the shelf for students, along with other science books and resources. Mr. Travers starts the lesson by having students think about and record what they know about the leaf as the food manufacturing site and encourages them to write down whatever comes to mind when they think about the term "photosynthesis."

After 2 minutes, he tells them, "Now turn to your partner and tell him or her your prior understandings about the word 'photosynthesis.' Take 2 minutes to share your thoughts and experiences about the word 'photosynthesis' with your partner." At the end of the "pair and share" activity, he asks several students to share their understandings about photosynthesis with the class. As students share their ideas, Mr. Travers writes and arranges their thoughts in a concept map on the front board. The rest of the period is spent having students work in groups to view a prepared section of a leaf cross section and compare it to the illustration in the book. As students are viewing the leaf section, Mr. Travers walks around the room answering their questions and posing his own to students.

The next day, students take notes from a brief presentation and overview on the cross section of the leaf as it relates to the first day's activity of exploration and sharing previous understandings. Mr. Travers now presents a question to the class: What would happen if you took away or changed one of the requirements for photosynthesis? This investigation provides an opportunity for students to choose an inquiry relevant to them and observe the changes in the leaf's food-making process. In the investigation, some students choose to cover one or both sides of the leaf with Vaseline, peanut butter, or even nail polish. Others choose to cover the leaf with aluminum foil, wax paper, or clear transparent wrap. Some want to find out how light affects the rate of photosynthesis, while others want to know how different colored light affects the rate of photosynthesis. Still others investigate how the availability of carbon dioxide affects photosynthesis. As students carry out their investigations, they document and record their daily progress and findings in their science journals.

Following the plant investigations, Mr. Travers reviews the process of photosynthesis and relates the process of photosynthesis as a "production system" in which ingredients such as carbon dioxide and water produce a sugar and a by-product—oxygen. He also reviews how the students' findings in their investigations relate to the food-making process. He then introduces appropriate concepts and vocabulary terms related to photosynthesis, including stomata, chloroplast, chlorophyll, phloem, and xylem. To apply their understanding of photosynthesis, students extend their investigations to new situations by explaining how pollution from cars affects the growth rates of plants. For the unit test, students are given an envelope containing 18 small cards, each with a word or words for a different part of the leaf or pertaining to the process of photosynthesis. The words are as follows.

Upper epidermis	Chloroplast
Lower epidermis	Chlorophyll
Palisade layer	Photosynthesis
Spongy layer	Autotroph
Xylem	Glucose
Phloem	Carbon dioxide
Vascular bundle	Water
Guard cell	Oxygen
Stoma	Light

The purpose of the assessment is to use the cards to create a concept map showing the interconnection of all the terms to the process of photosynthesis.

In this classroom, Mr. Travers's role is that of a facilitator rather than dispenser of information. In constructivist classrooms, teachers value the points of view students bring to the lesson and alter their agenda based on the prior knowledge and preconceptions of the students. In constructivist settings, emphasis is placed on the students working in groups and internalizing the information as they develop understandings of scientific phenomenon. Information is organized around holistic ideas and discrepant events that capture the students' interest. By using analogies and having students raise their own questions, constructivist teachers constantly connect the students' prior knowledge and experiences to new knowledge and concepts.

According to Brooks and Brooks (1999), traditional and constructivist classrooms differ by the following:

Traditional Classrooms	Constructivist Classrooms
• Curriculum is presented part to whole, with emphasis on basic skills.	• Curriculum is presented whole to part, with emphasis on big concepts.
• Strict adherence to a fixed curriculum is highly valued.	• Pursuit of students' questions is highly valued.
• Curricula activities rely heavily on textbooks and workbooks.	• Curricula activities rely heavily on primary sources of data and manipulative materials.
• Students are viewed as "blank slates" onto which information is etched by the teacher.	• Students are viewed as thinkers with emerging theories about the world.
• The teacher generally behaves in a didactic manner, disseminating information to students.	• The teacher generally behaves in an interactive manner, mediating the environment for students.
• The teacher seeks the correct answer to validate students' learning.	• The teacher seeks the students' points of view to understand students' present conceptions for use in subsequent lessons.
• Assessment of student learning is viewed as separate from teaching and occurs almost entirely through testing.	• Assessment of students' learning is interwoven with teaching and occurs through teacher observations of students at work and through student exhibitions and portfolios.
• Students primarily work alone.	• Students primarily work in groups.

Later, through the yeast investigation in Chapter 9, you will see how the notion of constructivism has implications for teaching and learning science. For now, how many of the following characteristics that portray a constructivist unit of study can you identify from the isopod investigation?

1. Knowing how adolescents learn has a bearing on how we approach teaching and learning.

2. Knowing educational theory gives meaning to our understanding about teaching and learning.

3. Demonstrating that it is essential to use concrete and manipulative materials to introduce formal concepts.

4. Starting with what the students know is an effective departure point for any science lesson.

5. Using explorations and time to "mess around" to introduce and sequence new knowledge, thus aligning with present learning theories.

6. Encouraging inductive and discovery learning that opens the doors to problem-solving and higher-level thinking skills.

7. Providing challenging activities stretches students' thinking and problem-solving skills.

8. Using active learning encourages students to discover and construct new knowledge.

9. Posing "What if . . ." and "I wonder . . ." questions facilitates assimilation and accommodation.

10. Allowing students to work in groups to share and communicate knowledge, and to test ideas and theories against one another, makes learning a personal and social experience.

HISTORICAL PERSPECTIVES
OF CONSTRUCTIVISM

At many science education conferences, workshops, and seminars on learning theory, one of the most talked about topics among science educators today is constructivism. Although the theory is not new, recent developments about how the brain works have strengthened the constructivist model. Aspects of constructivist principles date back to the works of Socrates, Plato, and Aristotle. Perhaps the first recorded constructivist was the Neapolitan philosopher Giambatista Vico, who worked in the field as early as 1710. Have you ever posed a question to a student and gotten the response, "I know it, but I just can't explain it"? According to Vico, we know something only when we can explain it (Yager, 1991).

John Dewey

John Dewey (1859–1952) was one of the first modern American constructivists. Dewey (1900, 1902, 1916) believed that learning and experience go hand in hand and that knowledge emerges from a personal interaction between the learner and the external environment. He felt that posing problems of significant interest that draw upon the student's prior knowledge activates the learning process. According to Llewellyn (2002), "Dewey felt that teaching should be an active process, including solving problems that interest students. He believed that problems posed to pupils too often involved the interests of the teacher rather than the interests of the students" (p. 42). Dewey's model for learning also incorporates the student's immediate surroundings. His teachings have had a profound influence on environmental and outdoor education. Because the lure of the outdoors and providing problems for students to solve go hand in hand with inquiry-based instruction, many inquiry teachers are aligned to Deweyian philosophy.

Jean Piaget

Probably the most influential 20th-century constructivist was Swiss psychologist Jean Piaget (1896–1980). Like Dewey, Piaget (1970) believed that knowledge is not "out there" somewhere, waiting to be discovered, but rather is a result of an interaction between the learner and the people or objects within the environment. Piaget was one of the first psychologists to shift the locus of learning from a behavioral aspect to a cognitive one. Piaget theorized that cognitive structures, called schemas, were the mental models that form by "acting on an object" and that schemas represent our ability to interpret incoming information. These schemas, in a sense, act as filters to assimilate new ideas. Unfortunately, one's mental models or schemas also can be a result of misinformation, resulting in presently held naive beliefs or misconceptions. We will address the significance of misconceptions and how they affect learning later in this book.

Piaget used the term "operations" to describe the way a child internalizes its interaction with the environment. The following is a brief summary of Piaget's four developmental stages:

Sensorimotor (birth–2 years): At this stage, the child learns to adapt to its environment and coordinate its motor actions through trial and error. Toward the end of this stage, the child begins to develop and use language to communicate needs and feelings.

Preoperational (2–7 years): At this stage, the child begins to become aware of its own actions through thinking. The child also develops the ability to plan solutions and actions to solve problems. Logic and contradictions are not yet part of the child's thinking. Often, the child solves a problem by focusing on one variable at a time. The solution to a problem is often judged by the child's illogical reasoning.

Concrete Operational (7–11 years): At this age, the preadolescent begins to develop the ability to think logically. Preadolescents can now perform many science process skills such as measuring, classifying, predicting, inferring, hypothesizing, and controlling variables. The preadolescent can also organize objects into sequences based on patterns and can explain the significance of the patterns to others. The student at this age can think about and provide reason to problems that involve using manipulative and concrete objects. At this point, however, little abstract thinking is experienced.

Formal Operational (12 and older): At this stage, the adolescent is able to think and to perform operations logically and abstractly. When faced with cause and effect relationships, the student can understand the interaction without the use of manipulative or concrete objects. At this stage, thinking goes beyond actual, personal experience, and reasoning about ideas not experienced can be understood.

In contrasting students at the levels of concrete and formal operations, Driscoll (1994) summarizes that

> Inhelder and Piaget (1958) presented children and adolescents with a chemistry problem, in which they were to mix clear liquid chemicals from four beakers until they achieved a yellow color. Concrete operational children

were rather random in their approach to the problem, sometimes repeating combinations of chemicals they had tried before. In addition, they typically combined only two chemicals at a time, or all four, without considering combinations of three. By contrast, formal operational adolescents generated a systematic plan of testing chemical combinations until they found the solution. Moreover, they kept records of their tests and generated appropriate observations concerning their results. (p. 178)

Piaget believed that although they progress at different rates, all humans go through these same four stages in mental development. Psychologists studying Piaget would later explain that the stages are not discrete and separate, but continuous, as humans often display behaviors characteristic of the "gray" areas between the "stages." Critics of Piaget's findings would also argue that children can manifest characteristics of more than one stage and that, at times, they may temporarily regress from one level to another.

According to Arlin (1987), there are several concepts that, when applied consistently by the student, differentiate concrete from formal operational learners.

- Multiplicative compensations: This concept relates when two or more dimensions constitute a situation. For example, when a student understands the volume of a solid block, he or she must consider three dimensions: length, height, and width. The concept of multiplicative compensations is required when a student studies a topic such as density or ecological life cycles, or whenever thinking about how one variable will affect another variable.

- Correlations: This concept relates when the student identifies a relationship between two events or variables. In science, students frequently are asked to describe a cause and effect relationship between the manipulated (independent) and responding (dependent) variables. As applied to inquiry, at the end of a plant investigation the teacher may pose the question, "What seems to be the relationship between the amount of fertilizer provided and the growth rate of the plant?"

- Probability: Probability is a formal operations skill that asks the student to develop the likelihood of a relationship. In genetics, the probability of a particular genotype or phenotype occurring serves as a typical example.

- Combinational reasoning: In combinational reasoning, the student is asked to give all the possible combinations of variables for a particular event. When a teacher poses the question, "What are the possible combinations of a specific phenomenon?," students utilize the skill of combinational reasoning. Combinational reasoning especially applies to topics in biology, chemistry, and physics.

- Proportional reasoning: Proportional reasoning incorporates the ability to discover the equality of two ratios that form a proportion. When students use map skills, draw models, balance chemical equations, or use scale structure, the skill of proportional reasoning is applied. Proportional reasoning is often used in earth science and chemistry.

- Indirect and direct verification: In earth science, chemistry, and physics, students often deduce the validity of an occurrence through indirect verification. For example, when students study black holes, the formation of molecules, or inertia, they deduce the existence of these phenomena by observing their effects, thus inferring their existence. More often, formal operations are equated with abstract concepts, such as forms of conservation, that are beyond direct verification.

- Mechanical equilibrium: Mechanical equilibrium requires the ability to simultaneously make the distinction between and coordinate two or more complementary sets. Physics problems regarding hydraulics and pistons require this type of thinking.

Hester (1994) states that these formal operations "represent a new level of abstraction, of thinking about the possible as well as the actual, of making predictions, forming hypotheses, and thinking scientifically, which sets the adolescent apart from the child with his/her dependence on purely concrete objects and referents for thinking" (p. 155). Although Piaget's research identified age 11 as the point at which children begin to move into formal levels of thinking, high school teachers know that many of their students still operate at a concrete level. As high school teachers use inquiry strategies and provide opportunities for students to test their predictions and hypotheses, describe relationships, describe possible combinations and arrangements, and use proportional thinking, they provide vehicles for students to make the transition from concrete to formal cognitive levels. During this transitional phase, preadolescents demonstrate inconsistent thought patterns concerning abstractions by showing evidence of using two or three of the formal operational skills cited earlier. As students progress in four or five of the concepts, they are making progress into formal levels of operations (Arlin, 1987).

What does Piaget's theory mean to high school science teachers? It means that every day, high school science teachers open their doors to students who may exhibit either concrete or formal operational behaviors, or both. By understanding Piaget's stages of cognitive development and being aware that students progress from concrete to formal operations during their middle and high school grades, high school science teachers can ease and accommodate the transition from one stage to another by providing a "concrete," hands-on, and motivational experience before introducing a new, "formal" or abstract concept. By sequencing a lesson or unit of study from a hands-on mode to a lecture mode, rather than the other way around, teachers provide a lesson in a sequence compatible with the student's cognitive development. This may seem, at first, counterproductive to a high school science teacher's normal practice because most science teachers introduce a new concept by providing background information and preteaching vocabulary terms *before* doing a hands-on lab. By using a constructivist approach to lesson design, however, science teachers can plan a lesson or a unit that first engages the learner, provides a hands-on exploration or initial motivational quick lab, then explains the concept, and finally extends the concept into an inquiry investigation or full laboratory experience. It takes time for high school science teachers to feel comfortable with this new notion of constructivist lesson design. After all, most of us were taught by high school and college teachers who lectured first, then did the hands-on experience sometime later. This constructivist lesson format is called the 5E Learning Cycle and will be introduced later in the chapter.

Thus, Piaget's theory has four key principles:

1. People develop through "stages" of cognitive growth.

2. Knowledge is a result of ever-changing social interactions between the individual and the environment.

3. Knowledge is constantly being constructed and reconstructed from previous and new experiences.

4. Cognition is self-regulating within the individual and the interaction with the physical and social environment.

Lev Semenovich Vygotsky

Russian psychologist Lev S. Vygotsky was born near Minsk in western Russia in 1896, the same year as Jean Piaget. He received a law degree in 1917 from Moscow University but later turned his attention to medicine and psychology, with a specific focus on learning disabilities. In 1924, the outspoken young psychologist took exception to Pavlov and Gestalt. With the prevailing behaviorist notion that animal behavior can be applied to understand how humans learn, Vygotsky (1924/1979) contrasted animal and human behavior by describing the abilities of humans as uniquely specific to the species. According to Bodrova and Leong (1996), Vygotsky's theories on cognitive development were unique and distinct from those of his contemporaries, and although under extreme pressure to be politically correct, he never gave in to that pressure. Although many of his theories on teaching and learning were never backed up with empirical data due to his early death in 1934, researchers recently have expanded on his theories and framework on preschool and early childhood education, applying them to innovation in teaching at all grade levels.

Vygotsky made a significant contribution to cognitive development and the theory of constructivism by writing frantically for his last three years before his death from tuberculosis at the age of 37. Most of his writings were still incomplete at the time of his death and weren't translated into English until the early 1960s. His work *Thought and Language* (1934/1962) did not capture the attention of Western constructivists until its translation in 1962. Vygotsky and Piaget shared similar thoughts on constructivism; however, Vygotsky was not concerned with identifying stages of mental development. He explored the influence of language and social processes on cognitive development, as well as the accomplishments a child could achieve when solving a problem alone as compared to accomplishments achieved with assistance from an adult.

Two basic principles from the Vygotskian framework include the role language plays in mental development and the importance of social interaction within the context of learning. Whereas Piaget's theory about learning focused mainly on the interaction with physical objects, Vygotsky believed that the construction of knowledge is predicated on manipulation, but additionally is socially mediated. In his work, Vygotsky emphasized the importance of social interaction between the learner and his or her peers; thus, he was labeled as a "social constructivist." According to Vygotsky (1978), an "important factor in social learning was the young person's ability to learn by imitating and modeling. Interacting with adults and peers in cooperative settings gave young children ample opportunity to observe, imitate, and model" (pp. 79–80).

One of his foremost known theories is the Zone of Proximal Development (ZPD). According to Vygotsky, students' ability and skills to solve problems or tasks can be categorized into two levels:

1. Skills the student possesses to perform tasks independently

2. Skills the student lacks (at an independent level) so that tasks can be performed only with assistance from another student or adult

The independent level is a lower or minimum level of performance where students can operate unassisted. The assisted level is a higher or maximum level where children can reach a more complex performance with the help or assistance from another. The zone is an arbitrary continuum or area between these two levels. Most of traditional teaching is focused more closely on what students can achieve independently, but a constructivist teacher teaches to the upper zone by providing assistance to students' performance through prompts, leading questions, hints and clues, or asking students to clarify their thoughts about the phenomenon being studied. Although this interaction can be interpreted as an "expert-novice" relationship, Vygotsky believed that all students could enhance their learning through social mediation with peers or an adult.

One instructional strategy based upon the idea of the ZPD is "scaffolding" (Wood, Bruner, & Ross, 1976), a metaphor to building construction. Scaffolding provides a level of support that enables the learner to accomplish a task normally beyond his or her current capabilities. In scaffolding situations, the teacher purposefully and intentionally designs a performance task just beyond the independent level. Providing guidance at first, the teacher then gradually decreases the assistance until the student can take more responsibility for completing the task. Vygotsky suggests that teachers provide problems and tasks just beyond the student's present capabilities; through cooperative learning groups and modeling from adults, the student is scaffolded to high levels of thinking and performance.

To provide an example of scaffolding, I'll use the day I taught my daughter, Janice, to ride a two-wheeled bike. She was the only one in her 4th-grade class who wasn't riding a bike without training wheels. That was enough of an incentive for Janice to ask me for help. We got the bike out of the garage and headed for the street. At first, she practiced balancing on the bike without the training wheels while I held the bike upright. Next, we moved on to short spurts where Janice pedaled and I ran alongside, holding the bike upright. With one hand on the back of the seat, I held the bike while she pedaled down the street. I can still recall her saying, "Daddy, don't let me go!" Well, what she didn't know, as I ran alongside the bike for what seemed an eternity, was that I was sporadically letting go of the bicycle seat, allowing Janice to ride on her own. "I've got you," I said. "Just keep pedaling!" Nearly out of breath, she began to gain confidence in balancing without assistance. After a few spills and some scraped knees, she gained more confidence and achieved the goal of riding the bike on her own. I think I lost a few pounds that day running up and down the street!

In many ways, good constructivist teachers teach in the same way. They are consciously aware of the prompts and assistance they need to provide to have their students achieve at higher levels of academic performance. Constructivist and inquiry-based teachers do not make the task easier; rather, they provide the appropriate level of support and assistance for students to acquire the necessary knowledge and skills in science. Constructivist and inquiry-based teachers are also constantly aware of shifting the onus of responsibility from the teacher to the student, enabling the student to become a more independent learner. Sometimes unknowingly, high school teachers use Vygotskian principles by implementing guided, semiguided, and independent approaches to providing tasks to students. The teacher begins by providing a mental challenge task to the student. With help from the teacher or a peer, the student is guided to the solution and begins to understand the nature of the concept. With the second problem, the student is provided a semiguided practice to gain confidence and control over the task. Presented with a third problem, the student functions independently at solving the task. The teacher models appropriate behaviors and assists students to work at levels that stretch their imagination, thinking, and abilities. As the communication exchanges between the student and the teacher continue, the student begins to construct and mediate understanding of the topic.

CONSTRUCTIVISM TODAY

Currently, many educators and cognitive psychologists carry the constructivist torch for innovation in teaching and learning for mathematics and science. They include David Ausubel, Jacqueline Brooks, Jerome Bruner, Catherine Fosnot, Linda Lambert, Joseph Novak, Phillip Sadler, Ernst Von Glaserfeld, Robert Yager, and many others. Science teachers interested in learning more about constructivism and its implications to inquiry-based learning are encouraged to do further reading on the topic by these authors (see Resource A).

Constructivism today is having an increasingly significant impact on educational reform and more frequently is viewed as a valid theory on how children and adolescents learn.

In summary, key points in constructivism include the following:

1. The senses are conduits to assimilating new knowledge.

2. The learner's existing or presently held understandings determine what new situations are accepted or ignored.

3. The learner's existing or presently held understandings determine how new situations are interpreted.

4. Knowledge is not transmitted from one individual to another. Communication is transmitted, but communication or incoming information is not knowledge. Knowledge is constructed in the mind by the learner attempting to make linkages between new and previously stored knowledge within the brain.

5. The learner uses linkages to construct new understandings.

6. The learner's understanding is constantly undergoing construction and reconstruction.

7. Learning is both personally (reflection) and socially constructed (testing one's model against peers).

8. Inquiry is a viable teaching strategy to test the "degree of fit" between one's previously held theories and the "scientific" explanation of how the world actually seems to be.

METACOGNITION

It seems appropriate to take some time to present a concept that underlies basic constructivism and inquiry philosophy: metacognition. Metacognition is a term many science teachers might have heard but seldom use in their everyday language. It is, however, a concept that is fundamental to what we do and say as inquiry-based science teachers.

Metacognition refers to the awareness and regulation of one's own learning process. It encompasses an internal conversation or reflective perspective in which an individual examines his or her own thinking and learning. Metacognition is of special interest to inquiry-based teachers because it focuses the responsibility of learning on the learner and the linkage of previously held notions to new information and understandings. According to the National Research Council (2000b), "a metacognitive approach to instruction can help students learn to take control of their learning by defining learning goals and monitoring their progress to achieve them" (p. 18). The NRC goes on to state, "children can be taught strategies, including the ability to predict outcomes, explain to oneself in order to improve understanding, note failures to comprehend, activate background knowledge, plan ahead, and apportion time and memory" (NRC, 2000b, p. 18).

Metacognition strategies can be promoted and implemented in the high school science classroom by providing time for students to engage in self-reflection and to make additions, corrections, and revisions to their work. These strategies are successful in helping students use previously known information and transfer it to new situations. Problem solving, when anchored with effective and strategic questioning strategies, also serves as a vehicle to foster metacognition and critical thinking. Other metacognitive strategies include the use of concept maps (Novak, 1990, 1998; Novak & Gowin, 1989). Concept maps serve as vehicles to illustrate the hierarchical connections among related entities in all areas of science. By using concept maps, high school students practice organizational skills and develop relationship patterns. Concept maps are also excellent tools for self-assessment.

Collaboration and reflection, two key components of metacognition, often are facilitated during the inquiry process through cooperative learning groups and students using journals to record their thoughts and ideas during the course of a scientific investigation. As an encouraging note to teachers, recent findings suggest that metacognitive skills can be taught to students regardless of their innate ability and result in higher achievement (Baird, Fensham, Gunstone, & White, 1989; Nolan, 1991; Novak & Gowin, 1989).

We will see in upcoming chapters how developing a culture of inquiry provides an excellent opportunity for teachers to have students engage in reasoning, decision making, and reflection—all important aspects of metacognition.

HOW ADOLESCENTS LEARN

Two Models of Learning

Have you ever heard a teacher say, "Those kids' minds are just like a sponge soaking up knowledge?" Although some educators frequently describe an adolescent's learning from a behaviorist/objectivist perspective, constructivist teachers view things quite differently. Constructivists perceive learning as a process by which the student is a "theory builder." In constructivist philosophy, one believes that knowledge is not imparted, accumulated, absorbed, or transmitted from one individual to another. Rather, knowledge and meaning is constantly being assimilated and accommodated in the mind of cognizant beings through interpretations of their experiences and from the communication of language with others.

Prior Knowledge

Adolescents bring many levels of scientific understandings to our high school classrooms. This can be simultaneously necessary and problematic. On one hand, their prior knowledge, along with their models and theories, shapes how they interpret the natural world and new scientific information; on the other hand, prior knowledge, in the form of misconceptions, can mask the way information is interpreted and lead to unacceptable explanations (Roschelle, 1997).

David Ausubel (1968) once said, "The most important single factor influencing learning is what the learner already knows; ascertain this and teach him accordingly" (p. vi). But how, you might ask, can I get inside the heads of 28 high school students to assess their prior knowledge? Before beginning a lesson on evolution, sedimentary rocks, organic chemistry, or quantum physics, consider trying a few strategies to assess their pre-understandings. Students' prior knowledge can be ascertained simply by asking, "What do you know about [a particular subject]?" Tell students to write down on a paper whatever they know about the subject you are about to introduce. They can make a list, write a short paragraph, construct a concept map, draw a picture, or use any method that is most convenient for them. After a few minutes, pair each student with a partner to share what each recorded. Tell them that they each get a minute to share what they wrote with their partner. Next, tell them to compare their statements and look for similarities and differences. After another 2 minutes, you can ask individual students to share their statements with the entire class while you record their comments on the board or overhead, making a list or a concept map. Review their presently held conceptions and, to yourself, make mental notes of any glaring misconceptions that need to be addressed later in the unit.

Usually, simply going around the room and listening to student conversations is a productive way to assess students' prior understandings. As you visit each group of students, be especially attentive to inconsistencies in their thoughts and conversations.

Another strategy to assess students' prior knowledge involves conducting misconception interviews. Pose a question or provide a task to three students at random a few days before starting a new unit. Have the students "think aloud" and verbalize their understandings as they perform the task. Again, listen attentively for any misconceptions or naive conceptions they raise during the interview. If misconceptions arise during the interview, anticipate that other students may have similar conceptions. This will allow you to adjust and plan your lessons accordingly.

Other preassessment strategies include giving a simple pretest or using a case study discussion to elicit prior knowledge. Teachers also can give students small cards each containing a vocabulary word that will be used in an upcoming unit. Have students arrange the cards to make a concept map. Tell them to write linking words that connect one card to another.

Understanding the prior conceptions of every student in your class is nearly impossible, but by using these suggestions, teachers can anticipate many or most naive conceptions and start a lesson from the students' point of view.

Misconceptions

Everyone has a set of beliefs, conceptions, and understandings. They are part of the models and theories we hold to make sense of the world around us. Duit and Treagust (1995) suggest that "at all ages students hold conceptions about many phenomena and concepts before they are presented in the science class. These conceptions stem from and are deeply rooted in daily experiences because they have proved to be helpful and valuable in daily life" (p. 47). These conceptions that students hold are sometimes grounded in scientific truth and other times are conceived through intuitive, yet incorrect, assumptions. Educators and cognitive psychologists often refer to these incorrect models as misconceptions, but because the conceptions are conceived from what the students believe to be reality, more appropriate terms may be naive conceptions, preconceptions, alternative conceptions, or intuitive conceptions.

Preconceptions play a major role in how students interpret new incoming information. Consider the case of an 11th-grade general physics class. Ms. Nolan is introducing the concept of pendulums and poses the question, "What affects the number of swings a pendulum will make in 30 seconds?" Let's listen as Ms. Nolan works with two students, Christy and Kara.

Ms. Nolan: Ladies, what factors do you think affect the number of swings a pendulum makes?

Christy: I think it's the weight at the end of the string.

Kara: Yeah, that sounds good. It's the weight.

Ms. Nolan: What makes you think that?

Kara: Because when you swing on a swing, some people can go higher than others. So . . . (pause) . . . your weight can affect how high you swing.

Christy: I remember swinging my sister. She couldn't go as high as I could because, I guess, I weigh more. That sounds right.

Kara: I think I remember talking about this in Mr. Farrell's science class in the eighth grade.

Ms. Nolan: Now, make a hypothesis about how the weight, but let's call it the mass—how the mass affects the number of swings the pendulum makes.

Kara:	The more mass, the more swings the pendulum will make.
Ms. Nolan:	All right, how could you design an investigation to test that hypothesis?
Christy:	We would have to set up the pendulum and tie a paperclip to the end of the string. Then we could open up the paperclip to form an "S" hook and add different amounts of washers to the paperclip. We could start with one washer and keep adding a washer until we had five washers on the hook.
Ms. Nolan:	Good! How far will you pull back the washers before releasing them?
Kara:	I'd say we should pull the washers back halfway, to a 45-degree angle.
Ms. Nolan:	Will you change the angle of release?
Kara:	No, that will be the same for each trial.
Ms. Nolan:	And how many trials will you do?
Christy:	One?
Kara:	No, I think we should do three and then take the average.
Christy:	Yeah, three. Sounds good.
Ms. Nolan:	Now what about the length of the string. Will that change?
Kara:	No, that will remain the same for all the trials.
Ms. Nolan:	Why is that?
Kara:	We can have only one variable in the experiment.
Ms. Nolan:	And what's that?
Christy:	The number of washers.
Kara:	Actually, it's the mass.
Ms. Nolan:	Very good. Nice job! Now set up your experiment, and call me over when you have your data.
	(Ten minutes later, Christy calls Ms. Nolan over to their table.)
Ms. Nolan:	Well, what did you find out?
Christy:	I think our calculations are wrong. We got the same number of swings for all three trials and with all the different washers.
Kara:	We must have made a mistake somewhere. We got 12 swings for all the trials and washers. What did we do wrong?
Ms. Nolan:	Did you time the number of swings the same for all the trials?
Kara:	Yeah. We used 10 seconds for each time.
Christy:	Something is wrong with our data.
Ms. Nolan:	According to your data, the mass had no effect on the number of swings the pendulum made.
Kara:	Is our hypothesis wrong?

Christy:	No, something is wrong with our data. Let's do it all over again.
Ms. Nolan:	Well, before you do the experiment all over again, what else might affect the number of swings the pendulum makes?
Kara:	I'm not sure.
Ms. Nolan:	Could it be how far you pull back and release the washers?
Christy:	That might be it, but I still think something is wrong with our data.
Ms. Nolan:	Try to test the effect of the release point on the number of swings the pendulum makes. Design an investigation to test the release point, and call me back when you're done. Be sure to write a hypothesis first before actually carrying out your procedure.
	(Ten minutes later, Christy again calls Ms. Nolan over to their table.)
Christy:	I don't believe this. We keep getting the same number of swings each time.
Kara:	We got 12 swings, the same as before.
Ms. Nolan:	Wait a minute. Are you saying you changed the mass and it had no effect, then you changed the release point and that still had no effect?
Kara:	Yup.
Christy:	This is very confusing. I don't know what's going on. Something's fishy!
Ms. Nolan:	Okay, Let's make sense of this. You tried the mass and no effect. Then you tried the release point and it still had no effect. What else can you try?
Christy:	I don't know. Something is really fishy here.
Kara:	What about the length of string? Can we try that?
Ms. Nolan:	Okay, that's a good idea. Go back to the drawing board and design a new investigation to see if the length of the string affects the number of swings the pendulum makes. What variable will you change?
Kara:	The length of string.
Ms. Nolan:	What will remain constant in your experiment?
Christy:	The number of washers and the release point?
Ms. Nolan:	Great! You got it!
	(Ten minutes later, Christy calls Ms. Nolan over to their table.)
Kara:	I think we got it. When we changed the length of string, it changed the number of swings the pendulum made. The shorter the string, the more swings. The longer the string, the fewer swings it made.
Christy:	That's weird. I thought it was going to be the mass, not the length of the string, that affected the number of swings.
Ms. Nolan:	Where did you get your original idea?

Christy: I don't know. I guess it was from watching kids play on the playground swing. It just seemed normal to say that the mass would make a difference. So, our calculations weren't wrong. It really was the length of the string.

Ms. Nolan: Now, when you came into the lab this morning, what did you think affected the swing of the pendulum?

Christy: I thought it was the weight or mass.

Kara: Me too!

Ms. Nolan: What do you think now?

Christy: It's definitely the length of the string, not the mass.

Ms. Nolan: Did you give up on your "mass theory"?

Kara: I know I did.

Christy: We both did.

Ms. Nolan: Now, let me ask you one more question. In the beginning of the lab, if I told you that the mass did not affect the swing of the pendulum, but it was the length of the string, would you believe me?

Kara: I don't think so.

Ms. Nolan: Why not?

Christy: We had to do it ourselves. We had to actually test it to change our minds.

Ms. Nolan: Great job today!

The case of the swinging pendulum reminds us that rote learning does not usually facilitate change in conceptual understandings, especially when the misconception is deeply held. Did you notice that Kara *read* about pendulums in the eighth grade? Keep in mind that misconceptions can be stubborn. In this case, Christy and Kara held, probably for 15 years, the naive conception that the mass affected the number of swings. The authority of a teacher is not often strong enough to change students' previously held conceptions and make accommodations in their cognitive structures. Combining a constructivist approach using both hands-on and minds-on strategies does have that strength.

Conceptual Change Theory

Now let's reflect on what we read about cognitive learning theory and apply it to the case of the pendulums. According to Piaget, people form networks or schemas within the brain to store information. Both Kara's and Christy's prior experience on the playground helped them to believe that mass affects the swing of the pendulum. All incoming information is now translated through the student's schema. When a new situation arises that is inconsistent with a child's present schema (such as the data from the mass experiment), the student may either disregard the new information because it doesn't fit with the presently held notion or he or she may change or give up the previously held notion and accept a new notion based on new evidence.

Driscoll (1994) points out that questioning one's beliefs and prior conceptions can be threatening to students and lead to defensive moves. In this case, Ms. Nolan was very careful not to ridicule their previously held models, but instead effectively posed questions and prompts to lead Christy and Kara to a new level of understanding.

When a child accepts a new model, it is probably more useful, makes more sense, or is more plausible than the previously held model. Keep in mind that children, adolescents, and even adults often are reluctant to give up their presently held models and misconceptions despite what their teachers or friends tell them. As you read before, misconceptions are stubborn and sometimes very resistant to change. Conceptual change is an integral part of cognitive development. Gunstone and Mitchell (1998) tell us, "When considered in terms of an individual learner . . . it is the learner who must recognize his/her conceptions, evaluate those conceptions, [and] decide whether to reconstruct the conceptions" (p. 134).

High school students often test their theories and models through the interactions with their peers, one of the most influential aspects of their life. When their observations and experiences continue to match their presently held theories and those of their peers, the experiences are *assimilated* and the model is reinforced. When their observations and experiences do not match their presently held theories, either the experience can be discounted because it doesn't align with their understanding or the model can be *accommodated*, by a conceptual change, to include this new experience. Adolescents then continue to test their ideas, beliefs, and models through ongoing observations. Assimilation is the filtering and integration of stimuli, concepts, and external elements within the context of existing knowledge and schema, whereas accommodation is the modification and adjustment of cognitive structures to new situations. Assimilation and accommodation influencing and working together results in equilibrium.

Posner, Strike, Hewson, and Gertzog (1982) suggest that students will undergo a conceptual change when the following conditions exist:

1. They must become dissatisfied with their existing conceptions.

2. The scientific conception must be intelligible.

3. The scientific conception must be plausible.

4. The scientific conception must be useful in a variety of new situations.

The history of science is a story with theories and models that are continually tested, refined, and changed over time. Youngson (1998) tells us that getting it wrong is often the way science advances. According to Youngson, "we are prisoners of our own experience" (p. 2). Consider Ptolemy, who placed Earth in the center of the solar system, or Lamarck, who proposed a theory of evolution based on the length of the giraffe's long neck. Do you remember the hoopla and fiasco about cold fusion? Yet probably no other theory has changed as much as that of the structure of the atom. In words that have been attributed to Thomas Huxley, "The great tragedy of science is slaying a beautiful hypothesis by an ugly fact."

Making Sense of Language

If we were to think that knowledge is imparted solely through language between teacher and students, why do teachers often find themselves teaching a concept one day and discovering the next day that the students just did not "get it"? If my teaching philosophy was based upon assumptive learning, I might assume that learning occurs because the students are listening to me, the teacher. But just because students are listening to me does not mean that they are always making sense of the words coming out of my mouth. Words are a sensory input that the learner must act upon.

Consider the case of a biology class just beginning a unit on the parts of the cell. On the first day of the unit, Mrs. Bell introduces the various cell organelles by writing their names and functions on the board. As students are copying notes, she is spelling out words and phrases such as mitochondria, ribosome, endoplasmic reticulum, Golgi bodies, and nuclear membrane. The words are part of the sender's (the teacher's) everyday language and experience, but not part of the receivers' (the students'). In this case, the terms make perfect sense to the teacher but may not mean anything at this point to the students. Thus, language is an important aspect of learning in a constructivist approach. The student needs a language connection, based upon his or her previous experience, to make sense of what is currently being said. We can see in the organelle lesson that the teacher had the cognitive structure (schema) to make sense of these terms. In the case of students without the cognitive structure to make sense of these terms, the words enter the brain through the ear, look for connections, and, finding none, get filtered out. Students are left with puzzled looks on their faces.

THE 5E LEARNING CYCLE

There are several implications to the constructivist learning model. The 5E Learning Cycle is one of them. Like constructivism, the 5E Learning Cycle is not new. It was originally proposed for elementary school science programs in the early 1960s by J. Myron Atkin and Robert Karplus (1962) and further documented by Lawson, Abraham, and Renner (1989), Beisenherz and Dantonio (1996), Marek and Cavallo (1997), Bybee (1997), Abraham (1997), and Colburn and Clough (1997). In the last 10 years, however, it has become a popular model for high school teachers too. Many articles in *The American Biology Teacher* refer to the learning cycle approach as an effective lesson format. In addition, the Biological Sciences Curriculum Study (BSCS), a premier curriculum developer in the area of biology, uses the 5E format for its instructional model. Unlike traditional three-step lesson plans in science that begin with introducing new vocabulary, then providing a step-by-step lab to verify the information presented, and finally finishing with an end-of-chapter problem or test, the 5E Learning Cycle model (see Figure 3.1) is a constructivist teaching strategy that includes five stages consistent with cognitive theories on how learning occurs:

- Engagement
- Exploration
- Explanation
- Elaboration or Extension
- Evaluation

Figure 3.1   The Learning Cycle

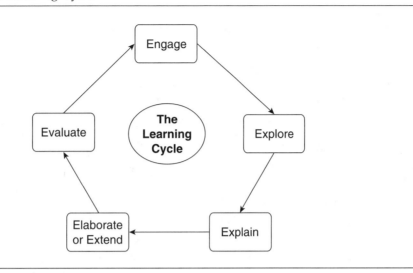

During the **Engagement** stage, the teacher sets the stage for learning. This is accomplished by stating the purpose of the lesson. Often, the teacher introduces the topic of the lesson and states the expectations for learning by explaining what students should know and be able to do by the end of the lesson or unit. The Engagement phase is also a means of getting the students' attention and focus. By using attention-grabbing demonstrations and discrepant events (Liem, 1987), the teacher creates ways to "hook" students into learning. Discrepant events generate interest and curiosity that set the stage for inquiring about a particular phenomenon. Discrepant events serve to create cognitive dissonance—or, in Piaget's words, disequilibrium—because the observation of such events does not readily assimilate into the student's presently held understanding. Because the observations made from discrepant events are counterintuitive to the students' prior experience, the students quickly activate questions.

From a constructivist perspective, the Engagement phase also provides an opportunity for the teacher to activate learning, assess prior knowledge, and have students share their prior experiences about the topic. During the Engagement stage, the teacher can note possible naive conceptions or misconceptions stated by the students. These misconceptions can be addressed during and after the students have an opportunity to work through the Exploration and Explanation stages. It should be noted that it is nearly impossible for any teacher to fully ascertain all the misconceptions held by all the students. The learning cycle, specifically the Engagement stage, does, however, provide the teacher with a means of assessing students' current beliefs and understandings.

The **Exploration** stage is an excellent place to engage high school students in inquiry-based labs or teacher-initiated inquiries. During the Exploration stage, students raise questions, develop hypotheses to test, and work without direct instruction from the teacher. They go about collecting evidence and data, recording and organizing information, sharing observations, and working in cooperative groups. The Exploration stage allows students to build on a common experience as they carry out their investigations. This common experience or exploration is essential because students will enter the classroom with different levels of experience and knowledge about the topic being studied. The Exploration stage allows all students to experience hands-on learning and helps "level the playing field" within a culturally diverse classroom. The Exploration stage also provides opportunities for students with diverse experiences to share their different understandings and broaden the perspective of the entire class.

During the teacher-directed **Explanation** stage, the teacher facilitates data- and evidence-processing techniques for the individual groups or entire class (depending on the nature of the investigation) from the information collected during the exploration. Information is discussed, and the teacher often explains the scientific concepts associated with the exploration by providing a common language for the class to use. This common (or scientific) language helps students articulate their thinking and describe their investigations and experiences in scientific terms. The teacher can continue to introduce details, vocabulary terms, and definitions to the lesson as students assimilate their understanding against the "scientific" explanation. This can be accomplished by using direct instruction/lecturing, audiovisual resources, online sources, and computer software programs. Here, the teacher uses the students' prior experiences to explain the concepts and attempts to address misconceptions uncovered during the Engagement or Exploration stages. The Explanation stage is sometimes called the "Concept Development" stage because evidence and newly developed concepts are assimilated into the cognitive structure of the student. During the Explanation stage, students may work to assimilate or accommodate new information as they make sense of their understanding, "constructing" new meaning from their experience and conceptual change.

During the **Elaboration or Extension** stage, the teacher helps reinforce the concept by extending and applying the evidence to new and real-world situations outside the classroom. This stage also facilitates the construction of valid generalizations by the students, who also may modify their presently held understandings of the phenomena being studied. During the Elaboration stage, teachers can provide follow-up, student-initiated inquiries and expand upon the teacher-initiated inquiry from the Exploration stage.

During the **Evaluation** stage, the teacher brings closure to the lesson or unit by helping students summarize the relationship between the variables studied in the lesson and posing higher-order questions that help them to make judgments, analyses, and evaluations about their work. Connections among the concepts just studied and other topics can be illustrated by using a concept map. Here, the teacher can compare the prior knowledge that was identified during the Engagement stage with the newly formed understanding gained from the lesson.

On the assessment side, the teacher will provide a means for students to assess their learning and make connections from prior understandings to new situations that encourage the application of concepts and problem-solving skills. Assessment strategies may include monitoring charts or checklists, portfolios, rubrics, and student self-evaluations. Later, in Chapter 8, we will address these assessment strategies.

The Biological Science Curriculum Study (BSCS) provides an excellent summary of the 5E Learning Cycle by indicating descriptors for the students as well as the teachers regarding consistency with the model. (See Figures 3.2 and 3.3.)

Figure 3.2   What the Student Does

Stage of the Instruction Model	What the Student Does . . .	
	That Is Consistent With the 5E Model	That Is Inconsistent With the 5E Model
Engage	Asks questions, such as: Why did this happen? What do I already know about this? Shows interest in the topic	Asks for the "right" answer Offers the "right" answer Insists on answers or explanations Seeks one solution
Explore	Thinks freely, but within the limits of the activity Tests predictions and hypotheses Forms new predictions and hypotheses Tries alternatives and discusses them with others Records observations and ideas Suspends judgment	Lets other do the thinking and exploring (passive involvement) Works quietly with little or no interaction with others (only appropriate when exploring ideas or feelings) "Plays around" indiscriminately with no goal in mind Stops with one solution
Explain	Explains possible solutions or answers to others Listens critically to others' explanations Questions one another's explanations Listens to and tries to comprehend explanations the teacher offers Refers to previous activities Uses recorded observations in explanations	Proposes explanations from "thin air" with no relationship to previous experiences Brings up irrelevant experiences and examples Accepts explanations without justification Does not attend to other plausible explanations
Elaborate	Applies new labels, definitions, explanations, and skills in new but similar situations Uses previous information to ask questions, propose solutions, make decisions, and design experiments Draws reasonable conclusions from evidence Records observations and explanations Checks for understanding among peers	"Plays around" with no goal in mind Ignores previous information or evidence Draws conclusions from "thin air" Uses only those labels that the teacher provided
Evaluate	Answers open-ended questions by using observations, evidence, and previously accepted explanations Demonstrates an understanding or knowledge of the concept or skill Evaluates his or her own progress and knowledge Asks related questions that would encourage future investigations	Draws conclusions without using evidence or previously accepted explanations Offers only yes or no answers and memorized definitions or explanations Fails to express satisfactory explanations in his or her own words Introduces new, irrelevant topics

Figure 3.3   What the Teacher Does

Stage of the Instruction Model	What the Student Does . . .	
	That Is Consistent *With the 5E Model*	*That Is* Inconsistent *With the 5E Model*
Engage	Creates interest Generates curiosity Raises questions Elicits responses that uncover what the students know or think about the concept/topic	Explains concepts Provides definitions and answers States conclusions Provides closure Lectures
Explore	Encourages the students to work together without direct instruction from the teacher Observes and listens to the students as they interact Asks probing questions to redirect the students' investigations when necessary Provides time for students to puzzle through problems Acts as a consultant for students	Provides answers Tells or explains how to work through the problem Provides closure Tells the students that they are wrong Gives information or facts that solve the problem Leads the students step-by-step to a solution
Explain	Encourages the students to explain concepts and definitions in their own words Asks for justification (evidence) and clarification from students Formally provides definitions, explanations, and new labels Uses students' previous experiences as the basis for explaining concepts	Accepts explanations that have no justification Neglects to solicit the students' explanations Introduces unrelated concepts or skills
Elaborate	Expects the students to use formal labels, definitions, and explanations provided previously Encourages the students to apply or extend the concepts and skills in new situations Reminds the students of alternative explanations Refers the students to existing data and evidence and asks: What do you already know? Why do you think . . .? (strategies from explore apply here also).	Provides definitive answers Tells the students that they are wrong Lectures Leads students step-by-step to a solution Explains how to work through the problem
Evaluate	Observes the students as they apply new concepts and skills Assesses students' knowledge and/or skills Looks for evidence that the students have changed their thinking or behaviors Allows students to assess their own learning and group-process skills Asks open-ended questions, such as: Why do you think . . .? What evidence do you have? What do you know about x? How would you explain x?	Tests vocabulary words, terms, and isolated facts Introduces new ideas or concepts Creates ambiguity Promotes open-ended discussion unrelated to the concept or skill

SOURCE: BSCS 5E Model reprinted from *BSCS Biology: A Human Approach*. Copyright 2003 by BSCS, published by Kendall/Hunt Publishing Company. Reproduced with permission.

CHALLENGES TO CREATING A CONSTRUCTIVIST CLASSROOM CULTURE

An obvious question arises at this point: If constructivism has so many valid attributes to enhance student learning, why aren't more teachers implementing constructivist strategies like the 5E Learning Cycle in their classrooms? The answer to the question may begin with the term *constructivist strategies*.

Constructivism should be viewed not as a set of teaching strategies, but rather as a theory about how learning occurs. To become a constructivist teacher, one needs to focus on developing and sustaining a *culture of constructivism* within the classroom rather than implementing a set of loosely coupled strategies or practices. According to Windschitl (1999), "before teachers and administrators adopt such practices, they should understand that constructivism cannot make its appearance in the classroom as a set of isolated instructional methods grafted on to otherwise traditional teaching techniques. Rather, it is a culture—a set of beliefs, norms, and practices that constitute the fabric of school life" (p. 752). Developing a constructivist classroom culture is an arduous process. It means taking on new challenges and unfamiliar norms. This new role does not occur overnight. Becoming an inquiry-based teacher takes years of sustained perseverance and reflection.

There are several challenges in transforming from the behaviorist-objectivist practices to a culture of constructivism. By examining these issues, we also question our own beliefs and values about good teaching and learning. Our journey to a constructivist culture begins with taking a risk to challenge our classroom norms and teaching paradigm.

1. Familiarity With Pedagogy: Despite its popularity in the research and journals, coupled with an increasing number of teachers embracing constructivist principles, many high school science teachers are still not familiar with the concept of constructivism. Most science teachers are well equipped in providing hands-on and problem-solving activities to students, but a lack of a philosophical foundation in learning theory often prevails. Looking back to their preservice education courses, many teachers cite the lack of constructivist role models, especially in college-level science content courses. Too often, teachers face lecture-centered college instructors in the science content areas who teach in a traditional, didactic format where learning is seen as externally motivated rather than internally motivated. This supports the notion that "teachers teach as they have been taught."

2. High-Stakes Assessments: Often the end-of-the-year, multiple-choice examination does not accurately assess achievement of all the goals of a constructivist teacher. With the increased emphasis on statewide standardized tests and the pressure teachers face to have their students perform at high levels of achievement, it is no wonder we hear the phase "teaching to the test." Constructivist educators constantly struggle with the balance between providing specific learning opportunities that best respond to the students' prior experiences and present understandings and the reality that high-stakes standardized assessments are not going away. For constructivist teachers to align their instructional goals with assessment goals, they need the flexibility to have students demonstrate their competencies using forms of assessment other than paper-and-pencil, objective-type examinations. Project-based

goals, critical thinking, cooperative learning, and problem-solving skills are not normally assessed on standardized tests. Thus, a shift toward the use of journals, portfolios, performance tasks with rubrics, and self-assessments becomes essential.

3. Curriculum and Standards: With the compliance to new state and national standards, the "one-size-fits-all" approach to curriculum does not always complement a constructivist culture. That does not mean that constructivist teachers do not have high standards for their students, but having standards, without flexibility, for differentiating individual instruction is not always compatible with a constructivist philosophy. Given the pressures of standardized instruction, many schools and teachers do not have the luxury of reducing the curricula load despite the call from some educational reform experts that "less is more." Constructivist teachers face the challenge of finding ways to do fewer topics in greater depth while still meeting national or state standards.

4. Daily Schedule: As teachers provide the opportunity for students to problem solve and design their own investigations, the daily schedule of 45-minute periods soon becomes constraining. For teachers to implement constructivist and inquiry-based strategies, block scheduling becomes a viable alternative for extended instructional time and opportunities for teachers across disciplines to integrate their curricula and develop team teaching partnerships. A block schedule may also give time for a team of teachers to redesign the curriculum and environment into theme-based and project-based units of study. Block scheduling also can provide common planning time for cross-content teachers to engage in discourse and reflection.

5. Textbooks: Textbooks are the greatest single source of information from printed materials used in high schools today. Look in any high school or college science classroom and you will probably find a single textbook being used. Because textbooks are written for a national audience, publishers fear swaying too far from the "middle of the road" from what schools expect in a textbook. With the exception of some authors like the BSCS and Paul Hewitt, writers of high school science textbooks preteach vocabulary and introduce concepts before students have an opportunity to explore a new phenomenon. To move toward a constructivist culture, teachers and administrators should consider a multitext approach while using primary sources of relevant information.

6. Professional Development: Although many agree that professional development is a continuous, lifelong process, too often teachers experience professional development as fragmented, one-shot workshops or in-services that center on the transmission of either content knowledge or classroom management skills presented from the speaker to the audience. In creating a constructivist and inquiry-based culture, according to the NRC (1996), "the conventional view of professional development for teachers needs to shift from technical training for specific skills to opportunities for intellectual professional growth" (p. 58). Such opportunities may include understanding the theoretical foundations for constructivism along with teaching strategies consisting of scaffolding, modeling, cooperative learning, and implementing performance assessments. The NRC goes on to say that "when teachers have the time and opportunity to describe their own views about learning and teaching, and to compare, contrast, and revise their views, they come to understand the nature of exemplary science teaching" (NRC, 1996, p. 67).

To cultivate a constructivist culture, teachers need to develop a new vision about teaching and learning founded on research-based knowledge and then work to change their practices to achieve their vision (Gallagher, 1993). Because visions are often met through collaboration, you need to realize that you cannot fulfill your vision effectively doing it alone. Transforming classroom norms and altering past practices requires a support system sustained over time.

Comparing Traditional and Inquiry-Based Science Classrooms

A TRADITIONAL CLASSROOM

Traditional high school science classrooms usually look different from inquiry-based classrooms. That is not to say that traditional classrooms are any better or worse than inquiry-based classrooms; it just means the behaviors of the students and the teacher, as well as the appearance of the physical environment of the classroom, are different. There are instances, such as the first week of school, or when making an expository presentation through direct instruction, or when presenting an imposing amount of information in a short amount of time, that a teacher might prefer a more traditional or teacher-centered classroom. In a traditional classroom setting, students usually sit in straight rows of desks (assigned by the teacher) and learn through rote memorization. Students attentively listen to the teacher, who is standing in the front of the room or behind a demonstration table "imparting" information, while passively taking notes from the blackboard or overhead projector. The recitation may be followed by a question-and-answer session in which students are presented with queries that summarize the lesson and evaluate the students' understanding of the concept presented. The lesson is structured around "teacher talk" and student responses. A single textbook usually guides the teacher's presentation and provides additional readings and questions for further discussion and homework.

In teacher-centered classrooms, demonstrations are often used by the teacher to arouse interest or reinforce a concept that was previously introduced. The demonstration also enables the teacher to model a particular phenomenon and provide all the students with an observable experience from which an explanation or a discussion may follow. Discussions are also an important aspect of traditional science classrooms; however, in teacher-centered classrooms, the line of communication is too often an interaction between the teacher and one student at a time. Toward the end of the unit, the teacher provides the students with a cookbook-type laboratory to verify that the information presented on previous days' lectures is correct. At the end of the lesson or unit, students' understanding is evaluated through an objective-type test containing true/false or multiple-choice questions.

The walls of the traditional high school science room probably show a periodic table of elements, commercially made pictures of scientists (no self-respecting science classroom would be without a picture of Albert Einstein), and safety posters to remind students of the proper conduct for laboratory behavior.

If inquiry is so publicly touted, why do we still find a large percentage of high school science classrooms to be so teacher-directed? The answer to the question may lie in the relative ease of expository teaching, the standards and assessment constraints that teachers face, and teachers' previously held beliefs about "good" teaching and learning. According to Jorgenson and Vanosdall (2002),

> despite the increasing numbers of schools and districts that are embracing inquiry-based science instruction, the vast majority of our public schools still rely on the traditional "drill and kill" model of teaching science: students study textbooks, watch videotapes on various topics, answer the questions found at the end of the chapter, and perhaps observe an occasional demonstration performed by the teacher. Ultimately, they display their knowledge on a paper-and-pencil test. (p. 603)

THE ENVIRONMENT OF AN INQUIRY-BASED CLASSROOM

Inquiry-based classrooms are quite different. We can differentiate the characteristics of traditional and inquiry-based classrooms by examining three areas: what the classroom looks like, what the students do, and what the teacher does.

To begin with, inquiry-based classrooms are often described as student- or learner-centered. That doesn't mean that traditional classrooms cannot be student- or learner-centered; however, there are some common features usually found in inquiry-based environments. In these classrooms, we usually find a culture that is friendly and facilitating. The atmosphere promotes an effective learning situation by making the students feel that their teacher and peers value their ideas, thoughts, and opinions. The classroom provides a positive socialization promoting active involvement along with inter- and intrapersonalization.

In inquiry and student-centered classrooms, we often find the following:

1. "What if . . ." and "I wonder . . ." questions posted throughout the room

2. Concept maps and graphic organizers displayed on the walls

3. Evidence of student work displayed and celebrated throughout the room

4. Students' desks arranged in a "U" shape or in groups of two, three, or four

5. Separate learning centers for extension investigations, as well as individual and small group work

6. A collection of fiction and nonfiction books, science magazines and journals, and other primary sources of information on the shelves

7. A box or a crate for student portfolios and reflection journals

8. A daily schedule that accommodates extended or multiple-period investigations through block scheduling or double periods

9. Materials and supplies readily available in bins or containers with areas set aside for storing projects and extended investigations

10. Videotaping equipment available for recording student presentations and analyzing students' performance

11. Computer resources available for accessing Internet sources and containing supplemental software to review or reinforce science topics

12. Classroom sets or collections of multiple textbooks for in-class usage and/or student sign-out

STUDENTS IN AN INQUIRY-BASED CLASSROOM

Like the classroom culture, students in an inquiry-based classroom demonstrate different behaviors and habits of mind from their counterparts in traditional classrooms. In an inquiry-based science classroom, high school students will do the following:

1. Show an interest and imagination in science by acting as researchers/investigators and viewing themselves as scientists

2. Engage in diligent investigations from their self-generated questions

3. Reflect on and take responsibility for their individual learning

4. Persist in asking questions to clarify and confirm the accuracy of their understandings

5. Work and communicate in thoughtful groups

6. Utilize higher-order thinking skills to solve problems and make judgments about their work

7. Consider skepticism and alternative models or points of view

8. Use unbiased data and evidence to form explanations

9. Connect new knowledge to prior understandings

10. Make decisions as to how to communicate their work

11. Demonstrate their science understandings and abilities in a variety of forms

12. Act as "reflective friends" through peer evaluation to seek other opinions and assess the strengths and limitations of their work

Students Acting as Researchers

Like the heart pumping blood, commitment, curiosity, and imagination pump questions throughout the learners' thought process. When students act as researchers, they take on a new role in an inquiry-based classroom. Action research leads students to using integrated process skills such as identifying variables, writing hypotheses, designing experiments and investigations, constructing data tables and graphs, and analyzing relationships between variables.

Having students act as researchers is a challenging endeavor for both the students and the teacher. For students to take on this new role, teachers must assume a new role too. Teachers must believe that students have the skills and interest to carry out their own investigations and generate their own ideas. When students act as researchers, they start taking responsibility for their own learning. That means students are given the opportunity to raise their own questions on a topic of their choice. Many students prefer answering their own questions to solving someone else's problems. It also means students can make decisions about their own work: how they will collect data, how they will organize the data they collect, and how they will communicate their findings to the rest of the class. By planning and designing their inquiries, students begin to use higher-level thinking skills, such as analyzing and evaluating, to guide the design and course of their investigations. Teachers will also begin to find that they need to provide fewer answers and more support to students. This support may include guiding the students to a location to search the Internet for a particular topic, suggesting they call a local expert on the topic, or recommending primary sources for the students to review.

According to the *National Science Education Standards*, in order to challenge students to accept and share responsibility for their own work,

> teachers [should] make it clear that each student must take responsibility for his or her work. Teachers also create opportunities for [students'] own learning, individually and as members of groups. Teachers do so by supporting student ideas and questions and by encouraging students to pursue them. Teachers give individual students active roles in the design and implementation of investigations, in the work with their peers, and in student assessment of their own work. (NRC, 1996, p. 36)

Students Working in Groups

According to the American Association for the Advancement of Science (1990),

> the collaborative nature of science and technological work should be strongly reinforced by frequent group activity in the classroom. Scientists and engineers work mostly in groups and less often as isolated investigators. Similarly, students should gain experience sharing responsibility for learning with each other. (p. 202)

There are many instances when students should work individually and other times when collaborative group work is most appropriate. This decision is often left to the discretion of the teacher, depending on the objective and nature of the lesson being studied. Group work can help students learn from each other, share and challenge their ideas, and distribute the work in an equitable fashion. This way, students learn to construct knowledge together and build positive peer relationships. Group work also allows students to build self-confidence while working collaboratively in a group to complete a common goal. Having students work in groups, however, always requires consideration of gender and cultural equity, as well as the interests, needs, and abilities of the group members.

According to Adams and Hamm (1998),

> cooperative learning is more than having students cooperate in a group activity or project. There is a set of strategies that encourage student cooperation while learning in a variety of settings, disciplines, and different grade levels. The process involves promoting positive interdependence by dividing the workload, providing joint rewards, holding individuals accountable, and getting students actively involved in helping each other master the topic being studied. Creative social engagement is paramount. (p. 2)

In high school settings, group work often becomes louder than traditional seat-time work. Because students are expected to communicate, debate, and move about the room while working in groups, classroom management techniques become essential. Students need and want rules of conduct to be established. They want to know the limits of classroom behavior. Problems often occur in inquiry-based classrooms when the teacher fails to effectively communicate group work expectations. The teacher can enhance the effectiveness of classroom rules by having students participate in deciding what rules need to be enforced while doing a scientific investigation. The students can agree to the rules and post them in the classroom. Classes can consider adopting rules of conduct by citing the positive behaviors that are expected (starting with the word *Do*) rather than rules written in a negative tone (starting with the word *Don't*).

Students Utilizing Higher-Level Thinking Skills

In a community of inquirers, utilizing exploration and discourse strategies stimulates students to think critically about the data and evidence accumulated during their inquiry. This motivates students to analyze and synthesize the data and to make judgments and evaluations concerning their evidence and conclusions. These types of thinking skills are far superior in developing scientific literacy than the lower-level, knowledge-type questions often repeatedly posed to students in traditional classrooms, where the recall of science fact is valued. In contrast, as students experience inquiry investigations, they use thinking skills that cause them to reflect about their work and pose logical arguments to defend their conclusions.

Students Showing Interest in Science

"Why do we have to learn this stuff anyway?" one 12th-grade girl asked in her physics class. "Because," the teacher responded, "it's going to be on the test." Have you been asked this question? It seems every teacher has, at some time in his or her career. From the point of view of the student, what does the question mean? Does it mean she doesn't like physics? Does it mean she doesn't like this particular lesson? Or does it mean she doesn't understand what she is expected to do? All we know at this point is that the student might not see the relevance of the content she's expected to learn.

Posing problems of importance and relevance to students is an integral aspect of inquiry and constructivist teaching (Brooks & Brooks, 1999). That does not mean that in inquiry classrooms the student decides what he or she wants to learn and when. Nor does it mean that we have to wait until the student wants to learn about Newtonian physics before the topic can be presented. It does mean, however, that in inquiry-based classrooms the teacher mediates relevance by engaging students in meaningful problem-solving investigations. According to Brooks and Brooks (1999), "The inquiring teacher mediates the classroom environment in accordance with both the primary concept she has chosen for the class' inquiry and her growing understanding of students' emerging interests and cognitive abilities within the concept" (p. 380). Making learning meaningful is another central theme in inquiry-based learning. Brooks and Brooks go on to say,

> It's unfortunate that much of what we seek to teach our students is of little interest to them at that particular point in their lives. Curriculums and syllabi developed by publishers or state-level specialists are based on adult notions of what students of different ages need to know. Even when the topics are of interest to students, the recommended methodologies for teaching the topics sometimes are not. Little wonder, then, why more of those magnificent moments don't occur. (p. 106)

In inquiry-based classrooms, students are engaged in investigations that interest them, through prompting and mediation from the teacher. As a result, students demonstrate open-mindedness and curiosity, and they gain an appreciation for and positive attitude toward science as well. Seeing themselves working as researchers and scientists does much to promote interest in science and encourages students to pursue further science courses in the years ahead.

TEACHERS IN AN INQUIRY-BASED CLASSROOM

The teacher's ABCs (attitudes, behaviors, and competencies) are paramount in inquiry-based classrooms. They set the stage for teaching and active learning. When observing inquiry-based high school teachers, we often see styles of presentation, organization, questioning skills, and even body language that differ from those observed in traditional settings. The following is a list of 40 attitudes, behaviors, and competencies that often accompany inquiry-based teaching. In high school classrooms, inquiry science teachers

1. use the *National Science Education Standards* and statewide standards to guide their long-range instructional plans;

2. select learning experiences that align with the national standards and the students' interests and abilities;

3. create a classroom culture that encourages positive scientific attitudes and habits of mind;

4. provide opportunities for metacognitive strategies;

5. stimulate and nurture students' curiosity;

6. limit the use of lecturing and direct instruction to occasions when the lesson cannot be taught through hands-on or inquiry-based instruction;

7. demonstrate flexibility by balancing and mediating their preplanned lessons and questions with the activities and directions prompted by students' questions;

8. assess students' prior knowledge at the start of a lesson or unit of study;

9. use students' prior knowledge as a basis for introducing new concepts and accommodating the lesson plan based on misconceptions;

10. make learning relevant and meaningful by exploring student interests, taking student interests into account, and basing lessons on students' prior suppositions;

11. use counterintuitive demonstrations and discrepant events to pose contradictions and challenge students' previously held conceptions;

12. use inquiries and investigations to "anchor" new information to previously held knowledge;

13. initiate classroom dialogue and discourse by posing essential or starter questions, offering prompts, and demonstrating thought-provoking discrepant events throughout the lesson;

14. ask questions that require higher-level and critical thinking skills;

15. use wait-time (Rowe, 1974, 1987, 1996) techniques appropriately and do not interrupt students in the middle of their questions and/or answers;

16. rephrase student questions and responses so students can begin to answer their own questions;

17. plan lessons utilizing the 5E Learning Cycle;

18. refrain from divulging answers and pose prompts to clarify students' questions;

19. say "Thank you" or "Great answer" in response to student contributions and give positive reinforcement for student contributions and exemplary work;

20. ask follow-up questions to student answers rather than saying "Okay" or just repeating the student answer;

21. maintain appropriate classroom management during hands-on investigations by displaying rules in a positive sense, providing expectations and structure, and creating a safe and well-organized room;

22. establish everyday routines for group interaction and when retrieving and returning materials;

23. arrange students' desks for collaborative work in small groups;

24. focus the lesson on engaging and relevant problem-solving situations;

25. move about the classroom and rotate among the small groups throughout the lesson;

26. encourage students to design and carry out their own investigations;

27. kneel to make on-level, eye-to-eye contact when speaking to students in small group settings;

28. value students' responses and view wrong answers as an "open door" to their naive conceptions or misconceptions;

29. keep students on task by having them support and debate their data, evidence, and conclusions;

30. use instructional classroom time effectively and efficiently by beginning the lesson on time and using the entire period for instructional purposes, not as time to do homework;

31. integrate science content with process skills and problem-solving strategies as well as mathematics, technology, and other subjects;

32. act as a facilitator, mediator, initiator, and coach, while modeling the behaviors of inquiry, curiosity, and wonder;

33. use primary sources of information rather than, or in conjunction with, commercially published textbooks;

34. encourage communication skills such as speaking and listening;

35. moderate classroom discussions so all students can share their points of view;

36. encourage students to use concept maps, graphic organizers, and drawings of models to explain and demonstrate newly acquired knowledge;

37. assess student performance in a variety of forms;

38. monitor student progress continuously on a daily basis;

39. assist students in assessing their own progress;

40. keep current in teaching methods by joining a professional organization, such as
    - the National Science Teachers Association,
    - the National Association of Biology Teachers,
    - the National Earth Science Teachers Association,
    - the American Association for Physics Teachers,

    and reading appropriate journals, such as

    - *The Science Teacher,*
    - *The American Biology Teacher,*
    - *The Physics Teacher.*

For more information on the attitudes, behaviors, and competencies of an inquiry-based teacher, see Chapter 3, "Science Teaching Standards," from the *National Science Education Standards* (NRC, 1996).

BECOMING AN INQUIRY-BASED TEACHER

Many teachers will admit that the journey to become an inquiry-based teacher is a very personal experience. Each of us makes the journey in different ways by constructing our own paths to instructional renewal and reform. Regardless of the path one takes, the transition to becoming an inquiry-based teacher usually follows four distinct stages: starting at *the traditional approach*, next *exploring inquiry*, followed by *transitioning to inquiry*, and finally *practicing inquiry* (Llewellyn, 2002). At each stage, teachers will exhibit and demonstrate increasingly effective inquiry strategies.

Becoming an inquiry-based teacher will require creating and sustaining reflection practices and discourse with other teachers. As Sergiovanni (1996) puts it, "good teaching requires that teachers reflect on their practice, and create knowledge in use as they analyze problems, size up situations, and make decisions" (p. 151). For that reason, teachers need to develop a network to offer encouragement and support. Forming inquiry support groups allows teachers to share their lessons, accomplishments, and frustrations. A local college or university science education department can be a source for developing and facilitating a teacher study and support group. Finally, the school administration must demonstrate trust that teachers can make the appropriate curricular decisions to bring inquiry-based instructional strategies and change to the classroom level. Lack of support from peers and administration has discouraged many teachers from building their capacity to develop inquiry-centered classrooms.

Regardless of how you plan to begin increasing your ability to teach through inquiry, my best advice is not to do it alone. Seek out a friend or a group of people who share your values and beliefs about teaching. Ongoing conversation with colleagues will help enhance your skills and development.

Regarding the impetus to change your instructional practice, the most effective results occur when motivation stems from both an internal and an external locus of control. Combining motivation from internally (yourself) as well as externally (peer support groups and administration) sources, teachers will find the journey exhilarating and fruitful.

Integrating Inquiry-Based Activities

PROMOTING STUDENT INQUIRIES

At this point, you have a good idea what an inquiry-based classroom looks like—what the teacher does, what the students do, and how the classroom environment may be arranged. We can now focus our attention on describing the investigations and inquiries that take place within and outside these classroom walls. This chapter will distinguish between typical science activities and laboratory experiences, on one hand, and those investigations that encourage students to pose questions and pursue their own answers, on the other.

High school science teachers new to inquiry usually ask three questions: What are the essential elements of an inquiry-based activity? How does an inquiry investigation compare and contrast to the typical textbook lab I do in class? and How do I get my students started in an inquiry activity if they have no prior experience in inquiry? Exploration of these three questions is essential for any teacher beginning to develop an inquiry-centered classroom. This chapter will answer all three questions.

At the high school level, every day teachers face daily prepubescent and "budding" adolescents whose bodies are filled with hormones and emotions that ride like a roller coaster. High school students are often self-conscious about raising questions and reluctant to give answers, because by doing so they risk the appearance of "standing out" in the class. For this reason, high school science teachers who have students with little prior experience in inquiry should introduce their classes gradually to student-initiated investigations. The "Invitation to Inquiry Grid" (Llewellyn, 2002) serves as a means to identify and categorize levels of inquiry-based instruction and guide more traditional-thinking students into reasoning and acting more like scientists and researchers.

INVITATION TO INQUIRY

Most laboratory experiments and activities that high school teachers do in science can be divided into three essential and distinct sections:

1. Posing the question

2. Planning the procedure

3. Formulating the results

Depending on whether each of the three sections is either posed by the teacher or completed by the students, the activity can result in different learning experiences. Picture, if you will, a high school science teacher posing a question to his or her students. Picture the teacher describing how the procedure of the "experiment" will take place, and picture the teacher actually performing the steps of the science "experiment." Also imagine the teacher guiding or providing the results of the "experiment" and then formulating the conclusions by providing an analysis and summary of the "experiment." We will call this scenario a *demonstration*. In a second situation, picture the teacher posing the question to the students and then providing a step-by-step procedure for answering the question. The students will then follow the procedure and formulate the results on their own. We will call this scenario a *lab* or an *activity*. In a third situation, picture the teacher posing the question to the students and then allowing the students to plan their own procedures and formulate their own results. We will call this a *teacher-initiated inquiry*. In our final situation, visualize the students posing their own questions, planning a procedure for answering the questions, and then carrying out the procedure and formulating the results. We will call this a *student-initiated inquiry*.

Figure 5.1 summarizes the four levels of instruction, with each higher level serving as a vehicle to further invite student-initiated questions and student-directed procedures that will encourage and fortify inquiry.

Figure 5.1   Invitation to Inquiry Grid

	Demonstration	**Activity**	**Teacher-Initiated Inquiry**	**Student-Initiated Inquiry**
Posing the Question	Teacher	Teacher	Teacher	Student
Planning the Procedure	Teacher	Teacher	Student	Student
Formulating the Results	Teacher	Student	Student	Student

SOURCE: Llewellyn (2002, p. 64).

DEMONSTRATIONS

According to Figure 5.1, demonstrations focus the attention and the control of the instructional situation around the teacher and the phenomenon being exhibited. Many science teachers are very familiar with doing demonstrations because they play an important role in teaching science-related topics. Some concepts and topics are best presented through demonstrations. Why? For the teacher, doing demonstrations captures the attention of the audience and keeps students engaged. For the students, demonstrations are usually interesting, thought provoking, and enjoyable to observe.

Why do science teachers do demonstrations? There are several excellent reasons. Teachers do demonstrations when

- all students need to observe a particular phenomenon;
- the procedure is complicated for students to follow;
- the results of the phenomenon need to be guided or controlled;
- dangerous, toxic, or flammable materials are used;
- an explosion may (or will) result;
- safety is a concern;
- materials or equipment are limited;
- expensive chemicals, equipment, or other supplies are being used;
- time is of the essence.

You probably can think of many other reasons to do demonstrations. Traditional demonstrations usually are done to show students a particular phenomenon. When a demonstration results in an observation or conclusion that is counterintuitive to a student's normal experience, the demonstration evokes "What if . . ." or "I wonder . . ." questions. Demonstrations that invite further questions and inquiries are often called *discrepant events.*

Discrepant Events

Discrepant events are mind-engaging demonstrations or activities in which the students observe unexpected results. Wondering why these unexpected things happen, contradictory to their normal or anticipated experiences, students experiencing the discrepant event have the motivation and interest to formulate questions to pursue. Discrepant events are especially useful to start a lesson or a unit and to capture student interest and promote curiosity. Teachers often use low-cost discrepant events that utilize everyday, household items to introduce a scientific concept.

Observing discrepant event demonstrations can serve as a springboard to scientific inquiry (Liem, 1987). Rather than introducing a new topic or concept and later providing the demonstration that proves the concept is correct, the discrepant event is used in the beginning of the lesson to capture the students' imagination and sense of wonder. Discrepant events are used successfully when they initiate a *wanting to know.* Several steps are recommended in incorporating discrepant events into a lesson:

1. Demonstrate the event. Present students with an opportunity to observe results that appear contradictory. Provide students with an opportunity to confront the questions being raised.

2. Allow students to investigate the event. Students should be allowed to test the event or discrepancy by using science process skills such as observing, inferring, recording data, formulating hypotheses, and generalizing. Allow sufficient time to "test" the event and form hypotheses or questions to test. Encourage students to raise "What if . . ." and "I wonder . . ." questions about the discrepancy. Provide guidance to introduce inquiry strategies without giving away the answer or providing a full explanation.

3. Allow time for students to test their "What if . . ." and "I wonder . . ." questions and share the results of their inquiries.

4. Discuss the causes of the discrepancy to introduce the topic being studied (density, pressure, heat, etc.). During the discussion, refer back to the demonstration to "personalize" the concept being presented.

5. Apply the concept being studied to an application level beyond the classroom. Provide a culminating activity or laboratory experience that extends the learning rather than proves that what already was said is correct.

LABORATORY EXPERIENCES AND ACTIVITIES

In traditional hands-on activities, the teacher or the textbook provides the question to be studied or tested, usually at the top of the activity or lab sheet. The students are also told what materials to use and what procedures to follow to generate data and results. These labs or activities are sometimes called *cookbook* science because, like following a recipe in a cookbook, students are expected to follow prescribed directions or procedures in which the results are predictably the same. Many high school science teachers subscribe to this type of *confirmation activity* because it provides direction for the students and tells them what to do to complete the "experiment." Most of the "experiments" found in science textbooks fall into this category, which is commonly called *structured inquiry.*

Teachers often "stick to what's in the textbook" and rely on prescribed activities as a source of involving students in science because they feel that activities are easy to follow and provide students with focus and direction on how to carry out the activity. Although activities do provide students with an opportunity to do hands-on, manipulative science, it is the teacher's role to promote and encourage further questions and pursue self-directed investigations—the goal of inquiry-based learning. The purpose of "cookbook" activities is to confirm what is already known.

Activities can become a means of inviting inquiry and can be used as a springboard into inquiry when, like discrepant events, they provide an opportunity for students to make observations or discoveries that are unexpected or unpredicted.

Providing extension or "going further" questions at the end of an activity is another way to engage students to inquire. For example, in a traditional activity from a 10th-grade chemistry class, the teacher poses the following question: "How can you test the hardness of water?" Then, the teacher provides each group of students the following materials to be used:

- Four samples of water (hard, tap, distilled, and bottled) labeled A, B, C, and D
- Four test tubes

- Four rubber stoppers
- A test-tube rack
- A graduated cylinder
- Liquid soap
- An eyedropper

Next, the teacher provides the following procedures for the students to follow:

1. Use the graduated cylinder to measure 50 mL of water sample A.

2. Label the test tube "Sample A."

3. Place the 50 mL of Sample A in a test tube.

4. Repeat the procedure for the other three water samples, B, C, and D. Place each sample in a separate test tube. Label each test tube according to the sample it contains.

5. Use the eyedropper to place two drops of liquid soap in each of the test tubes containing the water samples.

6. Observe and record your findings.

7. Now place a rubber stopper in each test tube and gently swirl each of the soap and water mixtures for 15 seconds. Again, observe and record your results.

8. Repeat the same procedure, but this time vigorously shake each of the soap and water mixtures for 1 minute. Observe and record your results.

9. Repeat the same procedure for 3 minutes. Observe and record your results.

Figure 5.2   Data Table

Sample	Observations before shaking	Observations after 15 seconds of shaking	Observations after 1 minute of shaking	Observations after 3 minutes of shaking
A				
B				
C				
D				

Although this is a relatively simple activity that most high school students can complete, you can see how teacher-directed it is. The original question, the materials needed, and the procedures are all provided to the students. All that the students have to do is follow the steps of the procedure and record the results in the appropriate column in the data table. You can see that this activity can be thought of as a type of cookbook activity, and although it is hands-on, it is not inquiry-based.

TEACHER-INITIATED INQUIRIES

The previous activity for testing hard water can be modified easily into a *teacher-initiated inquiry.* In a teacher-initiated inquiry, sometimes called *guided inquiry*, the teacher poses the original question and then allows time for the students to consider possible solutions, plan an investigation, and go about solving the question posed to them. Teacher-initiated inquiries align with problem-solving situations. Teacher-initiated inquiries also are appropriate when students are not accustomed to initiating questions on their own. This can be especially true in the beginning of the school year.

One step toward incorporating inquiry into the lesson would be to have several prearranged questions for students to answer on their own. The teacher could pose several *starter* questions, but the students are expected to write their own procedures and carry out their own investigations. The following are several starter questions:

- Using soap as an indicator, how can you design a procedure to test the hardness of water?
- What materials will you need?
- What different samples of water will you test?
- What steps will you follow?
- What will you look for to determine the level of hardness in the water?
- How will you organize and record your results?

In this way, a simple, traditional activity can be extended into an inquiry lesson.

STUDENT-INITIATED INQUIRIES

The highest level of inquiry occurs when students raise and initiate their own questions. According to the "Invitation to Inquiry Grid" (Llewellyn, 2002), in student-initiated inquiries, sometimes called *open inquiry*, students raise their own questions, formulate their own procedures, and determine their own results. In some cases, students may need prompting or an exploration experience to raise questions and engage them in inquiry.

Using the activity of testing for hard water, we can see how an initial demonstration or exploration can lead students to raising their own questions to investigate. Say, for example, that the teacher provides an opening teacher-led demonstration or a brief student exploration by testing one sample of water for hardness. From this initial experience, students would be given an opportunity to raise questions to investigate. Questions may include the following:

- What if we tested the water from the school drinking fountain?
- What results would we get if we tried the water from the locker room showers?
- Would different brands of bottled water give us different results?
- What results would we get if we tried distilled water?
- Or swimming pool water?
- What result would we get if we tried the water from our own homes?
- Or water in a local pond, stream, or river?
- What if we tested the city water versus well water?
- What causes water to be "hard"?
- What's the difference between hard and soft water?
- How can you make hard water "soft"?
- What do people do when they have hard water coming from their drinking water or well?
- Do some laundry detergents work best in hard water? Or soft water?
- Is prolonged intake of hard water harmful to humans?

We have seen that the levels of self-directed participation and involvement on the part of the teachers and the students vary significantly for each learning situation described. During a demonstration, the teacher plays an active role while the students are more passive. In contrast, during the student-initiated inquiry, the students' involvement is fully engaged while the teacher plays a less active teaching role. Figure 5.3 summarizes the participation level of each learning situation.

Figure 5.3   Student/Teacher Participation

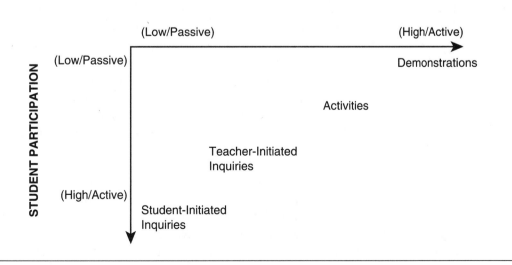

GUIDING STUDENTS INTO INQUIRY

Most students, and teachers for that matter, are not ready to begin with full student inquiries at the start of the school year. During the first few weeks of school, teachers need to set expectations for classroom management, discipline, classroom routines, grading procedures, and so on. Establishing and maintaining a healthy and safe classroom is a prerequisite for an inquiry lesson. Without rules, inquiry lessons become unruly and unmanageable. It is normal for teachers to wait until they grow accustomed to their classes before starting a full inquiry-based unit. This is especially true for teachers who have students coming to them without prior experience in inquiry learning.

For those reasons, the "Invitation to Inquiry Grid" (Figure 5.1) can also serve as a way to plan instructional units so that students are gradually but continuously encouraged to take on more responsibility for their learning. During the early months of the school year or when students are unfamiliar with inquiry learning, the teacher may choose to begin with the demonstration mode, focusing on having students observe and experience discrepant events. During the next several months, the teacher can then move into the activity stage, concentrating on providing sound hands-on activities that provide the opportunity for extension investigations. By midyear, a reasonable expectation would be to have students involved in one or more teacher-initiated inquiries, with the goal of evolving the students' expertise into several full student-initiated inquiries before the end of the year.

The "Invitation to Inquiry Grid" can also be used as a monitoring tool for teachers in designing their year-long instructional plans. As the school year proceeds, teachers can ask, "Am I moving my students from teacher-dependent to more independent experiences, and am I providing opportunities for student-initiated inquiries as the year goes on?"

By now, you should have a good grasp of the difference between doing hands-on science and inquiry-based investigations. You have read that although most inquiry investigations involve using hands-on and manipulative means of learning, not all hands-on activities are inquiry-based. When a hands-on activity poses the question to the students and also tells the students what materials to use and how to go about finding the answer to the question, it is not inquiry.

To further explain the differences between a demonstration, a traditional laboratory activity, a teacher-initiated inquiry, and a student-initiated inquiry, a lesson on soil permeability will be presented in four different ways. Using the same concept, we can then see how each stage differs from one another. Let's suppose, in a high school earth science class, we wanted to find out the drainage rates of different types of soil.

As a demonstration lesson, the teacher probably would be standing in front of the class behind a demonstration table, posing the question, "How does the type of the soil determine the drainage of water through the soil?" The teacher would then show and describe the supplies and materials to be used in the demonstration. Following the outlined steps of the procedure, the teacher would set up the materials as follows.

The teacher inserts a piece of filter paper in a large funnel that is held above a collecting beaker. The teacher then measures a given amount, say 200 grams, of a soil sample and places the soil sample into the funnel. Then the teacher uses a graduated cylinder to measure 100 mL of water and pours the water over the soil sample in the funnel. As the water seeps through the soil sample, some of the liquid will drain through the bottom of the funnel and drip into the collecting beaker. At the end of

5 minutes, the teacher measures the amount of water in the collecting beaker and records the results on the board. The teacher then goes on to test other samples of soil, clay, sand topsoil, and so on. At the conclusion of the demonstration, the teacher summarizes the data, plots it on a bar graph, then describes to the students the relationship between the soil and the amount of water that drained through the sample. Depending on the teacher and the class, questions from the students might arise from the demonstration. Because this demonstration does not represent a discrepant event, the teacher may choose to pose "going further" or extension-type questions to the class or may end the demonstration without further discussion. The demonstration may take from 30 to 45 minutes.

In a traditional laboratory activity lesson, the teacher would have the students at tables in small groups of three or four. A worksheet would be distributed to each of the groups, and the teacher would provide an overview or prelab the activity. The teacher would go over the procedure by reading the directions and answering any questions about the procedure. The question to be studied would be provided to the students on the laboratory worksheet, along with a list of the supplies and materials needed and the steps to follow in the procedure. A typical laboratory may look like this:

Question: How does the type of soil affect the drainage rate of water?

Materials:

- Four samples of soil (examples: topsoil, clay, sand, loam, peat moss)
- Ring stand and ring clamp
- 250-mL beakers
- Large funnel
- Filter paper or coffee filters
- Graduated cylinder
- Water
- Triple-beam or electronic balance

Procedure:

1. Set up the ring stand as shown.
2. Place a large funnel in the ring clamp.
3. Fold a piece of filter paper to fit within the funnel.
4. Place a collecting beaker under the funnel.
5. Measure 200 grams of topsoil.
6. Place the 200-gram sample of topsoil in the funnel.
7. Measure 100 mL of water.
8. Pour the 100 mL of water into the funnel over the topsoil sample.
9. Wait 5 minutes.
10. Measure the amount of water in the collecting beaker. Record your results.
11. Repeat the procedure for three other types of soil.

As the students work on the lab, the teacher circulates among the groups and provides assistance in answering their questions. In completing this activity, the students experience a hands-on science lesson with many opportunities to observe, make mathematical measurements, manipulate materials, record data, and draw conclusions. The activity is an excellent way to get students engaged in doing science and may take between 30 and 45 minutes to complete.

In a teacher-initiated inquiry, the teacher would pose the question, "Does the type of soil affect the drainage rate?" and challenge students to formulate a procedure to answer the question. The teacher would have four or five different soil samples available, some with large particles and some without. The students would be encouraged to write a hypothesis and a plan to test their prediction. Once the plan was completed, the students would be free to get whatever materials they needed to carry out their plan and collect evidence to test their hypothesis. The teacher may choose to substitute a 2-liter plastic bottle for more expensive equipment and glassware.

During this time, the teacher would circulate from group to group and listen in on their discussions. The teacher would be aware of comments made by the students that would reveal any misconceptions about drainage rates and provide additional prompts to test the misconceptions. The teacher would pose further questions for the students to consider and have additional inquiries available for those groups who completed their investigation early.

In a student-initiated inquiry, the teacher could assess prior knowledge and uncover misconceptions by asking students to share what they already know about soil and drainage rates. The teacher may choose to record their experiences by listing them on the board or on an overhead. Next, the teacher would allow time for self-directed exploration in which students observe drainage patterns with different soils. During this exploration stage, the teacher would encourage students to raise their own personal questions and inquiries about drainage rates and suggest that they phrase their inquiries as "What if," "I think," or "I wonder" statements. Depending on the preferences of the class, the teacher could again ask the groups to share their questions while making a list of their questions on the blackboard or on an overhead. Following this exercise, the teacher would identify each question as

- one that is ready to be answered through an investigation,
- one that needs to be revised and/or rewritten before it can be investigated, or
- one that requires an outside "expert" or resource to answer.

It is important for students to classify their questions into these categories to further understand the direction their questions will take them. For example, questions starting with "why" usually require an explanation to answer. These "why" questions often need to be revised into "what" or "what if . . ." questions before they can be investigated.

Sufficient materials and supplies should be available at a supply center for groups to use as needed. The students would brainstorm ways to solve their question and then go about carrying out their plans. The teacher would rotate from group to group, asking more questions and clarifying students' ideas and prior conceptions about the soil samples. The teacher would encourage the groups to write down and investigate other questions that come up during the course of their investigations. At the end of the lesson, the teacher would bring all the groups together so they could share their observations and conclusions. Each group would be given time to get up in front of the class and state the question they investigated and the results they discovered, as well as to apply the phenomenon studied to situations outside the classroom.

Each of the four levels of instruction has definite advantages and disadvantages, and of course each teacher could plan and implement the lesson differently from the way expressed here. Demonstrations greatly reduce the time requirement and ensure that each student has the same opportunity to observe the same concept being studied in the same way. The traditional laboratory format allows the teacher to have all the students arrive at the same conclusion together. This may be useful when introducing a specific concept when you want all students to come away with the same information. Activities usually are very structured and, except for any extension questions that may come about, are very straightforward and limit creativity. Teacher-initiated inquiry is a good instructional strategy for getting students to consider ways to plan and solve questions. Student-initiated inquiries take an extended amount of time. Often the teacher may not know where the students' questions will take them. These inquiries, however, provide a means for students to empower themselves by directing the course of their own work.

The four stages are summarized in Figure 5.4.

Figure 5.4   Expanded Invitation to Inquiry Grid

	Demonstration	Activity	Teacher-Initiated Inquiry	Student-Initiated Inquiry
Posing the Question	Teacher	Teacher	Teacher	Student
Planning the Procedure	Teacher	Teacher	Student	Student
Formulating the Results	Teacher	Student	Student	Student

++

	Demonstration	Activity	Teacher-Initiated Inquiry	Student-Initiated Inquiry
Starter Question	Predetermined	Predetermined	Posed by teacher	Generated by student
Plan or Procedure	Predetermined	Predetermined	Designed by student	Designed by student
Outcome	Predetermined	Expected	Guided toward a concept	Open-ended

(Continued)

Figure 5.4 (Continued)

	Demonstration	Activity	Teacher-Initiated Inquiry	Student-Initiated Inquiry
Time	5–30 min.	30–60 min.	45–60+ min.	60–120+ min.
Role of Teacher	Active	Provides direction	Guide/facilitator	Facilitator
Role of Student	Observer	Follows direction	Problem solver	Investigator
Materials	Provided	Provided	Suggested	Suggested
Content	Focused	Focused	Needs some focusing	Requires focusing

In this chapter, we have looked at ways to categorize science experiences ranging from demonstrations to student-initiated inquiries. As the teacher designs his or her year-long plans, the Inquiry Grid can serve as a way to move students toward more self-directed experiences. If the goal of your science program is to provide students with opportunities to engage in inquiry, planning a gradual shift from left to right in the Inquiry Grid will become a means to ensure that your students develop investigation skills throughout the school year.

EXTENDED INQUIRIES: A CASE STUDY IN BOTTLE ECOSYSTEM

Not all scientific inquiries are designed to be completed in one or two classroom periods. Inquiry investigations can be protracted and sustained over several months or even the entire school year. Knowing that biology students have an interest in plant and animal interactions, an experienced biology and environmental science teacher, Jay Costanza, uses and recycles 1-liter plastic soda bottles to engage his 10th- and 11th-grade biology students in designing environments for observing ecological interactions and succession over an extended time.

Jay is a veteran teacher of 15 years and has been teaching through inquiry-based strategies his entire career. With a background in project-based instruction, Jay teaches biology, environmental science, and Advanced Placement biology at School of the Arts, a midsized urban high school that specializes in the arts and drama performance. Bringing biological concepts and the human body, especially the muscular and skeletal systems, into the arts and dramatic theater has always seemed like a natural link to Jay. He also involves his students in an Adopt-a-Stream program; they take samples from a nearby creek to test and monitor water quality and assess the overall health of the creek over time.

At School of the Arts, building a *culture of inquiry* is an extension of the school's vision and philosophy. Because biological inquiries, like succession, are inherently longer, Jay designs the course curriculum from the macroscopic level (ecology) to the microscopic level (cell biology and genetics), with students beginning their extended inquiry into ecology during the first week of school. By beginning the biological and ecological inquiry in September, Jay feels he establishes a *tone* for the remainder of the year while introducing students to the theme of interdependency and succession.

Using the book *Bottle Biology* (Ingram, 1996), Jay introduces students to the idea of inquiry at the start of the school year. He initiates this low-cost inquiry with two essential starter questions: (a) What are the life processes that are essential to all living organisms? (b) What are the conditions to sustain life? He does this by first providing a scenario where students design a biosphere on the surface of Mars, then later has students apply their research in designing an actual plastic bottle ecosystem.

The Bottle Ecosystem unit aligns to the *National Science Education Standards* (NRC, 1996) for grades 9–12.

Science as Inquiry Standard

Students will

- Identify questions and concepts that guide a scientific investigation. (p. 175)
- Design and conduct a scientific investigation. (p. 175)
- Use technology and mathematics to improve investigations and communications. (p. 175)
- Formulate scientific explanations and models using logic and evidence. (p. 175)
- Communicate and defend a scientific argument. (p. 176)

Life Science Content Standard

As a result of activities, all students should develop an understanding that
- Energy flows through ecosystems in one direction, from photosynthetic organisms to herbivores to carnivores and decomposers. (p. 186)
- Organisms both cooperate and compete in ecosystems. The interrelationships and interdependence of these organisms may generate ecosystems that are stable for hundreds or thousands of years. (p. 186)

Science and Technology Standard

As a result of activities in grades 9–12, all students should
- Identify a problem or design an opportunity,
- Propose designs and choose between alternative solutions,
- Implement a proposed solution,
- Evaluate the solution and its consequences, and
- Communicate the problem, process, and solution. (p. 192)

To start the extended inquiry, Jay arouses students' curiosity by first posting a large picture of the surface of Mars in the front of the room. As students enter the classroom on Day 1 of the inquiry, a video from the Discovery Channel is showing mechanical robots collecting rock samples from the surface of the Red Planet. As the students settle into their seats, Jay begins. "What is life?" he asks. "What is a living thing?" Holding a rock in one outstretched hand and a piece of coral in the other, he asks, "Is this rock alive? Is this piece of coral alive?"

After a brief discussion on the meaning of life, Jay continues. "If you were to live on Mars for an extended amount of time, what would you need to survive? Can you think of a time in your life when you were far away from home and felt extremely cold, thirsty, lonely, or frightened? What did that feel like? Now imagine being an astronaut on the surface of Mars where there is no air, food, water, warmth, plants, or other animals. How could you survive? What would you need to stay alive?" As Jay walks about the room, he continues, "We have been given a special assignment by NASA. Your task is to design a biosphere that would sustain humans living on the surface of Mars for 18 months. I will now pass out the letter from NASA and you can read it quietly to yourself." The letter reads:

Date: September 10, 2003
To: The Biology Students in Room 246
From: Dr. Sharon Austin, Director of Destination Mars

Congratulations! Your class has been selected to participate in a secret program for NASA named Destination Mars. Because our government is considering the possibility of establishing a colony on Mars, your mission is to design a biosphere that will allow a group of ten astronauts to survive on the plant Mars for eighteen months. Your first assignment for Destination Mars will be to gather members of a team and form a "think tank." The objective of the think tank is to decide what is needed to sustain life on the planet Mars, ultimately making this program a success. You can submit your designs as a poster or electronically as a PowerPoint presentation.

During the project, you will be briefed by your biology teacher, Mr. Costanza, as to the specifics of the mission. Good luck, and remember, the success of this program depends upon you!

Jay now makes online resources and books available to students regarding climate on Mars. Several students use the following NASA Web sites for obtaining information about Mars:

http://mars.jpl.nasa.gov/classroom/teachers.html

http://mars.jpl.nasa.gov/odyssey/

http://mars.jpl.nasa.gov/odyssey/overview/index.html

http://mars.jpl.nasa.gov/index.html

The students are given several days to do their research. Although some time is spent in the classroom, most of the students' research is done in the school library, online, or at home as homework. In class, teacher-led discussions focus on the two initial questions: What are the life processes that are essential to all living organisms? and What are the conditions necessary to sustain life?

After several days of researching information, the groups are ready to share their designs. One at a time, the groups come to the front of the class and present their projects. As they compare and contrast the designs, students discuss the similarities and differences among the groups.

Jay now informs the students that they will use the research they discovered about the needs of living organisms from the Mars project to build an actual living model of an ecosystem from 2-liter plastic bottles. He tells the students that not only will they identify what living things need; they'll have to prove it! "Your next responsibility as a research ecologist," Jay continues, "is to use one or more 2-liter plastic bottles to design a living chamber that will keep a fish or other animal alive for 3 months. You can use sand; gravel; small rocks; soil; snails; aquatic plants like duckweed (*Lemna*), fanwort (*Cabomba*), or hortwort (*Ceratophyllum*); and pond water to build your mini-ecosystem."

Actually, Jay knows that most containers will last longer than 3 months. In fact, some may last as long as 5–6 months, but that is all part of the inquiry, to keep students engaged and involved.

"You mean we have to design a container using plastic bottles to keep something alive for 3 months?" Eugene asks.

"That's impossible!" Karen adds. "Come on, how can we do that?"

"Well," Jay says, "start first with a fish, say a guppy, and then later consider adding other organisms like a worm or a cricket."

Another student asks, "What do guppies eat? What are we supposed to feed them? How do I find out what a cricket eats?"

"Well," Jay responds, "that's all part of being a scientist. We have to do research just like in the Mars project."

Students begin by brainstorming various designs to construct their bottle ecosystems. One group decides to place a hole in the top of the bottle to monitor temperature and dissolved oxygen, while another group centers on how to measure the pH of the water. During the class's brainstorming and design sessions, Jay provides past copies of *Carolina Tips* (a product magazine from the science supply company Carolina Biological Supply) and the *Wisconsin Fast Plants* Web site (www.fastplants.org/home_flash.asp) as resources. Students also use other online resources to research their designs. For the remainder of the period and into Day 2, the teacher conveys additional parameters of the investigation. He tells the students they can experiment with their bottle designs for several weeks to determine what works and what doesn't work. Then, after 3 weeks, the containers will be sealed, with nothing new to be added. "That's when the 3-month clock starts ticking," he informs the class. Jay then provides aquarium books, Internet resources, scientific magazines and journals, biology textbooks, and other sources for the groups to research the needs of living things.

Students are instructed to place their research notes and designs in their journals, including a diagram and explanation of "How my bottle ecosystem works." The bottle designs vary. Some students choose conventional systems, while others choose to connect two bottles, with one ecosystem supporting another.

Each day, the students continue to enter their observations and drawings in their journals. As groups brainstorm their ideas, several students make concept maps to describe what a fish or a guppy needs to survive. One student's entry indicates, "I found out that fish feed on elodea. That may significantly improve its chances for survival." Students consider other fish they are familiar with, such as goldfish or betta fish.

After several days, students share their bottle designs by making posters from their journal entries. Their prototypes enable them to test their ideas and share their designs in front of the class. Jay tells students that by sharing their models and ideas, they should discuss limiting factors such as space, temperature, breeding concerns, and even the interactions among the organisms in the ecosystem.

Some groups choose plants like grasses, while one selects green beans as their food supply. During the discussion, one group mentions that it plans to place tap water in the bottle; another plans to get pond water. Other discussions center on the type of soil to use—dirt versus clay or sand. Others share research discoveries regarding the feeding habits of guppies, crickets, and earthworms. The teacher concludes the period by reiterating that the project is an inquiry into a design of trial and error.

Later in the week, the teacher introduces the class, by means of a formal presentation, to the carbon dioxide/oxygen cycle and nitrogen cycle. During the presentation, concepts including biosphere, abiotic and biotic factors, ecosystem, community, habitat, producer, and consumer are discussed. Jay asks the following questions: "Why is your ecosystem considered a closed system, why did we use a closed system for this activity, and why is light required in the bottle ecosystem?"

Now, the inquiry turns its attention toward discussing how students would monitor pH, temperature, and dissolved oxygen rates. Some students suggest using probes and spreadsheets to collect and record data over the 3 months.

By this time, students are eager to begin construction in their bottle ecosystems. At the start of Day 6, students use their scale drawings from their journals to cut plastic bottles and assemble their ecosystem structures, as shown in Figure 5.5.

Figure 5.5

Upon completion, the students add the fish, plants, and other organisms to the container, creating ecosystems similar to the one shown in Figure 5.6. For 2 weeks, the students daily observe the bottle environment, monitor the conditions, and record appropriate data. They update spreadsheets and record notes in their journals. The students now have 2 weeks to observe their structure and make modifications. During this time, students assess, through trial and error, the capacity of their structure to sustain life over an extended period of time.

Figure 5.6

During this 2-week experimentation period, some students discover that food supplies are not sufficient for all the organisms, and thus make revisions to their model. Others conclude that crickets have difficulty existing in a confined chamber without constant addition of a food supply. All these conclusions eventually result in revisions in the structure of the experimental chamber or changes in the choice of organism to be placed in the structure. Also during the 2-week experimentation period, Jay uses the ecosystems to introduce students to cloning. He conducts a lab using the Introduction to Cloning Kit: Duckweed, produced by Ward's Natural Scientific, because many of the students used duckweed in their bottle ecosystems.

Figure 5.7

After 2 weeks, the ecosystem containers are closed.

At the completion of the Bottle Ecosystem investigation, all students are expected to be able to do the following:

- Explain why their structure is considered a closed ecosystem
- Identify biotic and abiotic factors in their ecosystems
- Identify the following organisms in their ecosystem: producer, primary consumer, and decomposer
- Explain how carbon, oxygen, carbon dioxide, nitrogen, and water are cycled through their ecosystem
- Create a diagram of a food chain or energy pyramid and a food web from their ecosystem

AN INTERVIEW WITH JAY COSTANZA

How would you describe your approach to teaching?

Jay: In both my high school and AP biology classes, my approach focuses on piquing students' interest in science and having them enjoy learning science. I also want students to be able to apply what we learn in the classroom to situations in the real world and maybe even consider science as a career. What I keep in mind is that kids are often interested in science at the earlier grades, but that enthusiasm seems to evaporate at the secondary school level. I want to be sure they are as excited about doing science in high school as they were in their earlier grades. In my classroom, students are real busy. Kids are not sitting still for too long. You may see some of them sitting in groups having "pockets" of discussions talking while others are up doing a lab. It's a very active classroom. I use my instructional time guiding more than lecturing. I teach in a way that is quite the opposite from the way I learned science in high school. Times have changed. Or maybe they haven't. Back in high school, I sat down and took notes, I read and answered questions, and I did homework from the textbook. I don't remember learning much from those days or being very excited about science. Ironically, it turned me off from science. So in my classes, I try to give my students what I wanted when I was in high school, which was an opportunity to explore and be an active participant in science. I want to give my students a personal interest in finding the solutions to their questions.

I remember my first year of teaching. I was hired as a substitute teacher at an inner-city middle school to teach the dreaded 9th-grade general science. Since the previous two teachers quit after each teaching a month, I was the third teacher the students had in their science course that year. Needless to say, the class was out of control. I walked in the room and immediately discovered that they were not going to sit there and just listen to me. After all, it was the first week in October, and I was the third teacher they had. So the next day, I brought in a live snake, and they started asking what they wanted to know about snakes. That later led to doing activities and research about animals, and since that day, I always have had that hands-on approach. Back then, I didn't know it was called inquiry, but I know students were not going to learn unless they became active and engaged learners. The science teacher across the hall thought I was nuts. He advised me to get the class back in order by having the students do seat work. But my instincts told me otherwise. Each day, they began to look forward to coming to science. They didn't know what I was going to do each day, and that created an interest in what we were going to do that day. As the year went on, students did not want to be sent out of the room. Whereas before, that's all they tried to do, get thrown out of class. In short, I tried to develop a classroom that was interesting yet still meeting the needs of the curriculum while making it relevant to the students. In this case, I think I used an inquiry approach to get students involved in science which later brought the classroom management under control. In retrospect, it is probably the reverse way from which most teachers operate. Generally, teachers tend to get their classroom management under control, then move on to inquiry. For me, I knew if I used that same approach as the two teachers before me, I would probably suffer the same fate.

By the middle of the school year, I established a rotational station format for the general science course. I started by presenting a topic to the whole class through classroom discussion, then had the students move to five to seven stations. The students progressed throughout the station as they learned. This allowed students to move on at their pace when they mastered the material for that given station. It certainly was a different way for them to learn than they had previously experienced. I did get through that year in one piece. Looking back, it was one of the most rewarding years of my career.

To an untrained eye, it might appear as if the classroom you just described looked like a three-ring circus. How do you keep kids engaged, especially when there are different stations and different levels of progress going on in the room at the same time?

Planning ahead is the key. By planning ahead, the room is set up in a way where I check the progress of one group before they move on to the next station. I call it "directed movement." With different groups moving at their own pace, the directions at the stations need to be clear and explicit. There may be a unit with five different stations. At any one time, some groups may be at station #1, some at #2, and so on. And not all groups may complete all the stations, so I design stations where there are core versus enrichment topics. All groups are expected to complete the core stations, with some advanced groups moving on to the enrichment stations. I now use my time to rotate to the individual groups, and monitor and assess their progress. In this situation, groups self-pace themselves rather than moving on in a lockstep fashion. One of the benefits in this instruction is that after students are absent, they can continue at the station where they recently left off. In a traditional classroom, the teacher and the class have moved on to new information, and students who are absent assumingly get left behind. Keeping in mind certain instructional objectives, I continue to check groups to be sure they understand the purpose of the station and what understanding they should gain as a result of completing the station.

So it's really not a three-ring circus; it is quite structured and planned. If a visitor came into the room and stayed for 20 to 30 minutes, he or she could see how well "directed movement" works in a high school science class. Now, prior to the unit, it does take time to design and set up a station format; however, if it is well planned out, more of my energy is spent in organizing than managing classroom behavior. My guess is that a new teacher spends 20% of his or her energy in planning lessons and 80% in classroom management. In this case, I spent 80% of my time upfront in planning and 20% in classroom management. And now, for 3 or 4 weeks, I'm having a great time watching students learning and making decisions on their own.

In your classroom, students appear to be independent, self-regulating learners. What do you do to get students to this point?

Well, first of all, I believe that as teachers we have an obligation to create students who can enter the workforce with marketable skills. The science community needs creative thinkers and problem solvers. Ask business executives what are the most important skills and attributes that entering employees need to have for making a successful transition from school into the work setting, and many will say it's not content knowledge, it's problem-solving skills, working cooperatively in groups, and being a good critical thinker. People need to know how to work in a group and be a productive member of that group. It's a necessary part of life. What I like about inquiry-based learning is that it requires students to problem solve, to be independent thinkers, and so on.

Okay, now let's get back to the question. It starts with the premise that kids are resistant to work, whether it's physical or mental. So when presented with a problem, they often have difficulty coming up with a solution and they want the teacher to give them the answer, and often, without help from the teacher, they will "hit a wall" and be stymied. Some will say, "I quit." But I won't let them quit. Now I guide them to find their own answers. I hear, "Why don't you just tell us the answer, Mr. Costanza?" But I won't do it. Because once I do that, my answer becomes the crutch they never get rid of. And then they may never experience how much energy it really takes to resolve a difficult problem. I have to make them do it on their own and experience what it's like to think like a scientist. The urge for teachers to suppress is in always giving the answer students want. I have had to learn to restrain myself. I now know I want to provide the answers to their questions, but that doesn't help in fostering creative thinking. They can solve most of their questions on their own. There are only a few of their questions they need answered. I have since learned to sit back, listen, and allow them to figure out the answer on their own.

Now it may take a while into the school year for the students to deal with this new style that I don't answer all their questions. But sooner or later, they realize that is one of the goals of my course—to make them think for themselves.

Building a "community of learners" goes hand-in-hand with doing inquiry-based science. The students in your class seem to respect each other's work and ideas. In a way, they build on each other's strengths. Do you find that unusual for high school students?

No, it's not unusual for inquiry-based classrooms. In fact, it's quite commonplace. It's a great feeling to experience a classroom of 30 young kids, each operating at his or her own level, some listening while others are talking, working together solving problems. That's the joy of teaching. It takes time, however, to get to that point. When kids are enjoying the way they are learning and looking forward to coming to class, it's a great feeling.

To help foster this idea of a community of learners, once every 10 days I have a seminar period. In seminar, students are given questions or situations related to the unit we are studying. The questions can be a follow-up to previous homework, or come from a newspaper article. Their homework is to form opinions about the topic and be prepared to defend their positions in small groups the next day in class. While the students are in their groups, they are learning to listen and be respectful to others' statements and opinions. Part of the inquiry process is to have dialogues about topics relevant to students, to give opportunities for students to share their thoughts and opinions, and to test their opinions against their peers. These open-ended questions also allow me to assess individual understandings and become aware of what students are thinking while uncovering many of their misconceptions. This kind of feedback you can't get from a multiple-choice test. The seminar thus allows me to determine what students are learning and how they can apply what they are learning to everyday, real-world situations. The seminar period then ends with a reflection. During the reflection, students summarize the seminar proceedings and again express their ideas and what they got from the small group discussion. Often, students write about how their opinion changed after the seminar or how the discussion reinforced what they believe.

I allow the students to form their own small groups. Sometimes, the groups are functional; other times, they aren't. It becomes part of the day where they have some control. If the group is functional, I leave it alone. If a student is dysfunctional, rather than take that one disturbing member out of the group, I provide additional "assistance" on group cooperation and dynamics. It makes little sense to move a dysfunctional person to another group because chances are, he or she will only disturb the new group. Part of the seminar is to learn how to act respectfully and responsibly in a group setting. That's a lifelong skill.

We know that doing inquiry in a science classroom usually requires more time than traditional laboratory experiences. Given an extended inquiry like Bottle Ecosystem, which takes 4 to 6 weeks, how do you find time in the school year to do long-term investigations and still address district or state curriculum requirements?

What I especially like about extended investigations is the opportunity to integrate the topic with other areas of science. Thus, a 4- to 6-week unit on biodiversity also touches on metabolism, equilibrium, genetics, etc. Then, when I introduce the formal unit of genetics and heredity 2 months later, there is a reference point from the original investigation.

Inquiry-based science does require long-range planning. At the beginning of the school year, when I get my course assignments, I map out a pacing chart for each course. I know month by month, marking quarter by marking quarter, where I want to be in relation to each unit and investigation. I also have a matrix chart which monitors the district objectives for each course and where in each unit that objective is introduced and taught. That kind of organization, coupled with a strict sense of timing, allows me to work all my inquiry investigations into the course goals and objectives. Without the pacing guide and matrix chart, I would not be able to stay on track. Years ago, a unit that I thought would take 3 weeks suddenly got dragged out to 4. Before I knew it, the year was half over, and I was not halfway through the curriculum. If you are well organized and use your time efficiently, there is plenty of time for inquiry. I'm going to go out on a limb and say that teachers who say they don't have time to do inquiry probably lack planning and organization skills. If you really want to do something that means a lot to you, you'll find the time to do it, one way or another.

Last question: Do you find that high school students in inquiry-based science classrooms achieve at higher rates than students in traditional science classrooms?

I like to think that students in inquiry-based classrooms retain content and information longer because the process makes it more meaningful to them. And although students in my classes usually do well academically, even though I don't necessarily get assigned the "best" students, I can't attribute that exclusively to inquiry-based instruction. For example, the teacher across the hall, who is very traditional, generally gets the same passing results as I do. So I'm not sure that's the right question. What I do observe is that students in my class have fewer absences, arrive to class on time, have less classroom disruptions, and appear to be eager to find out what we are doing today in science. That, to me, is significant. I have a lot of students showing up at my room before school starts, during their lunch period, and after school, just to come in the lab and check on their investigations. I even have kids asking for a pass from study hall to work in the lab. It's rewarding to know that kids feel comfortable coming into my science class. In the end, I want them to like science class, not dread it. I want them to consider science, technology, or engineering as a career. And finally, I want them to be curious and ask questions about the world around them.

It's through long-term, extended investigations that students begin to find out what science is really like. The short, one-period cookbook labs paint an unreal picture of what scientists do, yet we use these verification labs as a way to show students what science is like. They show whether kids can follow directions or not. That's not what science is like. Science, and the work of scientists, is ongoing. It takes time.

QUESTIONS FOR REFLECTION

1. How would you describe Jay Costanza's approach to teaching?

2. What are the benefits of engaging students in extended investigations?

3. What are the benefits of engaging students in extended investigations that integrate biology with other areas of science, like space science?

4. In your experience, what helps students sustain engagement in extended, ongoing investigations?

5. In the Bottle Ecosystem case study, the teacher wanted to "set the tone" or "climate" for inquiry at the beginning of the school year. What are some advantages and disadvantages to using this approach so early in the school year?

6. What content and skills should be included in the student assessment at the end of the Bottle Ecosystem investigation? How would you assess the content and skills you identified?

7. How could you use the students' journal entries as part of an assessment?

8. How do you lead students through an extended investigation like the Bottle Ecosystem with little prior experience in inquiry?

9. Given that this is an extended inquiry lasting several months, would you assign pairs to work together, or instead have students choose their own partners?

Modifying a Lab Activity Into an Inquiry Investigation

THE ROLE OF THE LABORATORY IN SCIENCE

Despite the recent concern over science instruction, achievement levels, and the rising costs of education, doing laboratory work in high school science classes has a rich presence and history (DeBoer, 1991). As early as the end of the 19th century, Thomas Huxley embraced the importance of the laboratory experience. As Huxley (1899) put it (with apologies for the gender reference),

> In teaching him botany, he must handle the plants and dissect the flowers for himself: in teaching him physics and chemistry, you must not be solicitous to fill him with information, but you must be careful that what he learns he knows of his own knowledge. Don't be satisfied with telling him that a magnet attracts iron. Let him see that it does; let him feel the pull of the one upon the other for himself. (p. 127)

Today, however, with the cost of new technical and scientific equipment, the additional time needed to schedule labs, and the additional space needed for science labs, high school teachers are often called upon to defend the need for the laboratory experience. A majority of the students in your class may not aspire to become professional (career) scientists, so, in times of shrinking economies, many teachers are faced with the following questions: (a) Why should high schools provide students with laboratory-based science courses? (b) What role does the hands-on laboratory experience play in learning science concepts? Numerous arguments support laboratory-based instruction:

1. Laboratory experiences develop manipulative skills such as handling equipment, reinforcing hand-eye coordination, and practicing sensorimotor skills. By manipulating scientific equipment and materials, students learn to manage technical skills such as massing objects, using a microscope, staining samples on slides, techniques, and performing titrations.

2. Laboratory experiences reinforce science process skills such as observing, classifying, measuring, inferring, experimenting, and manipulating variables.

3. Laboratory experiences reinforce the use of the scientific method, by which students formulate hypotheses, control variables, design procedures, collect data, and analyze results.

4. Laboratory experiences enhance communication skills such as following directions, reading, speaking, listening, and writing reports.

5. Laboratory experiences develop inquiry and investigation skills.

6. Laboratory experiences reinforce organizational skills as well as group responsibility and collaboration.

7. Laboratory experiences reinforce concepts from the lecture/discussion portion of the class and extend learning to the problem-solving level.

8. Laboratory experiences support cognitive skills, critical thinking, problem solving, and higher-order thinking skills such as analysis, synthesis, and evaluation.

9. Laboratory experiences integrate science, technology, and mathematics.

10. Laboratory experiences develop habits of mind and scientific attitudes such as curiosity, risk taking, precision, and confidence.

Most important, the laboratory links the concepts being studied with real-world applications. According to the National Research Council,

> Designing and conducting a scientific investigation requires introduction to the major concepts in the area being investigated, proper equipment, safety precautions, assistance with methodological problems, recommendations for use of technologies, clarification of ideas that guide the inquiry, and scientific knowledge obtained from sources other than the actual investigation. The investigation may also require student clarification of the question, method, controls, and variables; student organization and display of data; student revision of methods and explanations; and a public presentation of the results with a critical response from peers. Regardless of the scientific investigation performed, students must use evidence, apply logic, and construct an argument for their proposed explanations. (NRC, 2000a, p. 166)

In the end, the laboratory experience is a multifarious and circuitous process. To become competent in experimentation and investigation, students need to understand the problem being posed, the concept on which the experiment is predicated, and the language in which the context of the procedure is based. When we talk about the *language of the procedure*, we refer to the process by which inquiry occurs. That frequently is referred to as the scientific method. Although inquiry seldom follows the step-by-step procedure prescribed by the regimen of the scientific method, it does provide a systematic and sequential framework for understanding the complexity of an investigation.

The following 13 steps describe the typical processes characteristic of a scientific investigation:

1. State the problem or question to be solved.

2. Identify all possible variables or factors that could influence the outcome of the investigation.

3. Construct a statement or hypothesis to test.

4. Identify the manipulating variable (independent), responding (dependent) variable, and controlled variables.

5. Design the procedure or steps to test the hypothesis.

6. Determine the supplies, material, and equipment necessary to perform the investigation.

7. Carry out the investigation and acquire data.

8. Record and organize data on a table or a chart.

9. Construct a graph, label the axes, and provide a title for the graph.

10. Describe the relationship between the manipulating (independent) variable and the responding (dependent) variable.

11. Draw a conclusion to determine the validity of the hypothesis.

12. Prepare a written report, PowerPoint presentation, or trifold poster of the data and conclusions.

13. Communicate your findings.

NEW APPROACHES TO TRADITIONAL LABS

Many teachers prefer doing traditional labs and prescribed activities with their students. They are often more comfortable with this type of lesson because it is the way they were taught. They may say, "I like that particular lab. I've been doing it for years," or "I do it because it's in the textbook." The purpose of this section is to provide the reader with suggestions on making traditional labs more inquiry-oriented. That is not to say that traditional labs don't have a purpose or place in the high school science curriculum. At times, such as the beginning of the school year, or when time is at a critical shortage, or when students have not had prior experience in designing labs on their own, or even when safety is an important issue, it may be more appropriate to provide students with a directed, hands-on laboratory experience.

Traditional labs are most often found at the end of the chapter in the course textbook. The purpose of the lab may be to verify or confirm through a hands-on experience a concept previously introduced in the chapter. Commonly referred as *cookbook labs*, these labs usually provide the student with the question to be investigated, the materials to be used, a step-by-step procedure, safety precautions, a guide on how to organize the data in a table or a chart, and leading questions to analyze the data. When students do cookbook labs, there is a degree of certainty and predictability in the conclusions. The amount of time it takes to reach an outcome is also unerringly anticipated. And the opportunity for individual dissimilarity is substantially curbed.

Writing for *The Science Teacher*, Colburn (1996) stated that "you don't have to abandon these [cookbook] activities to make your teaching more inquiry-based. There is a middle ground between activities that are teacher directed and those that are almost totally student centered" (p. 10). The teacher's understanding of instruction plays a key role in modifying labs (Bernstein, 2003; Clark, Clough, & Berg, 2000; Clough & Clark, 1994; Colburn, 1996; Colburn & Clough, 1997; Shiland, 1999; Volkmann & Abell, 2003). By making minor changes to the format and structure of the lab, teachers can provide a transition into inquiry-based learning, with more empowerment being granted to the students and with students developing more responsibility for their own learning.

As teachers modify their existing cookbook labs to create more open-ended labs, they encourage inquiry in the classroom. Changing a traditional textbook activity into an inquiry-based investigation can be relatively easy. It does not mean you have to give up favorite science activities you are already using. Shiland (1999) suggests that meaningful learning does not occur when students merely follow procedures identified in a prescribed activity. When you realize that cookbook labs and prescribed activities do not meet the instructional goals you have set for your students or that you are ready to adapt some of your (or your textbook's) existing activities, consider modifying your activities by referring to the Invitation to Inquiry Grid from Chapter 5 (Figure 5.1).

The following recommendations will assist high school science teachers in modifying their favorite "time-honored" labs that conform to the scientific method and will help teachers move from structured activities to teacher-initiated and student-initiated inquiries. These suggestions are presented in order, starting from the beginning of the lab and working toward the end.

Do a Prelab Assessment

Before actually starting the laboratory, constructivist and inquiry teachers want to know students' prior understandings about the topic or concept being investigated. In other words, you want to gauge before you engage! By assessing prior knowledge, you may discover many naive conceptions and misconceptions. Determining students' points of reference for a lab will allow the inquiry-based teacher to make modifications in the way the lab is presented so as to fit the students' past experiences. Because it is not unlikely that a high school chemistry class will have a mixed proficiency when using scientific equipment, knowing individual students' prior knowledge will also allow the teacher to make individual accommodations for a diversity of students' skills and abilities.

Do the Lab First

As previously mentioned, in most textbooks the lab is found near the end of the chapter. Resist the notion that you always need an understanding of certain concepts or facts to do the lab, and do the lab first. Begin by choosing an exploration or a lab that is nonthreatening and highly motivating. The lab should also require little prior knowledge as a prerequisite for its completion. Think, in advance, of the kinds of prompts and questions you will need to pose to students to lead them in the right direction. Use the results of the lab to stir excitement about the topic you are now about to present. Refer to the lab throughout your unit as a previous experience. The following is one example of a general chemistry lab that needs minimal prior knowledge about percent composition, solubility, mass, mixtures, evaporation, and filtration to complete the investigation. Most high school chemistry students have enough prior experience from their middle school science courses to complete the problem with little or no assistance from the teacher. The laboratory is called "Sugar and Sand."

The Objectives of the Laboratory:

1. To develop the ability to analyze and solve problems

2. To plan and perform a laboratory procedure to solve a problem

3. To select materials and equipment to carry out an investigation

The Task:

Given a 100-gram sample of a mixture of sugar and sand, the student will plan and perform a procedure that will determine the percent composition of the mass of the sugar and sand mixture.

The Problem:

What is the percentage of sugar and sand in a mixture?

The Situation:

You are a laboratory technician and are presented with the problem of determining the relative amounts of two compounds in a mixture. You are given a 100-gram sample of a mixture of sand and sugar. Design a procedure to determine the percentage of the mass of each of the two compounds in the sample. Once you have planned your procedure, carry out the procedure and report your findings.

Materials and Equipment:

The following materials and equipment are available for students. Additional materials, not needed to complete the problem, may be added as distracters:

- Triple-beam balance
- Filter paper
- Funnel
- Beaker
- Heat source or drying oven
- Evaporating dish

- Ring stand
- Stirring rods
- Water

At the conclusion of this lab, the teacher can give a presentation on percent composition, solubility, mass, mixtures, evaporation, and filtration. During the presentation, as the teacher introduces new concepts, he or she can refer back to the lab that the students performed and discuss their results.

Revise the Question Section

If the lab provides a starter question to answer, as it usually does, remove it. Start by demonstrating a discrepant event for students to observe. Allow the students to think of questions to investigate from the discrepancy. Provide prompts and explorations to lead students to the original question of the activity or lab. Allowing students to come up with the question or problem makes the investigation more personal and meaningful to them. This makes the activity more like a student-initiated inquiry. When designing a lesson around the 5E Learning Cycle, the Engagement or the Exploration stages can provide an excellent starting point for inquiry-based investigations. Inquiry can again be reintroduced during the Extension or Elaboration stage. Several excellent resources for demonstrations and discrepant events are listed in the back of the book.

Revise the Materials Section

If the lab provides a list of needed supplies and equipment, there are several alternatives to consider. In the beginning, cut the list of needed supplies and equipment into single strips or write them on small strips of paper (1 × 5 inches). Include several unnecessary items in the set. Students will determine which supplies and equipment are necessary and which are not. Later, you can provide a partial list of the supplies and equipment, perhaps four of the eight items. Students will write in the missing supplies and equipment. Eventually, students will list *all* the supplies and equipment for the materials section.

Remove the Safety Rules

Whether or not students design their own experimental procedures, they can always be encouraged to write the safety rules and guidelines for the lab. Consider having students align each safety rule to a particular step in the procedure. For example, if the lab calls for heating a substance in an open test tube, the students would write a safety rule connected to that specific step. You may find that students are more likely to follow a safety procedure if they suggest it. Safety rules that are imposed are often opposed.

Revise the Procedure Section

This is a key area in modifying traditional labs. If the lab provides a step-by-step list of procedures, there are several alternatives to consider to make it more student-centered. In the beginning, cut the list of the individual steps in the procedure into single strips or write the steps of a lab on small strips of paper (1 × 5 inches). Give a set to each group of students. Have the students read the steps and put them into a logical and sequential order. After a few labs, provide additional, unnecessary steps in the set. Students will determine which steps are necessary and which are not. Later, you can provide a partial list of the steps, say four of the eight steps. Students will write in the missing procedures and construct the lab. Eventually, students will design *all* the steps for the procedure section. Allow students to "brainstorm" how they would design an experiment or investigation to answer the original question, prediction, or hypothesis. This makes the activity more like a teacher-initiated inquiry.

Add Procedural Errors

Using the "Find My Mistakes" approach, Galus (2000) provides an incorrect experimental procedure and has students find the errors. According to Galus (2000), "Although students [are] not sure of the correct laboratory experiment necessary to test something that interests them, they [are] experts at pointing out someone else's mistakes. [Thus] students become experts in critiquing the process and determining the right way to complete an inquiry-based laboratory exercise" (pp. 30–31).

Take Away the Data Table or Chart

Another suggestion involves the data tables and charts. If the lab provides a predetermined data table or graph, remove it. Encourage the students to determine how they will collect and organize the data. Have students share their results in small groups and compare their findings. Students will have to construct meaning to the data in order to organize and record it into a table. If they cannot formulate a data table, they may not understand the significance and correlation of the data to the activity or may not have mastered strategies for organizing data. By designing their own charts and data tables, students demonstrate and reinforce their understanding of the difference between the dependent and the independent variables.

Redesign the Results Section

Traditional textbook labs often provide space for brief, one- or two-sentence summaries. As one means of improving students' observation and communication skills, consider replacing use of these questions with students writing a detailed, narrative description of what they observed in the investigation. In the results section, students can describe how their observations relate to the hypothesis and reflect on the significance of the observation phase. Students then can go on to predict what would happen if they changed one of the variables in the investigation.

Add "Going Further" Questions to the End of the Lab

By adding analysis and "going further" questions to the end of the lab, you extend the experience and use the activity as a springboard to inquiry. Allow students to raise "What if . . ." and "I wonder . . ." questions to investigate. Consider testing other variables in the original experiment. Encourage students to test different variables with an experiment. If, for example, a class of biology students were investigating how the amount of sunlight affected the growth rate of a plant, the teacher could prepare questions as prompts to start students thinking about other variables that affect the growing rate of a plant. Individual groups of students could design experiments to determine the effect of fertilizer on the growing rate. Others could test the amount of water or the type of soil on growing conditions.

Look at the questions at the end of your labs and the ones provided in the textbook. If the questions provide opportunities for students to analyze and evaluate the lab thoughtfully, but not through additional inquiries, consider adding questions that engage students in more investigations. With "going further" questions, students use the *initiating* or *starter* investigation to guide their design to plan the steps, what information/ data to record, how to organize the data on a chart, how to graph the data, and how to analyze the results. Although we are tempted to provide these "end of the lab" questions orally through a class discussion to save time, teachers will find that when students actually do the "going further" investigations, the concepts are solidified and students have opportunities to explore and extend their understandings.

THE HYDRATE LAB

The following lab is an example of how one high school chemistry teacher, Tom Mueller, took a traditional copper sulfate hydrate lab and revised it using the 5E Learning Cycle, making it more inquiry-based. The original lab provided the question to be studied, the materials to be used, the steps in the procedure, and a predetermined table to organize the data.

For the hydrate lab during the previous year, Tom's students completed a prelab assessment. As part of the assessment, students observed crystals of copper (II) sulfate pentahydrate and recorded their observations. After giving the class the prelab assessment, Tom determined that many of the students had difficulty believing that small blue crystals of copper sulfate could have any water content. Because he knew the phenomenon of hydration was an essential concept of the chemistry standards and curriculum, he decided this year to revise his approach to the lab based on the students' prior conceptions. He modified the lab through an extended 5E Learning Cycle. The following is a synopsis of Tom's revision.

Engagement

Anticipating that students would have difficulty understanding the notion that the blue crystals contained water, Tom showed the class an apple and posed the question, "Does this apple contain any water?" Taking a big bite out of the apple and squirting juice in all directions, he continued, "How do you know?"

Tracy answered by saying, "Sure, the apple is juicy, and some of that juice is made up of water."

"That's a great start," Tom suggested. "Now, how could you determine the percentage of water in the apple?"

Jason responded by saying, "You would have to weigh the apple to determine its mass. Then heat it to drive off all the water inside the apple and reweigh the apple to calculate the percentage of water."

After a bit more discussion, Tom pulled a dehydrated apple from his desk, held it up for the class to see, and gave the students its mass in grams before and after heating. Two minutes later, the students had calculated the percentage of water in the apple to be 65%.

Exploration

Now that the students had a concrete understanding of the percentage of water in an apple, it was time to move on to various other fruits. On his desk, Tom then placed a bowl containing oranges, grapes, plums, bananas, cherries, and a few exotic-looking fruits. "For homework tonight," Tom explained, "your assignment is to take one of these fruits and heat it gently in the oven at home to drive off all the water. Tomorrow in class, you will mass the fruit and determine the percentage of water in it." He had each student come up and choose a fruit. The students were instructed to mass their sample and place it in a clear plastic ziplock bag before the end of the class. The next day, they would remass their shriveled sample and determine the percentage of water.

Explanation

The following day, Tom presented a short lecture on the concept of hydration while students took notes. Later, he had the students remass their samples and share their calculations on the percentage of water. Jessica offered to share her calculations for the banana with the class:

Mass of the banana before heating = 110 grams

Mass of the banana after heating = 52 grams

Mass of water driven off = 58 grams

Percentage of water = 53%

Other students posted their fruits and percentages. The samples were then placed in sequential order from the greatest to the least amount of water. Some students then shared comments about using fruit hydrators and the benefits of freeze-dried fruits when hiking and camping.

Extension and Elaboration

With the fruit hydration example in mind, students now were given the task of designing a lab to determine the percentage of water in copper (II) sulfate pentahydrate crystals. By applying the formula from the previous activity, students worked in groups to develop a procedure and experiment for determining the percentage of water in copper (II) sulfate pentahydrate. They also used the example from the fruit investigation to design their own charts and tables to organize the data.

Many students decided to use the following materials:

- A sample of copper (II) sulfate pentahydrate crystals
- A heat source
- A test tube

- A test-tube holder
- A ring stand
- An electronic balance

The groups also had to record their own safety rules for the lab. With lots of ideas flying about, one group brainstormed the idea of using an evaporating dish versus heating the sample in a test tube. In the end, all the groups were able to design and carry out the experiment. At the conclusion of the data analysis, the percentage of error among the student groups was discussed.

Evaluation

As an evaluation of the hydrate concept, some students were given samples of other hydrates to calculate the percentage of water. Other students were given two samples and had to determine which sample was the hydrate and which is the non-hydrate. In either case, students had to use the knowledge and skills from the original investigation and apply it to a new performance task.

This is just one example of how teachers can revise a traditional lab and make it more inquiry-oriented and student-centered. As science teachers decide to use more inquiry-based investigations, there is no reason to discard the time-honored labs they have done over the years. Consider modifying aspects of the lab, and turn over more decision making and responsibility to the students. By following the suggestion made earlier in the chapter, you will find the transition into inquiry to be a smooth and evolving process.

Managing the Inquiry-Based Classroom

CHALLENGES TO INQUIRY-BASED TEACHING

Aside from the research that shows that inquiry-based teaching can be an effective means to engage students and increase academic achievement in science, the question still lingers: With the recent emphasis on the *National Science Education Standards*, why don't we see inquiry-based instruction in more high school science classrooms? This, of course, is not a new question for science educators. Back in 1986, Costenson and Lawson concluded—in an article for *The American Biology Teacher* titled "Why Isn't Inquiry Used in More Classrooms?"—that

> to implement inquiry in the classroom we see three critical ingredients: (1) teachers must understand precisely what scientific inquiry is; (2) they must have sufficient understanding of the structure of the (content) itself, and (3) they must become skilled in inquiry teaching techniques. Lacking this knowledge and skills, teachers are left with little choice but to teach facts in the less effective expository way. (p. 158)

Let's look at the 10 top reasons why teachers say they don't teach through inquiry.

10. I feel more comfortable teaching the traditional labs. That's the way I was taught.

9. When you teach through inquiry, you lose control.

8. Inquiry is not an emphasis in our science department. Besides, I have not had any professional development on teaching through inquiry.

7. Inquiry is not a focus of the textbook I am using.

6. Students need to be told how to do a science experiment.

5. I don't have enough supplies and equipment to do inquiry.

4. Students don't have the skills to do inquiry.

3. I have a final exam I have to teach to.

2. Students are accustomed to getting an answer from their teacher.

1. I don't have enough classroom time to do inquiry. I can teach a lesson quicker through a lecture or a demonstration.

High school science teachers often say the time constraint they experience is the number one reason preventing them from doing inquiry-based labs. Coupled with the number of content standards to be taught and the high-stakes assessment that frequently is associated with high school science curricula, finding classroom time to do scientific inquiry is a challenge to teachers. The question that faces us now becomes this: Knowing full well that open-ended investigations and unraveling students' misconceptions takes more time than traditional learning methods, how can science teachers recover lost time during the school day to do more inquiry-based instruction? This next section will attempt to answer that question.

MAKING TIME FOR INQUIRY

Effective management is the key to an inquiry-based classroom (Clough, Smasal, & Clough, 1994; Lawson, 2000). When teachers learn to be more effective and efficient with their time, they create more opportunities for students to engage in scientific inquiry. Increased engagement often can lead to increased achievement. Thus, reclaiming lost minutes in the school day has always been a priority for inquiry-based teachers. By being aware of their time management, teachers can find additional instructional time to do inquiry.

Benjamin Franklin is credited with saying, "Lost time is never found again." Consider the teacher who loses the first 2 minutes at the beginning of class in getting students settled down and another minute in taking attendance, and who also gives the last 2 or 3 minutes at the end of the period to do homework or get ready to pass to the next class. Not including additional lost time for other outside disturbances such as phone calls, announcements, and late students with or without passes, it is not uncommon for teachers to lose 6 minutes of instructional time per period! It may not seem like much, but when we figure 6 minutes over 180 school days, it calculates to 1,080 minutes, or 18 hours, a school year. Put another way, it becomes 24 45-minute periods. That's a whole month lost to noninstructional time.

In *The Tao of Teaching*, Greta Nagel (1994) suggests that it's not about finding time, it's about *making* time. Whereas *finding* time implies a passive search, possibly in a nonlinear, nonsystemic, or random process, *making* time involves the teacher in an active process of planning, and thus becoming more effective and efficient with the limited amount of time available.

Although typical approaches to time include lengthening the school year, reducing class size, or narrowing the curriculum (i.e., less is more), the purpose of this chapter is to provide science teachers with simple, practical suggestions for *making* time for inquiry. You are likely to discover that many of the suggestions are not new. However, we are remiss in implementing even the fundamental strategies for time management.

Time is the only phenomenon that is both a constant and a variable. Using the clock wisely means more instructional time for inquiry-based instruction. If you don't control the clock, the clock will control you! Teachers can implement several strategies to make time for inquiry, as outlined below.

Use Essential Questions

Write and post an essential (or starter) question on the board or on a separate piece of poster paper before the students enter the room. Posting the essential question avoids students asking "What are we going to do today?" Students will become accustomed to the routine of reading the question that identifies the objective of the lesson. Avoid writing the essential question on the overhead projector. When teachers write the essential question on the overhead, it is usually visible only for several minutes. Keep the essential question visible throughout the lesson. Posting the essential question also provides a means to bring the students to a clearer focus in the beginning of the period and to review and closure at the end of the lesson or period.

Develop a Sense of Urgency

At the start of the school year, begin instruction on the first minute of the first day. Don't use the first day for filling out attendance cards, distributing textbooks, or other trivial matters. Start the class by developing a sense of urgency and communicating the importance of learning.

Throughout the school year, use the entire instructional period by working bell to bell. In other classes, students may expect to have a few minutes in the beginning and the end of the period to socialize or do homework; but not in yours. Start your classes as soon as the bell rings even though all the students may not be in the room. Communicate to students that you begin on time and that they are expected to be in the room when the class begins. You will soon find that the first 2 minutes of class sets the tone for the remainder of the period. Do not allow students to "pack up" until the bell rings. Use the final 2 or 3 minutes of class to review the essential question or give an oral or written quiz to assess their learning, as well as the success of your teaching. That will provide suggestions for revisions. If you make concluding comments too soon, that becomes a signal for students that the lesson is over and it's time to get ready to move on to the next class. Soon the class will come to understand that working the entire period is part of the classroom culture and your effective use of valuable instructional time.

Develop Daily Rituals and Routines

Despite what students say, most want to know that there are classroom rules and routines to maintain order. Examples include passing back assignments as students come in the door or introducing the lesson by using an essential question. Except for the beginning of the school year, avoid using prime instructional time for taking attendance. Use a student to take attendance and spot check regularly.

The effective use of instructional time starts with sound classroom management strategies. Out-of-control behaviors cause the loss of instructional time. When calling on students, tell students to "raise your hand if you know the answer to this question." Insist on nonverbal behaviors for recognition. Don't call on students who shout out answers.

Design Your Lesson Plans Based on Time Allotments

Use your planning time to design lessons based on 10- or 15-minute time intervals. Balance your lesson plan with individual work, small group work, and whole-class instruction. Keep to the time allotted for each segment. With 3 minutes remaining until the end of the class, provide a brief summary, reflection, review, or closure to the lesson.

Teach to the Essential, Core Concepts

Educators always seem good at adding to the curriculum, but they seldom subtract from it. To make time for inquiry, cut the "fat" out of the curriculum and teach to the essential standards. Avoid adding extended topics that "eat up" prime instructional time and are not part of the curriculum. To maximize classroom time, consider selecting one or two topics or concepts that can be learned through independent study, by outside readings or homework, or by using the Internet. Additionally, many basic concepts in the curriculum can be learned through self-study or assigned study groups.

Pick Up the Pace

Confine lectures to shorter periods of time, usually 15–20 minutes, and limit off-task discussions during a teacher-led presentation. When a student raises a question, determine if the question stems from that one student, several students, or the entire class. If the question applies specifically to only one student's concern, it may be more appropriate to address that question individually with the student at the end of class.

Before beginning an activity or assignment, be sure the students understand its objectives or purpose. Limit the time used to read the directions aloud to the class. Have students read the directions silently to themselves, then ask several students to repeat the expectations of the lab. Having students correctly repeat the objectives, procedures, or expectations provides evidence that the directions were clear and the students know what to do during the investigation. It also puts the class design in another voice for other students to hear, perhaps more clearly.

To close the lesson, pose the question, "What are the two most significant points of the lesson?" or "What do you know now that you didn't know 45 minutes ago?" Ask a student to summarize the main points of the lesson and set the transition for the next day by saying, "Tomorrow we will . . ."

Use Organized Workstations

As an alternative to traditional labs, whenever possible, consider redesigning the lab so that students rotate to six or seven stations to complete a task on a particular concept. Stations may be appropriate when viewing various specimens under the microscope, testing samples of rocks or minerals, or conducting simple chemical tests.

Use Concept Maps or Graphic Organizers

Make the students' class time more efficient by using concept maps or graphic organizers for note taking. At the end of class, post the teacher's master copy, allowing students to compare their notes to it.

Assign Students to Work in Pairs

When students work in pairs, they are more likely to stay on task and use class time effectively. Larger groups open the opportunity for one or two students in the group to become inattentive and nonparticipatory members. When lab groups consist of three or four students, the responsibility often lies with one or two of the students in the group to carry out the lab. Larger groups also tend to produce added socializing and off-task behavior during the lab. Group size will, of course, be predicated on the supplies and equipment available.

Provide Time Limits

State the amount of time students have to complete a task, an activity, a lab, or an inquiry. Stick to the time limit. Don't allow a 5-minute activity to take 10 minutes. Asking "Who needs more time?" will only communicate to students that it's okay to waste time during the assignment. Consider using a stopwatch to announce the remaining time students have to complete an assignment or task. Help keep students stay on task by offering several time prompts, such as "You have 2 minutes remaining" and "You have 30 seconds remaining."

Limit Class Time for Test Review

Don't use instructional time for review in preparation for a unit test. Set aside after-school sessions for test review, and make it worthwhile for students to attend by providing additional credit or giving questions during the review session that are similar to those on the test. In some cases, teachers use 1 or 2 weeks at the end of the school year to review for the final examination. Save time by limiting the end-of-the-year reviews to after-school sessions. Use prior unit tests as the basis for the final and have students review unit tests for the final exam.

Consider Take-Home Tests and Quizzes

Unit tests and quizzes can consume up to 2 or 3 weeks of instructional time. Consider, as the test permits, occasionally using open-book tests to be completed at home rather than during class time. Determine when it is appropriate to provide the multiple-choice questions during class and open-book, take-home essay questions to answer outside class.

Limit Classroom Interruptions

Classroom interruptions are often a prime cause of lost instructional time. Classroom interruptions usually take the form of the school's public address system, phone calls during class, or students entering and being called out of the classroom once the lesson begins. How often have we heard, "Please pardon the interruption, but would Jackie Smith report to the office immediately?"

Every classroom interruption subtracts instructional time multiplicatively. After a 30-second interruption, it may take double the time, or 60 seconds, to get the students' attention back on track to the topic being studied. Teachers who experience constant interruptions should monitor daily occurrences and report the frequency to the principal.

Unfortunately, time is a limited, nonrenewable resource: There is only so much time available in the school day. Managing time is like managing money—you need to account for it. By developing a time management plan and spending your time wisely, you can generate 3 to 4 weeks of additional instructional time, time that can be used to engage your students in inquiry-based learning.

JUST TELL ME THE ANSWER

Aside from the challenges of making time to do inquiry, overcoming students' initial resistance to inquiry-based instruction also can be an obstacle to overcome. As we saw on the top 10 list, students are accustomed to getting an answer from their teacher.

When we were born, we were given two ears and one mouth. Do you think we were brought into this existence to listen twice as much as we talk? As a teacher, you may feel it's your job, even your professional responsibility, to provide answers for the questions that students ask. A good inquiry-based teacher, however, refrains from always providing the answer. A good inquiry teacher first listens to the question being asked and then, in his or her mind, pauses to determine if the student has enough innate ability to answer the question on his or her own. If the answer is "yes," then rephrasing the question or providing a "prompt" usually enables the student to get on track in answering his or her own question. Sometimes the prompt will help the student to clarify the concept that is puzzling to him or her. Sometimes the prompt can suggest that the student recall previously learned information to answer the question. Sometimes the teacher can simply respond with, "Well, what do you think?"

If, however, the teacher feels the student does not have sufficient background to answer the question given a prompt, it may be best to just come out and guide the student to the understanding desired or give the student the answer. Providing prompts to a student without adequate background can lead to frustration on the part of the teacher as well as the student. This explains why the teacher's pause at the end of the student's question is so essential. That brief, 2- to 3-second pause allows the teacher to assess the level of understanding the student has and provide an appropriate response to the question.

Practicing temperance in answering questions is not always as easy to do as it sounds. Students, even from their earliest grades, expect answers to their questions. That's why when students experience an inquiry-based teacher who wants students to try to solve their own questions, one hears, "Why don't you just tell me the answer?" Although telling students the answer might seem like the normal thing to do, for the inquiry-based teacher, helping students think inductively and logically is a first step in nurturing a *community of inquirers.*

QUESTIONING TECHNIQUES

One of the first skills teachers need to master on their journey to creating an inquiry-based classroom is the art of asking questions. In science, elementary school children seem to ask an infinite number of questions. As they reach high school, however, and peer relationships take a foothold in their life, their reluctance to ask questions in class often increases. During high school, students tend to become passive and are more accustomed to occasionally providing token answers to questions posed by the teacher. This situation can significantly interfere with the students' ability to formulate questions and conduct self-directed investigations (Edwards, 1997). Transitioning reluctant high school science students into the position of formulating their own questions for investigation can take several steps.

First, consider using nonfiction science articles from primary sources, magazines such as *Science News* and *Scientific American,* and local newspapers. Choose articles on current, relevant topics that interest adolescents. Have students summarize the articles for homework and write five questions for further discussion in class the next day. Encourage in-class student-to-student dialogues where they share their summaries and questions.

Second, use discrepant events that demonstrate a phenomenon that is counter-intuitive to students' prior experience. Have students observe the demonstration and then write several follow-up "I wonder . . ." and "What if . . ." questions. Begin a classroom discussion by having students propose answers to the questions they raised. As students attain more experience in planning and executing solutions to their own questions, they will develop the confidence to cultivate questions that nourish their interests.

Posing good questions is central to a teacher's instructional repertoire, especially in an inquiry-based classroom. The manner in which a question is posed and positioned is equally important as the question itself. Teachers with good questioning skills enhance the inquiry process and develop more opportunities for student-centered, self-directed learning. The following "tips" are tried-and-true suggestions useful in developing a culture of inquiry.

1. *Avoid "chorus" questions.* Chorus or group response questions are those questions the teacher asks to which anyone can shout out an answer. When teachers ask chorus questions for anyone and everyone to answer, they often get inappropriate answers. Suppose an earth science teacher asks the question, "What type of rock is limestone?" The entire class responds, "Sedimentary." Did all the students really answer correctly? Did some students quietly or to themselves answer, "Metamorphic"? The teacher doesn't know. It is nearly impossible to determine, through a chorus or class response, how many students actually know the answer to a question. Other students may answer correctly when they hear the correct answer from the class. As an alternative to chorus questions, pose questions to an individual student, not the entire class. Similarly, avoid asking questions that are directed to everyone in the

class, such as "Is everyone finished?" or "Does everyone understand?" Instead, have students respond with a nonverbal behavior, such as "Raise your hand if you are not finished" or "Raise your hand if you need more time." Asking for a nonverbal behavior for recognition decreases opportunities for students to shout out and maintains a quieter classroom environment.

2. *Think about when to use the student's name when posing a question.* Teachers can place the student's name either before or after the question. Each has its own specific purpose. By placing the student's name *before* the question, as in "Josh, explain the atomic exchange in a double replacement reaction," all other students may "shut down" as soon as they know that Josh, not them, has to answer the question. This immediately takes the rest of the class "off the hook." Another option is to pose the question, follow it with a pause of 3–5 seconds, and then state the name of the student you wish to call upon. During that brief amount of time, all students have to think of the answer, because they don't know who is going to be called upon. The brief pause invites all students to actively think about an answer, rather than the first student to raise his or her hand. By placing the student's name at the end of the question, *all* the students are kept "on the hook" a little longer. Pausing also gives students a chance to understand the question—not all students grasp the essence of a question immediately or at the same time. Sometimes teachers use questions as a disciplinary technique. If Josh is daydreaming or not paying attention in class, providing the question first and then adding Josh's name at the end of the question only serves to embarrass Josh because he has no warning a question is coming his way. Because his name doesn't precede the question, the teacher risks further alienating him from the class discussion. An alternative to getting Josh engaged in the class's discussion is to first get Josh's attention, ask him a question that you are sure he can answer, and then follow up the answer with positive reinforcement. "Josh, here's a question for you. Are you ready? Which of the following reactions represent a single replacement reaction?" After Josh's response, the teacher says, "Excellent, good job!" Directing questions to students for disciplinary reasons usually accomplishes little and is a poor use of questioning skills. This same strategy may also be useful when getting nonvolunteers to answer questions. Again, precede a question with the student's name, and then pose it. Over time, the nonvolunteer students will begin to feel more comfortable in answering questions, especially when they receive the teacher's praise.

3. *Apportion questions equally and equitably by gender.* Unknowingly, both male and female teachers often tend to pose more questions and take more responses to their questions from males than females in high school science classes. Also be aware that males are more likely to shout out an answer, thus receiving the teacher's attention. The teacher can also pose questions by gender to keep more students engaged by saying, "I'm going to ask one of the boys a question and then follow it up with a question to one of the girls." In this case, all the students are listening to the question in anticipation of being called on to answer it or the follow-up question. Again, remember to use the pause strategy between the question and the student's name.

4. *Avoid "guess what I'm thinking of" questions.* Teachers often pose questions with a particular desired response in mind. When this happens and the teacher does not get the answer he or she is looking for, the teacher may, through facial expressions or body language, indicate a "wrong" answer and call on another student until the "correct" answer is given. All the answers provided by the students may make

sense from the standpoint of the students who provide the responses; however, they just aren't the responses the teacher is searching for. Teachers should not ignore "wrong" answers. Most often, when a student gives a wrong answer, it points to a misconception the student has. Good inquiry teachers are just as concerned with "wrong" answers as they are with "right" answers.

5. *Avoid repeating student answers.* When a teacher poses a question and a student provides a correct response, what happens next? Usually the teacher (a) responds by saying "Okay," (b) says nothing and goes on to another student, (c) provides positive feedback for a correct response, or (d) repeats the student's answer. Observe any high school classroom, and far too often you will hear the teacher repeating the answer a student gives. Some teachers say they do it out of habit, while others say that students talk so softly that the rest of the class can't hear them. In either case, by repeating students' answers, teachers reinforce the notion that students do not have to speak up because the teachers will always repeat, in a louder voice, what they said. In this situation, the teacher is the conduit of the conversation. All the conversation goes "through" the teacher. Repeating student answers also communicates to the class that the students do not have to listen to other students' responses, just what the teacher says. In creating a classroom culture of inquiry, everybody's responses are important and should be heard. When the teacher repeats the student's answer, he or she, in a sense, is communicating to the class that "I will call on a student, the student will tell me the answer, and then I'll tell the rest of the class what the student said." Consider this as an alternative.

Teacher:	"What are the three types of rock? [Pause] Gino?"
Gino:	[Speaking softly] "Sedimentary, metamorphic, and igneous."
Teacher:	[Pointing to a student across the room] "Michael, did you hear that answer?"
Michael:	"No."
Teacher:	[Allowing a pause]
Gino:	[Speaking louder this time so Michael can hear him] "Sedimentary, metamorphic, and igneous."
Teacher:	[Giving a thumbs-up sign] "Correct. That's great!"

By doing this, the teacher is prompting Gino to speak up and communicate to the entire class, not just the teacher. The pause that the teacher provides is a nonthreatening prompt for Gino to speak up so everyone can hear him. With enough practice and consistent use, the voices of the students will rise so they will respect each other's contributions, thus creating a community of learners.

6. *Rephrase the question when a student can't provide an answer.* Not all questions that teachers pose result in immediate answers. There are times when students may have the background knowledge for a concept but just don't understand the question being asked. Frequently, the tendency for the teacher is to repeat the question as originally stated or ask the same question to another student. Neither of these options models good questioning strategies. When a student cannot answer a question, first consider rephrasing it. The question may make sense to the sender (the

teacher) but not to the receiver (the student). Second, consider asking another student to rephrase the question to the class. It might be that the manner in which the teacher asks the question does not make sense to the students. Sometimes students are great at "translating" teacher questions into forms that adolescents can understand. Third, don't be too quick to let the student "off the hook" by calling on someone else. Continue to rephrase the question or provide prompts to help the student answer the question. If the teacher goes on to another student, he or she communicates to the class that students can avoid answering just by claiming "I don't know."

7. *Follow up a student's response by asking for supporting details.* After posing a question and receiving a correct response, what do you do next? The teacher has several alternatives. She could go on to ask another student another question. She could ask the first student to support the answer with additional supporting details. She could follow up the student answer with the question "Why do you think that?" Or she could ask a second student to respond to the first student's answer. Depending on the situation, any of these alternatives may be appropriate. In creating a classroom culture of inquiry, consider the importance of interstudent communication where students react and respond to other students' answers. This encourages everyone to be active listeners and respect other participants' points of view.

8. *Know when to answer a student's question.* What is the first thing you think of when a student asks a question? The answer? Before answering the question for the student, the teacher should think, "Does the student have enough background information to answer his own question?" If you think the answer is "yes," consider posing prompts back to the student to assist him in answering his own question. By doing this, you encourage students to think critically and for themselves. Learning to answer your own questions is an essential aspect of inquiry-based classrooms. Often, the teacher can turn the question back to the student or to the entire class by asking, "What do you think?" According to Dyrli (1999), "If you always serve as answer-giver in your classroom, you lose important opportunities for students' thinking to take place" (p. 63). If you decide, however, that the student does not have the appropriate background information to answer the question, providing prompts and rephrasing may further frustrate both the student and the teacher. In this case, it may be more reasonable to provide the student with an answer.

9. *Don't interrupt a student's answer in the middle of the response.* Too often, a teacher poses a question that a student begins to answer correctly, and realizing the answer is correct, the teacher interrupts the student in the middle of her answer and provides further elaboration of the response. Over time, this communicates to students that their opinions are not as important as the teacher's. When a student provides an answer to a question, be patient and wait until she completes her response. Doing this will encourage the student to give a complete, thoughtful response and encourage higher-order thinking skills at the analysis and synthesis levels.

10. *Move about the classroom when asking questions.* A teacher's position in a classroom can have a profound effect on student participation in answering questions. When a teacher positions himself in the front of the class, the tendency is to acknowledge students in the immediate area, also being the front of the class. A teacher can enhance his questioning skills by walking about the room during a discussion-based

lesson and consciously calling on students across the room. Try calling on a student while you are standing behind her and encourage the student to answer and make eye contact with the other students in the class, not you. This helps students respond to each other rather than directly to the teacher, encouraging the development of a community of learners.

11. *Avoid rhetorical questions that require students to confess to the class that they do not understand a particular concept.* Questions that fall under this category usually include the following:

- Does everyone understand that?
- Who doesn't understand what I just said?
- Isn't that right?
- Who didn't get that down?
- Who doesn't get it?

12. *Plan three to four discussion questions in advance to direct the conversation and stimulate critical thinking skills.* By choosing levels of questions that require higher-level thinking skills (application, analysis, and synthesis), the teacher prompts the classroom discussion to challenge students' thinking. For example:

- What is the phenotypic proportion of offspring for a cross AABB × AaBb? (application)
- What is the relationship in a pond community between the food supply and the population size? (analysis)
- Given the data collected, how do you determine if your hypothesis is valid? (synthesis)

Careful planning of classroom questions can foster an inductive thinking model and whole-class discourse. As inquiry-based teachers hone their questioning skills, they provide opportunities to internalize learning, motivate students to challenge their models and thoughts, and provide thoughtful, engaging discussions around topics that are relevant to students.

Assessing Inquiry

THE CONCERN ABOUT ASSESSMENT

As science teachers, we understand the need to determine what our students are learning. But just the sheer mention of a unit test or a final examination can strike fear in the hearts of high school students. To most students, tests and exams are a necessary evil of school. The threat of an examination can also cause even the best of students to freeze up, a phenomenon known as *test anxiety*. Yet standardized tests, end-of-unit assessments, and midterm and final examinations have become a routine part of the school's instructional program. Some estimates report that schools devote as many as 20 days, or approximately one tenth of the academic year, to district, statewide, and national testing. Besides these formalized tests, teachers constantly make informal judgments and assessments in their classrooms all day long to monitor student progress toward achieving curricular standards. It is no wonder that assessment is a major concern to teachers today.

"Not everything that counts can be counted and not everything that can be counted counts." This maxim, reportedly posted in the office of Albert Einstein, summarizes the recent controversy over standardized testing and the use of alternative assessments. Although inquiry may seem, at first, difficult to assess, there are useful means to measure students' competence in scientific inquiry. Whereas traditional, paper-and-pencil multiple-choice tests are best in assessing content knowledge, teachers can use alternative strategies such as rubrics, performance tasks, concept maps, structured interviews, and self-evaluation to measure students' competence in inquiry. Before probing such strategies, let's first look into the importance of assessment and its alignment to standards and instruction.

Assessment is the process of using on-demand written tests and/or alternative performance tasks to collect evidence and data to make judgments regarding students' work and progress over time and to draw conclusions about the effectiveness of the teacher's instruction, leading to possible modification of the lesson or unit of study. In short, assessment has a twofold goal: determining the level of competence of the student and the effectiveness of the teacher's instruction. Although assessment and testing are often used interchangeably, assessment refers to making judgments about performance and instruction, whereas testing refers to the administration and mechanics of the examination instrument itself. Assessment is an integral aspect of teaching and learning science. According to the National Research Council (2001), assessment includes "making judgments about the students' quality of work and designing the necessary steps for improvement" (p. 7). Thus, assessment includes a multiple focus—determining the criteria for learning and quality of student work, monitoring student progress, and adjusting and improving instruction.

CURRICULUM ALIGNMENT

Curriculum alignment is a concept referring to the interrelationship among standards, instruction, and assessment. The concept of curriculum alignment is often represented in the form of a triangle.

The top point of the curriculum alignment triangle identifies the learning standards. The standards may originate or be guided from the national, state, or district level and may be defined as learning goals, frameworks, benchmarks, syllabi, or any document that identifies what students should know and be able to do. The standards are the starting point in designing any instructional or assessment program. The second point of the triangle identifies the instructional program. The instructional program includes the scope and sequence, units of study, learning strategies and activities, print and computer resources, and other teaching materials. The third point of the triangle identifies the assessment program. The assessment program includes both formative and summative assessment. When the curriculum is "aligned," the three aspects complement each other. In other words, the instructional and the assessment programs are in congruence with the implementation of the standards. If the goal of science literacy is to develop active, engaged learners, then the instructional and the assessment components of the science program should align to the standards by also being active and engaging to students.

In any instructional program, high school science teachers need to clearly and specifically identify to their students the goals and standards for their courses. Teachers then need to design appropriate assessment strategies that measure whether the goals and standards have been attained. Finally, teachers need to create and implement an instructional program that guides students through a sequence of learning opportunities and leads to success in attaining the standards.

A problem with curriculum congruence usually arises when there is a mismatch or misalignment between the instructional strategies used by the teacher and the assessment techniques employed. For example, if high school chemistry students are learning, through student-initiated inquiry, methods in which they are solving problems based on observed evidence and are later tested solely through multiple-choice items, the instruction and assessment aspects of the program are out of alignment. If you want to know if students learned a specific concept, a multiple-choice assessment can quickly determine that. If you want to know if students can complete a process, then a performance assessment is most appropriate.

Figure 8.1   Curriculum Alignment

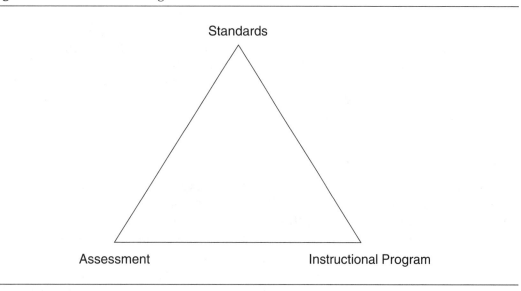

According to Audet and Jordan (2003),

> the central questions addressed by the principle of congruence are 1) how does the teacher take a learning goal and use it to design an assessment that provides valid and sufficient evidence that this goal has been achieved by students? and 2) How does a teacher then use this assessment to guide his or her selection of learning experiences that enable students to demonstrate that they have attained the learning goals? (p. 51)

To have standards, instruction, and assessment aligned and consistent, teachers can ask themselves three questions:

1. What do my students need to know and be able to do? (standard)

2. How will I know whether the students meet the standard? (assessment)

3. What learning opportunities will I provide for students to meet the standard? (instruction)

DESIGNING ASSESSMENTS

Unfortunately, most high school teachers have been taught to use the learning standards to *first* design an instructional unit *and then* write the unit test. In this way, the sequence of planning units of study starts with the standards, moves to the instructional strategies, and finally arrives at the assessment procedures. Although this may sound logical, McTighe and Wiggins (1999) offer a "backwards design" approach to curricula planning. They suggest first sequencing the design of units of study with the standards, then moving to the assessment method, and last forming the instructional strategies. In the "backwards design" approach, McTighe and Wiggins suggest that teachers first be extremely clear in identifying the unit's goals and expectations (what the student is expected to know and be able to do), then decide how to determine the level of achievement in achieving the standards. By placing the assessment up front, before the instructional strategies, the teacher avoids writing the test the night before it's given. In a "backwards design" approach, the planning of the unit progresses from standards, to assessment, to instructional strategies. As the teacher designs the assessment procedures, she asks herself, "What am I interested in measuring? What do I value? What are the essential content areas, skills, and attitudes that students need to know and be able to do as a result of this unit?"

Choosing the Right Test Item

Given the vast amount of content students are expected to amass during today's high school science courses, it is not difficult to understand the role that traditional, on-demand tests play in assessing student achievement. Test items of this type share the advantages of ease in administration and scoring, reliability, and availability. Objective question formats such as multiple-choice, true/false, matching, and fill-in-the-blank frequently can be found at the end of a chapter in biology, earth science, chemistry, and physics textbooks. Objective test items also work well for assessing large numbers of students in a short amount of time. Although objective-type items serve the specific function of assessing content, they generally are inappropriate for assessing inquiry and science process skills.

Assessing inquiry skills is best done over extended periods of time rather than during a test in a single class period. Inquiry assessment should mirror the work students do in school. According to the National Research Council (2001), "for an assessment to make valid claims about a student's ability to conduct inquiry, the assessment would need to assess the range or abilities and understandings comprised in the construct of inquiry" (p. 55). Think of an assessment of inquiry skills like practicing for a diving competition. The competition (or test) is completely known to the diver (or student). The diver (or student) gets to practice a particular dive (or task) and knows both what he or she is expected to do during the competition (or test) and the criteria for a high score (or grade). With a standards-driven, inquiry-based assessment, the teacher's goal is to balance objective testing with authentic performance tasks that mirror or apply the work completed during the investigation. An appropriate inquiry-based assessment will test not only content knowledge but also science process skills, scientific reasoning skills, and metacognitive skills. The assessment would also include the standard to be achieved, the criteria for accomplishment, and examples of exemplary, high-quality student work. In scientific inquiry, teachers develop a new paradigm for assessing students' work. It includes not only the answers they give but also the questions they raise.

Given the subjectivity of inquiry-based assessment, without specific measurements much of the assessment depends on the judgment of the classroom teacher. After all, it is the classroom teacher who knows his students' work the best. The National Research Council (2001) suggests that "inquiry is difficult to assess in a one-time test. A teacher's position in the classroom allows for personal judgments of one's abilities over extended investigation that cannot be matched by any feasible external testing procedure" (p. 17). For that reason, teachers need to constantly use multiple assessment measures to monitor and record students' interactions.

What is important is that assessment is an ongoing activity, one that relies on multiple strategies and sources for collecting information that bears on the quality of student work and that can be used to help both the students and the teacher think more pointedly about how the quality might be improved. (NRC, 2001, p. 30)

Using Multiple Assessments

Many of us have heard the phrase "teaching to the test." The phrase refers to the notion that assessment drives instruction. Well, if it's a *good* test, there is nothing wrong in teaching to the test. Because inquiry-based teachers consider assessment alternatives that align to the philosophy of inquiry, their decisions often lead to multiple, standards-driven assessments rather than reliance on one single test. It is, however, more difficult to assess learning through inquiry. What verifiable evidence exists that learning has occurred? By correctly answering a multiple-choice question, does a student truly indicate that he or she has mastered the information? By using a wide range of assessments, including multiple-choice items, constructed response questions, performance tasks, rubrics, portfolios, monitoring charts, concept maps, self-evaluations, and structured interviews, inquiry-based high school teachers can gain a better understanding of whether or not the student truly has constructed an understanding of the content.

AUTHENTIC ASSESSMENTS

The term *authentic* (or *alternative*) *assessment* is often used when describing measurements to assess inquiry. Authentic assessments are embedded tasks that are similar in form to tasks in which students will engage outside the classroom or are similar to the activities of scientists (NRC, 2001). They are designed to measure what students know as well as what they can do. Authentic assessments and performance tasks have an advantage over traditional objective assessments. Besides assessing content and high-order thinking skills, they also provide opportunities for students to demonstrate creativity, problem solving, and decision making. Although it takes time to develop accurate, dependable, valid assessments that measure inquiry, having assessments that align to the standards and instruction is a step further in curriculum alignment. This section will provide several types of assessments high school science teachers can use in an inquiry-based classroom:

Performance Tasks

In a performance task, students engage in collecting information to solve a given problem and often construct a model based on the evidence collected. Performance-based assessment can take the form of open-ended investigations, station-to-station laboratory tasks, or structured tasks.

For an example of a performance task, David Stevens, a high school earth science teacher in Maryland, encourages problem solving in his classroom (see Stevens, 1991, p. 359). This task assesses geologic understandings, manipulation, and science process skills, as well as the ability to construct a model. According to Stevens, students start the exam by spending two to three days measuring, identifying, and recording data taken from meter-long plastic tubes that have been placed at specific locations around the classroom. Each tube represents a hypothetical core sample of material taken from that location. The tubes contain various rock and fossil specimens that will be used to draw conclusions about climate, geologic age, geologic events, and geologic history. Students may collect their data individually, in pairs, or in small groups. The data collected and the method by which the student represents the data comprise one-third of the final exam grade. (p. 359)

In the second part of the final exam, each student takes his or her data home and constructs a "model" of the area represented in the classroom. (Previous examples of models are withheld from the students.) Finished models usually take the form of geologic maps, topographic maps, cross sections, or three-dimensional replicas. The model constitutes another third of the final grade.

Last, each student is required to write a geologic history of the area. The theoretical geologic history must be plausible, and the history should identify as many of the area's unique geological features as possible. There is no required length for the theory, which constitutes the remaining third of the final exam grade (Stevens, 1991, pp. 359, 361). In this case, the assessment provides an opportunity for students to demonstrate mastery of their understanding of earth science in a variety of ways. The task allows students to (a) use knowledge to solve problems, (b) use performance and science process skills to complete the task, (c) collect data and evidence based upon their observations, and (d) construct an explanation, in the form of a written report, based on the evidence collected. In addition, the task reinforces the development of scientific dispositions and attitudes that empower students to make decisions on their own.

For other excellent examples of high school–level performance tasks for biology, earth science, chemistry, and physics, see Resource A (Print Resources on Assessment) for *Science Educator's Guide to Laboratory Assessment* by Doran, Chan, Tamir, and Lenhardt.

Rubrics

Rubrics or scoring guides, when used in conjunction with projects and performance tasks, provide a means for all students to achieve high standards by communicating what exemplary, high-standard work looks like. Rubrics articulate explicit performance descriptions and criteria for specific areas at different levels of competence. They distinguish proficiency from above-standard (or exemplary) and from below-standard (or unacceptable) work. Rubrics, when used throughout the inquiry investigation, foster conversations about what constitutes quality work. When a student asks the question "What are we supposed to do?" the teacher can refer to the rubric. The rubric also answers the student question, "What do I have to do to get an A?" For students, rubrics takes the "game" out of guessing what the teacher is looking for and provide a means for self-reflection when evaluating their own work. For teachers, rubrics communicate the classroom standard for excellent work. Many teachers who use rubrics in the classroom admit that they help students both make better judgments about their own work and strive for the highest possible standard.

Sources of both analytical and holistic rubrics can be found through an Internet search. The Northwest Regional Educational Laboratory, Mathematics and Science Center, provides an excellent analytical rubric for an inquiry investigation, in both a student and a teacher version, for the secondary school science level at its Web site, www.nwrel.org/msec/science_inq/guides.html.

A second excellent resource for an inquiry rubric can be found at http://col-ed .org/smcnws/scientific.html. You may find that each rubric you use will need revision and "tweaking" to modify it to your specific classroom needs.

The holistic rubric shown in Figure 8.2 is applicable for scoring the planning and performance of a laboratory procedure such as the "Sugar and Sand Task" in Chapter 6.

Figure 8.2   Holistic Rubric for Scoring the Planning and Performance of a Laboratory Procedure

---

The Sugar and Sand Task

Levels of Performance

Level 3: Exemplary (above standard)

- Needs no prompting or assistance to begin or complete the task
- Demonstrates complete understanding of the nature, conditions, and limits of the question or problem
- Designs and describes in depth the logical order of the procedures
- Carries out the plan with accurate quantitative measurements
- Manipulates equipment and materials safely
- Uses appropriate techniques in collecting data
- Records data and measurements accurately and concisely
- Communicates findings and results effectively
- Demonstrates precise and accurate solutions to the question or problem
- Performance results in precise and accurate solution to the question or problem

Level 2: Competent (at standard)

- Works cooperatively with partner to complete task
- Considers the nature, conditions, and limits of the question or problem
- Designs acceptable and appropriate procedures
- Carries out quantitative measurements
- Uses apparatus safely and with good technique
- Records measurement correctly
- Communicates findings in a satisfactory manner
- Performance results in solution to the problem

Level 1: Limited or inadequate (below standard)

- Requires assistance or prompting to begin the task
- Fails to consider one or more conditions and limits of the question or problem
- Plans inappropriate procedure to solve the question or problem
- Uses unsafe laboratory techniques or procedures
- Makes errors in recording data
- Commits errors in calculations
- Records result incompletely
- Performance does not solve the question or problem

Application Questions

Application questions allow the teacher to conduct assessments in situations where students use data and evidence from their original inquiry investigation to solve a problem in a related situation. This can be accomplished by referring to an investigation the students just completed and testing their understanding by providing a new, similar situation. The teacher can have students design another investigation using a different manipulated or independent variable. As an example, in an 11th-grade general physics class, Ms. Clark uses Nasco's Rubber Band Cannons to answer the question "How does the angle of the cannon affect the distance the rubber band will travel?"

Figure 8.3a

Figure 8.3b

Figure 8.3c

Figure 8.3d

During the inquiry phase of the lesson, students have to

- identify the manipulated variable (the angle), the responding variable (the distance the rubber band travels), and the controlled variables (the size of the rubber band, the amount of force applied to the rubber band, the classroom environment, how the rubber band is released, etc.);
- write a hypothesis for the investigation;
- design an appropriate investigation to test the question;
- carry out the investigation and record the data on a chart or a table;
- create a graph, using a computer, to represent the data;
- draw a conclusion that describes the relationship between the manipulated variable and the responding variable;
- determine whether the hypothesis is correct;
- complete a summary of the investigation and communicate the findings.

During the assessment phase of the lesson, Ms. Clark gave the students a two-part test. Part 1 included 10 multiple-choice questions that measured their understanding of physics concepts, including trajectory and potential and kinetic energy. The second part of the test included an application question where some students had to design an experiment to determine how the *force or pull back* will affect the distance the rubber band travels, while other students had to determine how the *size* of the rubber band affects the distance traveled. By using multiple assessment measures, Ms. Clark can determine not only what students know about forces, energy, and trajectories but also their abilities to use information gathered from an investigation and apply it to similar situations.

Monitoring Charts

Observing day-to-day performance is an informal and practical means of assessment in an inquiry-based science classroom. Through the use of monitoring charts (Llewellyn, 2002), teachers can observe and monitor a predetermined set of behaviors, including the following:

- Brainstorms possible solutions to questions and problems
- Makes careful observations
- Follows directions

- Interacts positively with peers
- Uses equipment properly
- Acts responsibly
- Uses the Internet and computer software to collect, organize, and present data
- Makes positive constructive contributions during group work
- Collects data and evidence in a journal or research notebook

A teacher can move about the room, observe students' behavior, and carefully note individual actions on a chart. Specific behaviors can be indicated with a *check plus* (✓+) for above-standard performance, a *check* (✓) for at-standard performance, or a *check minus* (✓–) for below-standard performance. High school teachers are also encouraged to make anecdotal records of daily observations and notations in a daily running record by using a notebook or chart on a clipboard to record students' comments, questions, ideas, misconceptions, problems, and achievements. When using monitoring charts, remember to document the student's name, date, time, and title of lesson. Teachers are also encouraged to observe and monitor all students equitably, make observations regularly, and make multiple observations to ensure reliability (Hart, 1994). Figure 8.4 is an example of a monitoring chart.

Capstone Projects

Capstone projects are final inquiries, investigations, research projects, or presentations usually completed toward the end of the school year. When students complete a capstone project, they model the inquiry process by

- identifying a worthwhile and researchable question,
- planning the investigation,
- executing the research plan, and
- drafting the research report (NRC, 1996).

Capstone projects offer teachers a unique opportunity to judge how well students can integrate the knowledge from a science course and apply it in a research setting. Like an extended performance task, capstone projects enhance speaking and listening skills, including making eye contact, projecting voice, and speaking clearly.

Some high schools have separate courses or electives for juniors and seniors, such as *Research in Science*, that are completely inquiry-based. In these courses, students choose a research question to investigate. The teacher or a community scientist acts as a mentor in guiding students in writing a proposal that carefully frames the question. Working as individuals or in groups of two, students develop a set of procedures to carry out the inquiry, a list of materials and equipment needed, and a means for collecting and organizing the data. When the plan is completed, it is approved either by the classroom teacher or by a committee of other science teachers and/or peer reviewed by other students in the class.

During the actual inquiry, students may need the assistance of a local college professor or might benefit from using a college's laboratory facilities or library. For this reason, coordinating research with a nearby college or university may be helpful. The contact may also lead to the higher education institution offering college credit upon successful completion of the investigation.

Figure 8.4   Science Inquiry Monitoring Chart

Stage / Behavior	Investigation #				
	1	2	3	4	5
Exploring					
makes observations					
records observations in journal					
takes careful notes					
draws illustrations/sketches					
records "what if . . . " questions					
Stating a question					
sorts and revises questions					
states an investigation question					
brainstorms possible solutions					
Identifying a statement to test					
makes a statement to test					
records statement					
Designing a procedure					
brainstorms possible steps					
arranges steps in sequential order					
identifies manipulated variable					
identifies responding variable					
identifies dependent variables					
determines materials to use					
Carrying out a plan					
obtains supplies and materials					
follows written procedure					
follows safety guidelines					
shares/respects ideas with group members					
assumes responsibility for group role					
makes constructive contributions to group					
Collecting evidence					
gathers data					
makes accurate measurements					
organizes data in tables or charts					
plots data on a graph					
describes relationship between variables					
draws conclusion					
analyzes results					
determines validity of hypothesis					
Communicating results					
prepares trifold poster					
makes contribution to presentation					
uses appropriate terminology					
makes eye contact with audience					
speaks clearly					
answers questions from audience					
reflects on investigation					

Concept Maps

Concept maps are schematic organizations that identify multiple concepts and their interrelations with each other. Concept maps usually have either a radial (or weblike) orientation, with the main idea in the center of the map, or a hierarchical orientation, with the main idea at the top of the map. Connecting words, cross-links, or short phrases are used to show the relationship between concept and subconcepts. Software programs such as *Inspiration* provide a step-by-step tutorial guide to show how to create concept maps and templates for other graphic organizers. Figure 8.5 is an example of a concept map with radial orientation.

Concept maps have been widely used in assessing presently held knowledge and documenting the acquisition and progression of new knowledge (Edmondson, 2000). This is accomplished by simply having the student create a concept map citing his or her preunderstandings about a particular topic prior to the start of a unit of study. As the student completes the concept map, the teacher can determine what the student knows about the topic. As the unit progresses, the student can return to the map and make corrections (from prior misconceptions) and additions, citing newly acquired information. Using a different colored pencil or pen for each revision makes it easy to visualize how knowledge is constructed and modified. The concept map then acts as a vehicle for initiating a discussion on the student's pre- and post-knowledge.

Structured Interviews

Although some students can demonstrate their competence in writing, others can best explain concept by expressing themselves verbally. Structured interviews can be a viable means to assess students' understanding (Southerland, Smith, & Cummins, 2002) and are especially effective for students with test anxiety.

During a structured interview, the teacher provides several probing questions or visual prompts to elicit the student's understanding of a concept. The questions can center on the student solving a problem, making a prediction, or drawing an inference about a particular situation or phenomenon. The teacher may also choose to provide two or three questions in advance so that the student can prepare responses for the upcoming interview. In this case, the student researches the answers to the questions but will not know which specific questions will be asked during the interview. The advantage of this one-on-one interaction is that the student can then blend his or her jargon with scientific terms to express an understanding. This process also provides flexibility for the teacher, who can assess a student's understanding of the inquiry process by individualizing and tailoring the questions posed based on the student's responses. Because structured interviews are very time-intensive, a teacher can use the interview process on a sample of students in the class to gauge the entire class's understanding and modify instruction accordingly.

While planning for a structured interview, consider the following steps:

1. Select questions based on goals and objectives of the lesson/unit. Include actual objects, diagrams, pictures, materials, or equipment whenever possible to assist in posing questions.

2. Design questions that provide students an opportunity to explain and elaborate their understandings. Avoid questions with "yes" or "no," or "one-word" answers.

Figure 8.5   Concept Map

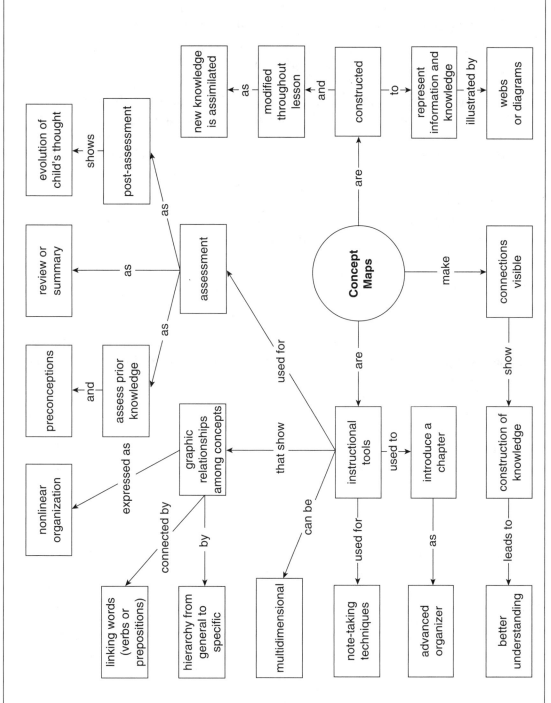

3. Start the interview with an "easy" question to make the students feel comfortable. The success of the structured interview lies in the comfort level of the students and their ability to provide supportive details to their responses.

4. Employ wait-time strategies (Rowe, 1974, 1987, 1996) for the student to respond. Do not interrupt the student in the middle of his or her answer.

5. Make recordings of the student's responses by taking notes or using an audio-tape recorder or a videotape machine.

Interviews can be either formal (structured) or informal. In structured interviews, according to Dana, Lorsbach, Hook, and Briscoe (1991), "teachers and students are jointly responsible for determining what the student knows. Through personalized communication, both teacher and student negotiate the meaning of what is being said, with the student empowered to make sure meanings are expressed thoroughly and understood" (p. 336). Interviews with students, however, can also be informal and day-to-day.

In this more familiar case, the teacher circulates around the room, sits down with an individual student or group of students, and discusses the investigation, the procedure, and the evidence being recorded. The teacher carefully listens to students' interaction, values their comments, and poses diagnostic questions to determine how well the individual or group is mastering the concepts being studied. During the informal interview process,

> the teacher makes judgments about the students' level of understanding by assessing the student during the course of the project and carefully observing the student's work, asking key questions along the way, and responding to the student's questions. The teacher continually probes the student to ensure how well the student understands the concept, to determine how he approaches the problem, and to find out the assumptions that underlie a student's response. During the process, the teacher has a unique opportunity to make considered judgments, based on the concrete evidence collected about the quality of student accomplishment. (NRC, 2001, p. 8)

Self-Evaluations

Self-evaluations are vehicles in which students assess their performance and metacognition skills through reflection on their own strengths and weaknesses. Self-evaluations are especially useful in inquiry-based instruction because the student provides individual feedback on his or her performance. Although students tend to rate themselves favorably, the self-evaluation can be an effective assessment instrument when it challenges students to reflect on the task and identify how they might improve their performance if they were to repeat the inquiry or engage in a similar task.

Self-evaluations usually contain a set of statements and a rating scale. The statements can describe proficient levels of behavior, while the rating scale can vary from 5 (the highest) to 1 (the lowest), or include descriptors such as *Always, Usually, Sometimes, Rarely,* and *Never.* Figure 8.6 is a self-evaluation about the assessment system in your classroom. Complete the self-evaluation by circling the appropriate number/response for each statement.

Figure 8.6 Assessment Self-Evaluation

Circle an appropriate number/response for each of the following statements about your assessment system:

My assessment system . . .	Always 5	Usually 4	Sometimes 3	Rarely 2	Never 1
1. Includes various measures, both traditional and authentic, to assess students' understandings.	5	4	3	2	1
2. Includes assessing students' understandings prior to the beginning of a new topic or unit.	5	4	3	2	1
3. Provides students with essential information that progress is being made toward reaching learning goals, standards, and course expectations.	5	4	3	2	1
4. Assists in planning teaching and making adjustments to the instructional program as well as students' understandings.	5	4	3	2	1
5. Assesses group as well as individual work.	5	4	3	2	1
6. Assesses what students know, what they can do, and their scientific attitudes, attributes, or habits of mind.	5	4	3	2	1
7. Includes day-to-day as well as end of the unit assessments.	5	4	3	2	1
8. Provides students the opportunity to demonstrate their understandings, competencies, and accomplishments in a variety of ways.	5	4	3	2	1
9. Addresses "core" content and science process skills.	5	4	3	2	1
10. Is aligned to learning standards and instructional strategies.	5	4	3	2	1
11. Is based on clear, communicated criteria (e.g., rubrics).	5	4	3	2	1
12. Applies to relevant and real-life situations that are extensions of in-class performances.	5	4	3	2	1

(Continued)

Figure 8.6 (Continued)

	Always	Usually	Sometimes	Rarely	Never
13. Allows for at-home as well as in-class assessments.	5	4	3	2	1
14. Allows for students to engage in ongoing assessments of their work and that of others.	5	4	3	2	1
15. Allows for the assessment to be written at the beginning of the unit rather than the night before it is administered.	5	4	3	2	1
16. Is free of bias and ensures that all students are assessed fairly and equitably.	5	4	3	2	1
17. Incorporates higher-order thinking skills such as appraising, critiquing, hypothesizing, and analyzing as well as recalling, describing, and explaining.	5	4	3	2	1
18. Addresses the nature of science, social perspectives, and history of science.	5	4	3	2	1
19. Includes students manipulating equipment and using laboratory techniques learned in the classroom.	5	4	3	2	1
20. Includes review of written responses from other science teachers to ensure interrater reliability.	5	4	3	2	1

Rubrics can be considered a form of self-evaluation. Using rubrics in the high school science classroom provides a unique opportunity for students to self-assess their work and strive to achieve at the highest standard. Through using a rubric to guide performance, students know what constitutes exemplary work. Rubrics allow students to reflect on their work and attain the highest possible level.

The most important point of this chapter is to clearly demonstrate that inquiry-based teaching is predicated on a different form of assessment. It is not always practical to use objective-type, multiple-choice items to assess scientific inquiry. High school science teachers can use concept maps to preassess students' understanding, along with monitoring charts and rubrics during the inquiry. At the conclusion of the inquiry, they can use self-evaluations, performance tasks, concept maps, structured interviews, capstone projects, and application questions. Given the challenges of class size, with some teachers having as many as five classes with 25–30 students in each, the question often asked is, "How do I make the transition into new assessments while I'm still trying to understand how to teach through inquiry?" It is true that alternative assessments demand more time to construct and correct. Some may question their subjectivity. Others may question their reliability. Because teachers are not assessment specialists, they need to work in teams and support groups to develop inquiry-based units and the appropriate assessments. It may take time for teachers to develop appropriate assessment tools, but when you use them, you will have true alignment among the standards, the instruction, and the assessment.

Teaching Biology Through Inquiry

INVESTIGATING YEAST

In this chapter, we will examine a 10th-grade biology class carrying out laboratory investigations involving yeast. The investigations in this case study lead students from teacher-initiated inquiries into student-initiated inquiries. In addition, the case study will further our understanding of how teachers can use a constructivist lesson format, the 5E Learning Cycle, to sequence instruction.

This lesson correlates to the *National Science Education Standards* (NRC, 1996) for both inquiry and content standards, which are quoted below.

Science as Inquiry Standard

Students will

- Identify questions and concepts that guide a scientific investigation. (p. 175)
- Design and conduct a scientific investigation. (p. 175)
- Formulate scientific explanations and models using logic and evidence. (p. 175)
- Recognize and analyze alternative explanations and models. (p. 175)
- Communicate and defend a scientific argument. (p. 176)

Life Science Content Standard

As a result of their activities in grades 9–12, all students should develop (an) understanding that

- Cells have particular structures that underline their functions. Every cell is surrounded by a membrane that separates it from the outside world. Inside the cell is a concentrated mixture of thousands of molecules which form a variety of specialized structures that carry out such cell functions as energy production, transport of molecules, waste disposal, synthesis of new molecules, and storage of genetic material. (p. 184)

A Day at the Life Sciences Learning Center

Sara McClane has been teaching general and college preparatory biology at Penport High School for 8 years. This past July, she participated in a 2-week summer professional development workshop sponsored by the Life Sciences Learning Center (LSLC), located in the University of Rochester in Rochester, New York, to engage secondary school science teachers in inquiry-based instruction. As a follow-up to that workshop, participating teachers are encouraged to bring their biology classes back to the LSLC for a full day of laboratory investigations. The LSLC is a unique hands-on science inquiry center serving middle, high school, and Advanced Placement students and teachers throughout central-western New York State. The LSLC is devoted entirely to precollege science education and providing hands-on, inquiry-based, and laboratory-based investigations for students aligned to the state's science learning standards. The LSLC also provides ongoing professional development, such as the workshop Sara attended, on laboratory-based life science instruction and biotechnology for secondary school teachers. For more information on the LSLC, visit http://lifesciences.envmed.rochester.edu/.

Dr. Dina Markowitz, LSLC director, and Ms. Jana Penders, LSLC science educator, lead the lessons for students attending the center. Dina is an associate professor and Director of Community Outreach and Education Programs at the University of Rochester's Department of Environmental Medicine. With a background in molecular biology from Columbia University, Dina also is a research geneticist at the university. Jana is a former high school biology and chemistry teacher with research experience in microbiology and molecular biology. She is presently fulfilling requirements for a master's degree in secondary science education.

The day's agenda for the yeast investigation follows the 5E Learning Cycle format. The morning session includes the Engagement and Exploration stages. Following lunch, students return for the Explanation and Extension stages. The Evaluation stage will be completed by Sara the next day, when the class returns to school.

Engagement Stage: What Is Life?

Sara and her students arrive by bus at the center at 8:30 A.M. They are greeted at the door by Dina and Jana, then are led upstairs to the laboratory. As the students put on their white lab coats and settle onto the stools at their assigned lab tables, the lesson opens with a 20-minute introduction by Jana. She initiates a discussion to assess the students' prior understanding of the characteristics of living things. "What do you know about living things?" she asks. "Do you think this is living?," she asks as she points to a potted geranium near the window. Nora, a student in the class, tells Jana that living things carry out certain functions such as respiration and reproduction, and also respond to external stimuli. "Since the geranium performs these functions," Nora says, "it is a living organism." Jana then shows the class a picture on the television monitor and continues. "How about these bacteria? Are they alive? How do you know?" Several students provide responses to indicate that bacteria, like the geranium, are living organisms.

"Today we are going to act like scientists and detectives," Jana says. "In a sense, they both do the same kind of work. They both make observations and draw inferences based on their observations." She then holds up two identical-looking vials, one labeled "A" and the other labeled "B." The vials contain equal amounts of tan-colored granules.

"We have a mystery to solve," Jana continues. "I have two vials, but I don't know what is in them. I'll need your help in finding out which of the granules in the vials are living organisms or nonliving." Although the contents look nearly identical, vial A contains sand and vial B contains common baker's yeast. The students are told that their task is to perform several laboratory techniques to determine which vial contains living organisms, be able to substantiate their evidence, and be able to provide a logical explanation. "You will be making both qualitative and quantitative observations," Jana tells the students. "All your data should be accurately recorded in your science journals." The students then pair up and move on to the Exploration stage, during which they begin to test the samples in the vials.

Exploration Stage

During the next 2.5 hours, students design their investigations through prompting and guidance by Jana and Dina. The students are provided with the following materials and equipment to help them collect evidence and draw their conclusions:

- One vial of sand (labeled Sample A)
- One vial of baker's yeast (labeled Sample B)
- One transfer pipette
- One small beaker containing 100 mL of warm water
- Two test tubes
- Two large ziplock bags
- One plastic teaspoon
- One permanent marker
- One ruler
- One 100-mL graduated cylinder
- Two packets of sugar and artificial sweeteners (Equal, Sweet'N Low, Sugar Twin)
- Microscope slides
- Microscope cover slips
- One container of methylene blue
- One magnifying lens
- Paper towels
- One dissecting microscope
- One compound microscope (with oil immersion)
- Oil for immersion objective
- One incubator (set at 37°C)

"Because all good scientists and detectives start with observations," Jana explains, "your first step is to use your senses, with the exception of taste, to observe the two samples. Although they are both safe, it's recommended not to taste anything in a laboratory. You can observe the samples first with your naked eye and then by using a magnifying lens."

"Later," Dina adds, "you can put the samples under the microscope and see if there is a difference in the samples. I suggest you start with the dissecting scope first, and then use the compound microscope later. This way, you are always increasing in magnification." The groups take the next 15 minutes to observe both vials and record observations in their science journals.

Figure 9.1

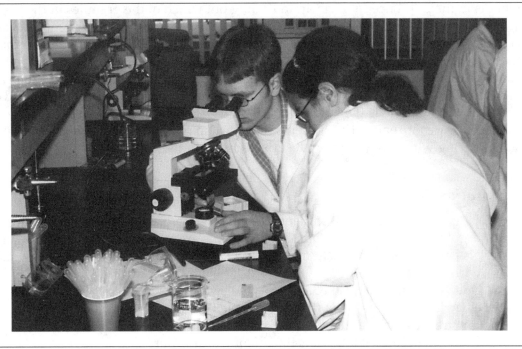

In one group, Ann records that Sample B looks like fish food. Michael adds that Sample B looks like little capsules and smells like pizza dough. In another group, Michelle says, "Sample A doesn't smell at all, and B smells like yeast." As the students are busy making their preliminary observations, Jana encourages students to use a two-column chart, similar to Figure 9.2, to record their observations and questions.

Figure 9.2   Two-Column Chart

Observations	Questions

Once the groups have made their initial observations, they are ready to move on to Step 2. Jana begins the discussion by asking "What can we do next to further our investigation?"

A student suggests, "I think we should put each sample in some water and see if it dissolves, floats or sinks, or changes color." With minimal guidance, each group now takes a small sample of the unknown granules, places each in a separate test tube, and adds equal amounts of water. The students then observe the test tubes with a magnifying lens and note that Sample A rests at the bottom of the test tube and water, while Sample B forms a suspension. One group asks if they can prepare a wet mount of each sample, and Dina encourages the entire class to do so. The students observe the two samples under both low and high magnification. For the first time, the groups distinguish significant differences between the two samples microscopically, using both flat and depression slides. Students now include in their journals illustrations of granules for Sample A and cell-like objects for Sample B.

Figure 9.3

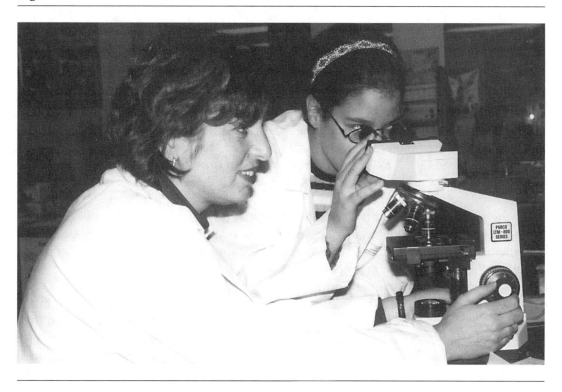

As Dina continues to circulate among the groups, Jana places slides of Samples A and B, similar to what the students prepared, in the micro-viewer for the entire class to see. She uses the samples in the micro-viewer to compare and contrast the two samples and what the students have in their own microscopes. She suggests the students construct a Venn diagram in their notebooks, similar to Figure 9.4, to record the similarities and differences of Samples A and B.

Figure 9.4 Venn Diagram

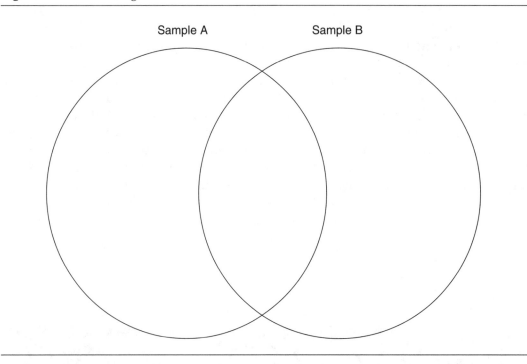

By the end of Step 2, most of the groups conclude that the samples are sand and yeast. Although many of the groups come to this conclusion, they are reminded that they need substantial data to prove their case and that their observations alone are not sufficient. They need more evidence!

Jana now leads the class into a discussion about the staining techniques for Step 3 of the investigation. She tells the class that when they add methylene blue to each slide sample, the stain will indicate the presence of a cell membrane. "How, then, does the methylene help you to answer the question—is it alive?" she asks.

Maria answers, "If the methylene blue stain is absorbed by the sample and the cell membrane is highlighted, we have additional proof that the sample is a living organism." Jana now demonstrates how to add a drop of methylene blue to the slide. By placing a drop of stain at one end of the cover slip and by placing a piece of paper towel at the opposite end, the stain is drawn across the slide, through the sample, and into the paper towel. After students perform the technique on both slides, they view the samples under 100X magnification with oil immersion and soon discover that the sand, Sample A, does not absorb the indicator, whereas the yeast in Sample B does, highlighting the cell membrane. They conclude that Sample B consists of living cells.

The students are now ready to begin Step 4. Dina begins this section of the investigation by asking, "Do you think the yeasts will grow in water alone?"

"No," one student suggests. "You'll need a food supply."

Dina then asks, "What food supply would you add to the water to help the yeast grow?" Some students suggest sugar; others suggest molasses or corn syrup. "All of you are right," she says. "Now let's design a way to determine the effect of sugar, or any another sweetener, on the samples." During this part of the lesson, students are led through a teacher-initiated inquiry: Are yeasts living things, and do they need a food supply, like sugar, to grow? Students are given two ziplock plastic bags, and they place a teaspoon of yeast in each bag. A packet of sugar is added to one of the bags and labeled "Sugar." The second bag, to which no sugar is added, is labeled "Control." One hundred milliliters of warm water is added to each bag. (Some students decide they want do the identical procedure with the sand sample just to compare.)

Figure 9.5

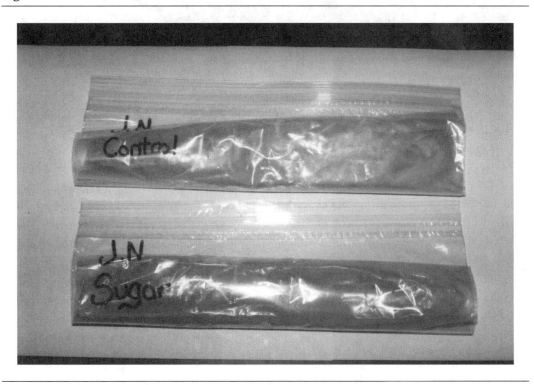

The students squeeze all the air out of the bags, seal the tops, and roll the bags tightly. They now place their paired bags in an incubator set at 37°C for 15 minutes.

After 15 minutes, the students remove their bags from the incubator, measure any vertical rise in the bags, and return the bags to the incubator for another 15 minutes.

After 30 minutes and again at 45 minutes, the students repeat the procedure, removing the bags from the incubator and measuring any change in height. The students continue to make observations and record their measurements in their science journals. One student makes a notation in her journal with the following results:

When I add sugar to the yeast and then place the bag in an incubator for 30 minutes, fermentation occurs and a gas, probably carbon dioxide, is produced. The bag inflates because the gas being produced is trapped within the bag. The yeast metabolizes the sugar and produces the gas (carbon dioxide) as a by-product.

Figure 9.6

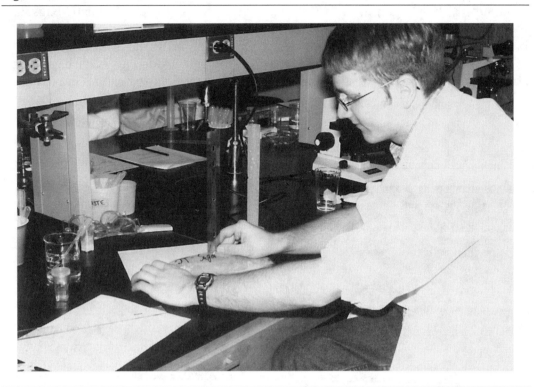

| | Bag Height (in centimeters) | |
Time (in minutes)	Control	Sugar
15	0	1
30	0	2
45	0	5

Explanation Stage

After the groups record their data from the yeast exploration, Jana brings the class together for a teacher-led discussion. A handout accompanies her comments. "Yeasts," she explains, "are unicellular and belong to a group of microorganisms called the ascomycotes, or *sac fungi.* Their scientific name is *Saccharomyces cerevisiae*, meaning sugar-loving. They are quite common and can be found naturally in the soil, in animals, including humans, on locker room floors, or just about anywhere there is moisture. Yeasts are especially noted for their ability to ferment carbohydrates, like sugar, and produce alcohol and carbon dioxide. This makes them important in the production of beer, wines, and bread. Yeasts usually reproduce by budding. That means that they reproduce asexually by producing small budlike outgrowths from the parent cell. Yeasts, however, can also reproduce sexually by producing spores called *ascospores*."

Figure 9.7

As the students take notes for their presentations, Jana shows yeast cells and their rigid cell walls on the monitor using the micro-viewer. She continues her presentation by explaining that yeasts, although living, are neither plants nor animals. "They belong to a separate phylum of fungus," she adds. "And since mycology is study of fungi, today you have been working as mycologists!" She goes on to explain why yeasts are eukaryotic and describes both the fermentation process and the life cycle of yeasts.

At the end of the Explanation stage, the class concludes that yeasts are indeed living organisms because they reproduce, use respiration, and repair and grow new cells. The class also concludes that Sample A is sand and Sample B is yeast. After a full morning of laboratory work, the class breaks for lunch.

Elaboration Stage: What Do Yeast Live On?

When the students return from lunch, they are ready to begin the Elaboration stage, in which they design their own student-initiated investigations. Jana tells the students to work in their groups to brainstorm questions to investigate. She suggests they refer to their two-column charts from the Engagement section and their data from the Exploration section to consider questions for further investigation.

After a few minutes of brainstorming, Tim and Carrie decide to test regular sugar versus artificial sweeteners. They want to see if the amount of carbon dioxide produced during fermentation varies among natural and artificial sweeteners such as table sugar, Equal, Sweet'N Low, and Sugar Twin. They design their investigation so that equal amounts of each sugar or sweetener are placed in a plastic bag with yeast and warm water.

Brian and Brandon want to find out how the amount of sugar affects the rate of fermentation and production of carbon dioxide. To do this, they propose adding varying amounts of sugar (10, 20, 30, and 40 grams) to the plastic bags. They also hope to determine how the amounts of food available affect the growth of the yeast cells.

Donnell and Willis want to know if baker's yeast metabolizes differently in varying types of sugars. To do this, they design an investigation to test sucrose, dextrose, glucose, and fructose. They inform Dina that their manipulating variable in the investigation is the type of sugar used and the responding variable is the amount of carbon dioxide produced as measured by the height of the bag after fermentation.

Sandy and Sharon's question is "What is the optimal temperature for yeast growth?" They decide to investigate the ideal conditions for yeast growth and metabolism by growing yeasts at three different temperatures: 27°C, 37°C, and 47°C.

When Carol and Ron placed the methylene blue stain in the slide from the morning investigation, that stirred three new questions: What would happen if we place a sugar solution under the slide of yeasts? Will gas bubbles form under the cover slip? Will the carbon dioxide bubbles look different from air bubbles?

For each investigation, Jana and Dina encourage the students to identify the manipulated (or independent) variable, the responding (or dependent) variable, and the controlling (or constant) variables. Once the students design their experiments, they bring their plans to Dina or Jana for approval. After an hour of investigation, each group has 10 minutes to share with the class the question they investigated and communicate their findings.

Before they know it, it is time for the class to board the bus and return to school. As the students make final notations in their journals and clean up their lab stations, they all agree that the day was worthwhile and rewarding. Many of the students comment that they felt they were actually doing real science!

Evaluation Stage

In class the next day, Sara uses the data collected at the Life Sciences Learning Center to introduce a genetics lesson on haploid and diploid life cycles. The purpose of the lesson is to extend the Elaboration stage and apply what the students learned at the LSLC to the district's science standards and curriculum. At the completion of the Elaboration stage, Sara gives the students a unit test. The unit test includes multiple-choice questions, several short answer response questions, and a performance task to assess their progress in meeting the learning standards. Here is the task the students are given:

The task: A student wants to demonstrate how the rate at which a balloon inflates is proportional to the growth rate of the yeast cells. Use the materials listed below to:

1. Design an investigation to solve the problem.

2. Provide an appropriate table to record your data.

---

3. Carry out your investigation.

4. Fill in the data table.

5. Make a graph of your results.

6. Draw a conclusion from the data collected.

Materials:

- 100 mL of warm water
- Sugar cubes (or packets)
- A package of yeast
- One medium-size plastic bottle or flask
- One balloon
- One metric measuring tape

A sample procedure may look this:

1. Place the three sugar cubes (or packets) in the plastic bottle and pour in 100 mL of warm tap water.

2. Swirl the bottle until the sugar has dissolved.

3. Pour the entire contents from the package of yeast into the bottle.

4. Squeeze all the air from the balloon and stretch the balloon over the top of the bottle.

5. Observe what happens. Every 5 minutes, use the measuring tape to measure the circumference of the balloon.

Time (in minutes)	Circumference of balloon (in centimeters)
5	_____
10	_____
15	_____
20	_____
25	_____
30	_____

To assess the students' progress on the performance task, Sara develops her own analytical rubric, similar to others she found posted on the Internet at the following sites:

www.col-ed.org/smcnws/scientific.html

www.nwrel.org/msec/images/science/pdf/secondaryteachers.pdf

http://resources.yesican.yorku.ca/trek/assessment/r8_inq.html

In this case study, we see how teachers can use the 5E Learning Cycle to design investigations and units of study. We also see how a teacher-initiated inquiry can lead to a student-initiated inquiry. (Note: For references on artificial sweeteners, see www.sweetnlow.com or www.equal.com.)

AN INTERVIEW WITH DINA MARKOWITZ AND JANA PENDERS

From the perspective of a university researcher and a science educator, what is your definition of inquiry? Is inquiry any different for the researcher than it is for the high school science teacher?

Dina: I think inquiry has multiple meanings. It can be both similar and different things for the researcher and the science teacher. In both cases, inquiry centers on asking questions, which leads to some answers and which lead to more questions. There are, however, limited numbers and types of inquiries that can actually be completed in a secondary school lab. Teachers are often limited by time, whereas research is often limited only by money. Researchers often need many months or years to come up with the answers, whereas science teachers need to be sure that students complete most or all of the inquiry activity in the time allowed by a classroom period. Teachers may also be constrained by the resources and equipment available to them, whereas in the research laboratory, that is usually a smaller concern. At the Life Sciences Learning Center, we need to make sure that students work on a question or problem that is answerable and that they are able to complete all or most of the investigation in the time they are here. We also need to be sure that all students meet a level of success while they are here and that they leave with very positive attitudes about science.

Jana: Here at the LSLC, I often say that every day is like the first day of school. That means that each day, we face the challenge of getting to know the kids as quickly as possible so they trust us in guiding them through their inquiry, thus leading to achieving success. Part of the approach we use here tries to make students feel confident in their own inquiry abilities and have ownership in the questions they pose.

Recently, I was at a high school and asked students who they felt was the best inquirer of all times. One student said it was Galileo. Another thought it was Isaac Newton. Then, when I suggested that newborn babies are perhaps the best inquirers, the kids agreed. We discussed how, with no means of communicating (except screaming or crying), babies have to figure out what they need, what they want, and how to get it. Babies have to figure out their whole new world, devoid of any preconceived notions. The infant discovers by putting objects in her mouth and touching and grasping things with her hand. So I suggested that all the students in the class have already been the best inquirers ever, just by experiencing life.

Are all your programs inquiry-based?

Dina: Most are inquiry-based. There are, however, some science activities that don't lend themselves to an inquiry orientation. Some are what I would term "directed inquiry" because the procedure, like in the case of most of our biotechnology programs, such as "DNA Fingerprinting," must be sequenced in a particular order. There is no other way to do it. In other cases, where students are mixing reagents, we don't have enough time for them to discover this on their own, so the question, materials to use, and procedures of the technique are provided to the students. With wanting to have all students be successful when coming to the center and given the limited amount of time we have with the students, it becomes necessary to provide the structure that will lead to their success. I'm sure this is as true in the high school lab as it is here at the Life Sciences Learning Center.

Jana: In the case of the yeast investigation, there isn't much that can go wrong. Even with some errors in the procedure, the yeast is probably going to grow and metabolize. But with the biotechnology activities, it's different. There are the sequenced procedures that Dina mentioned. As engaging as inquiry is, you just can't do it *all* of the time. Some activities and labs require structure. Others do not. It's the teacher's challenge to analyze the lab and determine when and where more decision making and student ownership can be placed.

You mentioned the importance of "trust" in an inquiry-based classroom. How do teachers build trust with their students?

Jana: First of all, you have to communicate that everyone in the room has something to contribute and that no one will be teased, ridiculed, or laughed at for anything that's said. We remark that every comment that students make is valuable and adds to our discussion. Also, by practicing "wait-time" strategies, we tell students that they will have ample time to completely think out their responses. I often borrow the phrase "lifelines" from the show *Who Wants to Be a Millionaire*, by giving students an opportunity to "phone a friend" when they need help answering a question.

Dina: When students come to the center for the first time, they often have no previous relationship with us. We have found that by visiting their classroom one or two times before students come to the center, we introduce ourselves on "their turf," and that makes the transition to the LSLC and the level of trust more comfortable. These skill-building, previsitation lessons help us to prepare the students for their investigations at the center and to introduce specific laboratory techniques, like using a pipette or gel electrophoresis equipment, which students will be using at the center.

What are some of the skills you find students need to have in order to be successful in completing an inquiry investigation?

Jana: Surprisingly, some of them are not science related at all. I find that life skills are just as essential as science process skills. Self-confidence and self-esteem are very crucial to success in inquiry-based classrooms. Once you develop the life skills, they lead to success for the manipulative skills. I once heard a teacher say his students may not be able to do the investigation because they don't have the necessary organizational skills. I posed the question, "How will students ever learn and develop organizational skills if teachers don't first give them the opportunity to do inquiry?"

The yeast investigation provides a means for students to learn through scientific inquiry. How difficult is it having students come into the lab with varying prior experiences with hands-on and inquiry-based science?

Jana: Before a science class actually visits the center, I make one or two classroom visits to the high school to meet the teacher and students and communicate the purpose of the visit. Communication is essential. During the previsits, the teacher and I discuss the individual needs of students and tailor a program specifically to that class. This way, I can anticipate what each class's needs will be. There are some prerequisite skills students need before coming to the center. For example, in our "DNA Fingerprinting" lesson, students need to know how to use certain equipment. I can preteach those certain skills during the previsits, thus increasing the chances of success for every student.

The Life Sciences Learning Center is an excellent example of a university reaching out to the community and supporting middle and high school science teachers. How important is it for higher education institutions to form partnerships with secondary school teachers to ensure that all students meet rigorous national, state, and local standards in science?

Dina: It's essential that universities tap into local high school students who may in the near future be their own students. Universities today see the need to attract local students and keep them in the community to fill prominent positions in math, science, and technology. And with shrinking high school budgets, science teachers are looking to nearby community colleges and universities, as well as local businesses in science and technology, for additional support and resources. Coupled with the spiraling cost of laboratory equipment, more and more high school science teachers are turning to colleges and outreach centers to develop partnerships.

What suggestions would you give to a high school science teacher seeking to form a partnership with a local college or university?

Dina: First, look to a college or university with an undergraduate or graduate-level science education program and find out what resources it has to offer. Often, colleges have outreach grants and programs to support local and regional public schools; especially schools with high need and at-risk students. There are several federal grants available for higher education specifically to partner with public schools around needs in math, science, and technology. Many federal granting organizations, like NSF [the National Science Foundation] and NIH [the National Institutes of Health], now specify that up to 10% of the awarded amount must be set aside to support public educational programs. Although some partnerships are initiated by one science teacher approaching a college or university, the school should form a team ideally consisting of the principal, science department head or curriculum coordinator, and classroom teachers to identify their needs and explore possible avenues for assistance and resources.

What knowledge, skills, or attitudes do you expect students to walk away with after visiting the Life Sciences Learning Center?

Dina: Our goals are not different from the majority of high school science teachers. We want students to learn how scientists do their work and what it means to do a science investigation. Not everything scientists do is "Hey, wow!" exciting. And sometimes, science experiments don't always work. We want them to discover that two scientists, working side by side, may not necessarily come up with the same answer. That's true too for any pair of students working together. Or even if they get the same data, they may interpret the evidence differently. That's the nature of science.

Jana: It's important for students to realize that most scientific investigations evolve over time.

Dina: We also want them to know that science is not a solitary, isolated process. When students act like scientists, they must work cooperatively together, discuss and share their results, and present their information. We want them to know that real science is not "cookbook" style.

Jana: Having students leave with a feeling of self-confidence is important to me. I want them to feel science is fun and not all scientists are stereotypic of the images they see on television or in cartoons. I want them to leave feeling that they are scientists and can pursue scientific, technical, and engineering careers in the years ahead.

Given the evolving nature of science investigations, is there some fallacy in the scientific method? It seems so many teachers and science textbooks place a high priority on introducing this.

Jana: When you leave it in the singular sense, yes, there is some fallacy. But in the plural form, scientific methods, it is not. That means there are many methods of doing science. So using *the* scientific method is different from using scientific methods.

Dina: The second fallacy lies in the "H" word. There are not always hypotheses in an investigation. Sometimes you go into an investigation and you have no clue what you are going to get. I'm sure this is true for some high school students. You are collecting data because you are interested in studying a phenomenon, but you really have no idea or preconceived notion about how it will work out. So those inquiries have no hypothesis. And yet the scientific method that teachers espouse often emphatically states that you *must* have a hypothesis and follow a linear, sequential format.

What knowledge, skills, or attitudes do you expect teachers to walk away with after visiting the Life Sciences Learning Center?

Jana: It's important that science teachers return to their schools being excited and eager to transplant and follow up on any or all of these activities in their own classrooms and labs.

Dina: I would like teachers to understand that it's okay to occasionally let students go off on the wrong path. Much of what we learn is from our own mistakes. I also would like them to realize the amount of time it takes to do a scientific inquiry properly.

Jana: Given the reality of the amount of content teachers need to cover (or should I say uncover) during the school year and the amount of instructional time available to teachers, the challenge lies in finding and scheduling longer periods to do engaging and extended inquiries. Most inquiries do not lend themselves to a 45-minute period. In a short 45-minute lab period, how can anything be accomplished that resembles real-life science? Inquiry-based labs usually take more time than traditional labs, which can often be completed in one period. That's a very real challenge to high school science teachers.

QUESTIONS FOR REFLECTION

1. When having students design their own investigation, what precautions should the teacher take before allowing students to begin carrying out the procedures?

2. How can teachers anticipate the kinds of supplies, materials, and equipment that will be needed when students design their own inquiries?

3. If the teacher decides to use a rubric in this lesson, where would it be most appropriate?

4. What other examples of student-initiated inquiries can you suggest?

5. What other examples of assessments can you suggest for the evaluation phase of the lesson?

Teaching Earth Science Through Inquiry

TOILET PAPER TIMELINE

In this case study, we will observe Tom O'Brien, an associate professor of Graduate K–12 Science Teacher Education at Binghamton University in Binghamton, New York, lead an earth science class through an investigation of constructing a toilet paper timeline and geologic scale while using Internet resources for researching topics in geologic history and fossil formation. This case study, although fictitious, is based on O'Brien's article "A Toilet Paper Timeline of Evolution" (2000).

A researcher in inquiry-based instruction and constructivist teaching strategies, Tom has years of experience with National Science Foundation (NSF) grants focusing on teachers implementing the 5E Learning Cycle. Prior to teaching at Binghamton, Tom was a high school chemistry teacher in Kentucky and one of the original contributors to Chemistry in the Community (known as ChemCom), an interactive, community-based high school chemistry program.

The "Toilet Paper Timeline" inquiry aligns to the *National Science Education Standards* (NRC, 1996) for grades 9–12, which are quoted below.

Science as Inquiry Standard

Students will

- Formulate and revise scientific models using logic and evidence. (p. 175)
- Recognize and analyze alternative explanations and models. (p. 175)

Life Science Standard

- The great diversity of organisms is the result of more than 3.5 billion years of evolution that has filled every available niche with life forms. (p. 185)

Earth and Space Science Standard

- Observing rock sequences and using fossils to correlate the sequences at various locations can estimate geologic time. (p. 189)
- Evidence of one-celled forms of life—the bacteria—extends back more than 3.5 billion years. (p. 190)

Introduction to the Lesson

The historical perspective of time, as it relates to the geologic past, creates an intriguing scientific lesson. A change in the age of the planet Earth, from a few thousand years to hundred of millions, first proposed in the early 1800s by Charles Lyell, created a major paradigm shift in the minds of many believers and nonbelievers. This newly proposed model was "based upon indirect evidence from fossils and rock formations and supported the even less acceptable concept of biological evolution" (AAAS, 1993, p. 246). Nearly 200 years later, biblical literalists still challenge the scientific perspective on the age of Earth. The notion of time and scale provides students with an engaging vehicle for understanding how models and theories come to be accepted within the science community.

The concept of scale as a unifying theme is not new to most students. Since their earliest years, children have experienced scale models of cars, trucks, planes, trains, dolls, and other toys. Children know that the toy model they hold in their hands represents a smaller version of the original. The reality of scale seems to make sense. Even as elementary school students learn to read maps, they begin to understand the significance of scale. Often maps include a scale key (for example, 1 inch = 1 mile) to show the relationship between the illustration and reality. Today's high school students, however, are faced with understanding scientific scales ranging from hundred of billions to the microscale concept of a nanometer.

When studying the cosmos, earth science students need to comprehend the immensity of a billion. When studying our sun, we find it is just an average star in size, brightness, and age among 100 billion other stars in the Milky Way galaxy. The concept of a billion also arises when we consider the population explosion of Earth. With the population reaching 6 billion in 2000 and rising each year, some scientists predict that Earth can support only between 10 billion and 15 billion inhabitants. Thus, whether it is vast numbers of bodies in the universe or the population of humans on Earth, the notions of time, scale, and using models become important scientific themes for high school students.

According to the *National Science Education Standards*:

in studying the evolution of the earth system over geologic time, students develop a deeper understanding of the evidence . . . of the Earth's past and unravel the interconnected story of earth's dynamic crust, fluctuating climate, and evolving life forms. . . . They will discover that while certain properties of the earth system may fluctuate on short and long time scales, the earth system will generally stay within a certain narrow range of millions of years. . . . Many students are capable of doing this kind of thinking, but as many as half will need concrete examples and considerable help in following multi-step logic necessary to develop the understanding described in this standard. Because direct experimentation is usually not possible for many concepts associated with earth and space science, it is important to maintain the sprit of inquiry by focusing the teaching on questions that can be answered using observational data, the knowledge base of science, and processes of reasoning. (NRC, 1996, pp. 188–189)

The evolution of the earth system, including both geological and biological factors, is more challenging for students to understand because of a number of conceptual, methodological, philosophical, and secular factors. One of the most difficult issues for high school students is geologic time, partly because we have difficulty fathoming numbers larger than a thousand, much less a million or a billion. Textbooks also contribute to this problem by showing a timeline with squiggly or broken lines for an era too large to fit on one page. Unfortunately, truncated scales are a necessary evil given the size dimensions of a textbook. Teachers, however, do not have to be limited to the scale drawing from textbooks. They can provide alternative and authentic performance tasks for students to help them grasp the reality of time, scale, and models. The following case study shows how one college professor presents a series of lessons to a high school earth science class and wipes away misconceptions about geologic scale. The lessons came about when Tom was discussing with his graduate-level science education students the 5E Learning Cycle. Toward the end of the class, Joanna Moore, a student in Tom's course, came up to him and asked if he would be interested in teaching a class for her 11th-grade earth science students at Thomas Edison High School. He agreed, thinking that he'd design the lessons to introduce students to the scale age of Earth while modeling for Joanna the 5E Learning Cycle. The "Toilet Paper Timeline" is presented in five separate lessons spanning several days. He uses the Engagement stage to introduce the concept of a scale and models, the Exploration stage to make the timeline, and the Elaboration stage to extend the lesson into an inquiry-based investigation. Arrangements were made, and 2 weeks later Joanna's college professor found himself facing a class of eager young minds in Room 214 at Edison High.

Engagement

"Let's begin by thinking and reflecting what we know about the age of Earth," Tom begins. "How old is Earth?" he asks the class while writing the question on the board. "Is it 10,000, 500 million, 1 billion, or 4.6 billion years old? Make an estimate as to the age of Earth and write that number down on a sheet of paper." He then asks the students to *pair and share* their estimate with someone sitting next to them and give a reason why they chose the number they did. As the students work in pairs, Tom and Joanna circulate about the room, listening to the comments being made and mentally noting possible misconceptions. Of the 24 students, 11 choose 4.6 billion years, 6 choose 1 billion, 5 choose 500 million, and 2 choose 10,000 years. After recording the estimates on the board, Tom asks several students to provide a rationale for their answers. One student, Lisa, responds by saying she read in a magazine that Earth is more than 4 billion years old, so that seemed like the best answer. Rather than giving the class an immediate answer, Tom probes further by asking, "How do scientists estimate the age of Earth?" A discussion develops in which students receive a brief background on radiometric dating. Students later are told that, based on scientific testing, geologists now date Earth's origin to be 4.6 billion years ago.

"How can we understand such a large number? How much is a million? Or a billion?" Tom asks. "To understand the concept of a million, look at this jar." Holding up a 1-gallon glass jar, he says, "It contains 1,000 jellybeans. Now, how many jars would we need to represent a million jellybeans? How about a billion jellybeans? Figure it out and tell Ms. Moore and me your answer." The professor also challenges students to come up with other representations of a million or billion and poses the question, "Suppose you wanted to put 4.6 billion jellybeans in this classroom. Is it possible? How much room would 4.6 billion jellybeans take up?" By the end of the first half hour, students are beginning to construct a concrete understanding of the concepts of a million and a billion. Tom concludes this portion of the lesson by saying, "Now it is time to move on and design a geologic timeline."

Exploration

"Open your earth science textbook to page 205. What do you see? That's right, it's a geologic timeline. But is the timeline drawn to scale?" Tom asks. "No," he answers, after a brief pause. "You can see that all the eras are pictured equally in size; however, the time spans of all the eras are not equal. Suppose we use this meter stick for the entire age of Earth. The combination of the pre-Archean (pre-Cambrian), the Archean (Cambrian), and the Proterozoic eras," he says while holding up the meter stick, "would extend from the beginning of the meter stick to 89 cm, the Paleozoic era would extend from 89 to 95 cm, the Mesozoic era from 95 to 99 cm, and the Cenozoic era would be in the last centimeter of the meter stick. So you can see that all the eras are not equal in length of time."

"In this 2-day investigation, each group will create a geologic timeline drawn to scale. To do this, you will use a roll of toilet paper to represent time and determine what data and information you need to complete the timeline. Knowing Earth's history is actually 4.6 billion years old, read the outer wrapper to determine the number of sheets a roll of toilet paper contains. Then you will have to mathematically calculate how many years each square sheet represents." For information about the age of Earth, relative geologic timelines, and major divisions in geologic time, Tom directs students to the U.S. Geological Survey's Web site, http://pubs.usgs.gov/gip/geotime.

As students begin their investigation, Tom places several different brands of toilet paper on the front table. Students now decide which brand to use for their timeline. Some brands are single-ply, others are two-ply. Some are smooth, and some are quilted, with an imprinted design. Some are plain, and others are scented. Cottonelle contains 264 two-ply sheets, and other brands contain 170 or 300 sheets. Both Charmin and Quilted Northern have 400 two-ply sheets, while Scott has 1,000 single-ply sheets on a roll.

Some students ask if they can manipulate the number of sheets used in the timeline to represent Earth's 4.6 billion years. One group wants to round off the number of sheets used to 230, figuring that number can be divided easily into 460, making each sheet equal to 20 million years. Another group wants to increase the number of sheets it uses to 460, making each sheet equal to 10 million years.

Figure 10.1

Once the time span is determined, students then identify sheets on the timeline for each of the four eras. Some students choose to use colored markers to distinguish among the four eras. Students also identify specific sheets to represent when life begins, the rise of marine invertebrates, the development of flowering plants, the age of dinosaurs, and the time when humans first appeared on Earth. Upon completion, the groups carefully post their toilet paper timelines, ranging from 40 to 80 feet, on the hallway and cafeteria walls, with Tom and Joanna Moore leading a discussion comparing and contrasting the different models. The discussion guides the class into the next phase of the lesson: the Explanation.

Explanation

By the fourth day, students develop a good understanding of the unifying themes of scale and models. Tom begins this day's lesson by saying, "It is now time to provide some background information to our timelines." By using simulations, discussions, videos, and virtual Internet field trips, he presents a lesson that focuses on fossil evidence for the appearance of various life forms on Earth and the stories that fossils tell us. As a homework assignment, students are directed to the U.S. Geological Survey Web site for research on index fossils (http://pubs.usgs.gov/gip/geotime) and for fossil formation and succession information (http://pubs.usgs.gov/gip/fossils/).

The second part of the Explanation stage centers on scientific notation. According to Tretter and Jones (2003), "in order for students to appreciate the vast differences in size of various biological or physical systems, they need a firm grasp of scientific notation" (p. 23). The presentation on the age of Earth now evolves into a lesson on scientific notation and its application to geology, space science, biology, chemistry, and physics. To complement the discussion, students view a Web site, www.wordwizz.com, based on the 1970s film *The Power of 10*. At this site, which integrates space science with biology and chemistry, students observe images from the subatomic quark (10^{-16} m) to the galactic quasar (10^{25} m).

Extension/Elaboration

On the fifth and final day, students critically evaluate other scales and timelines in their science textbook. Students determine if they are to scale, and if not, how they can be revised to represent an accurate scale. Several students bring up additional illustrations in other chapters of the book that inaccurately illustrate the relative sizes of Earth and the Moon. These students discuss and analyze the actual size and distance relationship between the two bodies. Other students find similar illustrations showing the solar system or universe out of scale because of the size limitations of the textbook page.

To provide more details to their geologic timeline, students are given a take-home assignment. During this Extension/Elaboration stage, students can choose any topic to investigate that applies to their timeline. Tom and Joanna provide suggestions, including the following.

- For any one of the geologic eras—Paleozoic, Mesozoic, or Cenozoic—choose one plant or animal fossil and research its geologic record. Place the fossil accurately on your timeline.
- Analyze other timelines and models in the textbook that encourage a misconception. Design an accurate version of the scale or model.
- Design a geologic timeline or scale of the solar system based on the dimensions of a football field.
- Design a geologic timeline based on the 365 days of a year.
- Design a geologic timeline based on a 24-hour clock.
- Design an accurate scale drawing of the size of various dinosaurs relative to a human.
- Use an inflatable beach ball and a Styrofoam ball (or other appropriately sized ball) to represent the relative size of Earth and the Moon. Determine the correct amount of distance to place between Earth and the Moon to represent the correct span between them. (A 16-inch inflatable ball would be placed approximately 40 feet from a 4-inch Styrofoam ball or softball.)

The projects are to be completed outside class time and are due in a week.

Evaluation

A week later, for the final stage or Evaluation, each student has 5 minutes to present his or her research and findings to the questions and inquiries chosen during the Elaboration stage. Students are assessed on their ability to accurately present correct scientific information as well as their ability to communicate the information clearly to the class, including making proper eye contact and speaking clearly.

AN INTERVIEW WITH DR. TOM O'BRIEN

What does scientific inquiry mean to you?

Tom: Inquiry is the essence of science. Science starts with a base of prior knowledge, which in some cases may be partially correct or a misconception, and leads to an interaction with the world and having to test the data collected against reality. Inquiry, on the other hand, often involves encountering discrepancies that don't make sense in light of what we know. Thus, we must engage in the Piagetian process of accommodation to reconstruct our prior understandings in light of new data when we synthesize both concepts. Inquiry is the evolution of our understanding. The metaphor of evolution is a very accurate one, because in evolution you have competing organisms and in different contexts. Sometimes a given theory becomes extinct because it is no longer suitably adapted to a changed environment that new data presents. Thus, our own personal mental theories and models about how the world operates constantly change to better fit a changing external reality.

What is the connection between inquiry and the 5E Learning Cycle?

We see inquiry throughout the entire 5E Learning Cycle. In the engagement phase, students are presented with a particular phenomenon that presents a challenge to what they know or believe to be true. In a sense, you are shaking up their present understandings and notions. Inquiry also involves generating questions at the start of a unit rather than saving them to the end. So much of our traditional high school teaching provides students with the answers to questions they never ask. In the Engagement stage, the discrepancy leaves questions that hopefully won't be answered for a while. In contrast to verification lab work done in high school, the Exploration stage starts with a question, and you go about finding out how nature works. The conceptual piece lies in developing an answer after phrasing the question and doing the work to tease out of nature how it does work. The Explanation stage synthesizes and clarifies the range of results a class generates from the exploration. It's natural for teachers to expect a range of students' results because students' technique of collecting data varies. Then there is still variation on what the data means and the students' interpretation of the evidence. That's an important idea to be highlighted during the Explanation stage. The Explanation stage also functions to relate the new phenomenon back to the students' prior knowledge and make an assessment as to the validity of that prior knowledge. During the Explanation stage, you should have the opportunity to challenge some of what they know. Then, when we get to the Explanation stage, it is the teacher who provides a good interactive, multisensory lecture. There is a very good purpose for lecture when done at the right time. And that too is an inquiry process. So it becomes a dialogue more than a lecture. It becomes interactive teaching with a lot less "teacher talk." So the Explanation stage is not just telling them the answers. Because if you did that, it would invalidate their work and students would get on to that real quick . . . Why put in the energy when the teacher is going to tell you the answers anyway?

Do you think some science textbooks unintentionally foster misconceptions on scale and structure? How does the "Toilet Paper Timeline" differ from other timelines in earth science textbooks?

There are some areas where you cannot show pictorially what the actual number represents. Take, for example, the concept of a mole. How could you possibly fit 10^{23} in a textbook? Or how about the relationship between the sizes of or distance between Earth and the Moon? I have not yet seen any textbook that accurately portrays the scale of relationship correctly. It is possible, however, to show the relative size and distance of Earth and Moon on a two-page spread. So all the pictures students see of the planets and the solar system are incorrect, yet as teachers we seldom take the time to tell students this. If you look at the timeline, it should read "Not to Scale" because equal distances on the timeline do not mean equal amounts in time. We need to supplement this diagram with activities that present a realistic relationship of scale and structure. That's where the "Toilet Paper Timeline" is so good. It lets students discover the truth! Let's say we wanted to introduce the notion of a million. The teacher can begin by placing a hundred marbles in a jar and then ask, "How many jars do we need to represent 10,000 marbles? 100,000 marbles? A million marbles? A billion marbles?"

Most textbooks underestimate the awesomeness of reality, and that essentially creates misconceptions. They actively teach something that is not true. Interestingly enough, the scale, as wrong as it is, can become a perfect evaluation instrument. For many teachers, the textbook becomes the bible, even though there are many things that are downright inaccurate. Sometimes graphical inaccuracies are a necessary evil, given the constraints of textbook dimensions. An eight-and-a-half by eleven-inch page does not do justice to a geological timeline. But that's what the authors ought to challenge students to think about. Sometimes all we are given is a squiggly line to represent some span of time not represented on the page. An essay question that leaps out at me is "Compare the timeline in the book to your toilet paper timeline. How are they alike, and how are they different? And specifically, what are the problems associated with the textbook?" To analyze the difference between reality and what they see in their textbooks. Plus, look at the animals represented in each of the eras. Each animal is represented as the same size. A dinosaur looks the same size as a tree shrew. And all of that would be fine if you provided the natural limits of the drawings. In a very real sense, the textbook lied, but it didn't tell you it lied. If a picture is worth a thousand words, a wrong or incorrect picture is worth a thousand misconceptions. How does it misrepresent reality? And why do you think the publishers did this? Is it possible to provide anything to scale in the confines of a textbook page? You might be able to do that if you devoted the entire textbook to just showing the historical timeline. I suspect the timeline would run the entire length of the pages. If evolution is an important theme in biology and earth science, can you run an accurate scale in the entire textbook? We need to help students toward critiquing the limitations of any science textbook to capture the true wonders of the physical universe.

Is a billion a difficult concept for high school students to understand?

Well, first of all, so much of what we try to do in science is to take a concept or idea that took thousands of years to develop and try to present it overnight. We think that we give students this one-shot presentation and they're supposed to get it. My argument on this would be that the notion of scale, which is important in all sciences, which helps explain how the world works, is well outside the range that people commonly conceptualize. And even though, at the high school level, we use exponents and power to the nth degree, many students don't truly grasp that idea. And so what students need are multiple experiences with the concept, which ought to be dealt with in both math and science. There are, fortunately, many ways of doing that. I feel it's unusual for any middle school students to get a sufficient understanding of scale at the middle school level to prepare them for high school science. You seldom find any articulation in the K–12 curriculum to prepare students for the kind of thinking they will do to handle the meaning of such large numbers. Some schools are struggling to develop curriculum maps just for this purpose, but for the most part, it is not formed by research. The bottom line is that scale is an absolutely pivotal concept in math in multiple sciences. And for the most part, we don't teach the themes of scale very well.

QUESTIONS FOR REFLECTION

1. How can high school teachers use the theme of *evolution* to integrate biology and earth science?

2. Why is the age of Earth so important to the theory of evolution?

3. What religious and/or political issues surround the concept of a geological timeline and evolution? How would you deal with them?

4. Why do students have difficulty conceptualizing large numbers such as a billion?

5. What are the essential knowledge and skills students should have after studying the geologic timeline?

6. How can teachers use textbook inaccuracies to develop scientific habits of mind and understanding the nature of science?

11

Teaching Chemistry
Through Inquiry

THE PEANUT LAB

In this case study, we will observe Teresa Gerchman, a veteran teacher of 17 years, as she leads her 10th-grade students through a lesson on calculating energy and caloric content. Teresa teaches Advanced Placement and college preparatory chemistry at Spencerport High School. The class in this case study contains 21 regular education students and 3 special education students. A teacher aide assists Mrs. Gerchman 2–3 days a week by providing resource help in the room to the three special education students.

After participating in several professional development workshops on inquiry 5 years ago, Teresa shifted her instructional methodology to an inquiry-based approach. She now incorporates inquiry into all phases of her instruction. Teresa is also the head of the science department and places a high emphasis on inquiry-based instruction throughout the department, which she reinforces by modeling scientific inquiry in her classroom. Teresa's chemistry labs usually involve students writing their own investigations, designing procedures, and choosing what kind of data to collect. Over the course of the school year, students will plan and design 10–15 of their chemistry labs. Her chemistry course culminates with students designing and carrying out a full research project in May. This lab focuses on decision making and determining the amount of energy stored (caloric content) in a peanut. Although many high school chemistry teachers undoubtedly are familiar with the infamous "peanut lab," during this experience, students, not the teacher or the lab manual, decide how to plan the procedure, what materials to use, and how data will be collected and represented.

This "peanut investigation" is divided into 4 days; the odd days, 1 and 3, each comprise a 90-minute, double period. The even days, 2 and 4, are single 45-minute periods. During Day 1, students review the previous day's lesson and the joule concept. They are also introduced to a teacher-initiated inquiry, the peanut lab, in which they plan and carry out the lab procedures, as well as record and analyze the results based on a question posed by the teacher. Day 2 involves a brief review lecture, an introduction to new material related to heat energy, and the extended, student-initiated inquiry lab in which students design a lab based on questions they raise. On Day 3, students carry out their investigation, organize their evidence and data, and make graphs and charts to communicate the results. To communicate the results and conclusions of their investigations, each group is required to make a 5-minute oral presentation using either a trifold poster board or a PowerPoint presentation on Day 4.

The peanut investigation aligns to the *National Science Education Standards* (NRC, 1996) for grades 9–12, as quoted below.

Science as Inquiry Standard

Students will

- Identify questions and concepts that guide a scientific investigation. (p. 175)
- Design and conduct a scientific investigation. (p. 175)
- Use technology and mathematics to improve investigations and communications. (p. 175)
- Formulate scientific explanations and models using logic and evidence. (p. 175)
- Communicate and defend a scientific argument. (p. 176)

Physical Science Content Standard

As a result of activities, all students should develop an understanding [that]

- Chemical reactions may release or consume energy. (p. 179)

Life Science Content Standard

As a result of activities, all students should develop an understanding [that]

- The chemical bonds of food molecules contain energy. (p. 186)

Day 1

Mrs. G., as her students call her, starts the class by reviewing the previous day's homework. "Which unit is used to express the amount of energy absorbed or released during a chemical reaction?" she asks.

"A joule," one student responds.

"If two systems at different temperatures have contact with each other, how will the heat flow from one object to another?" is the follow-up question.

Another student answers, "From high to cold temperatures."

One of the students who's also on the football team then asks, "If placing a cold pack on a swelled ankle feels cold, how is the heat moving from the ankle to the cold pack? Isn't it the other way around?"

Teresa thinks to herself, "This presents one of those teachable moments to apply the laws of thermodynamics beyond the classroom and into the student's real life." After a brief explanation on the cold pack question, she moves on and poses two questions as a "warm-up" quiz.

How much heat is needed to melt 50 grams of ice?
and
How much heat is needed to vaporize 10 grams of water?

Mrs. G. suggests that students use their notes from the previous day's class and their *Chemistry Reference Tables* (The University of the State of New York. (2002) to apply the appropriate formula to answer the questions.

While students work on the problems individually, Teresa and the special education aide walk about the room, assisting those students who need help. The students are then told to "pair and share" their solutions with a partner. While Teresa walks about the room, she chooses several students to come up to the board and share their solutions with the class. The teacher and students discuss the various ways to solve the problem. The class comes to agreement on the correct solution.

How much heat is needed to melt 50 grams of ice?
Heat of fusion: MHf = q = 50 grams × 334 J/g = 16,700 joules or 16.7 KJ
How much heat is needed to vaporize 10 grams of water?
Heat of vaporization: MHv = q = 10 grams × 2,260 J/g = 22,600 joules or 22.6 KJ

As part of the prelab discussion, Teresa introduces the lab by saying:

Energy that is produced when plants go through photosynthesis is stored in the leaves, roots, and stem. We eat food to get that stored energy. When food is "burned" during the process of digestion, the energy is released as heat energy in our bodies. The amount of energy is measured in calories. One calorie is equivalent to 4.2 joules. The amount of energy released by the food can be calculated, and the amount of energy stored in the food determined.

In this lab, you are to determine how much stored energy, in joules, a peanut has. You all have regular laboratory equipment available for your use as well as peanuts and matches. Your job is to write out the equation to calculate the heat energy released by the peanut as it burns. Identify what variables you will need to measure in the lab, and then write a safe procedure to determine the amount of heat energy released by the peanut as it burns. Include a drawing of how your lab equipment will be set up. For today's lab, you are going to design a way to determine the amount of energy in a peanut.

Teresa then tells students to take out their chemistry lab journals and record all their information in their notebooks.

After the students pair up, each group begins to work on brainstorming the design of the lab.

Figure 11.1

While students are doing their work, the teacher takes attendance and returns the previous day's homework assignment. After 15 minutes, Teresa asks several groups to come up to the front of the class and share their lab designs with the class.

In Model #1, Jessica and Kara thought about using a Bunsen burner to heat the water in a beaker, allowing the steam from the water to heat the peanut being held above the beaker. They thought they would take the temperature of the peanut before and after heating and then calculate the change. But they weren't quite sure how they were going to take the temperature of the peanut.

In Model #2, Samantha and Josh thought they would heat the peanut with a Bunsen burner and then place the peanut in a beaker of water and see how many degrees the water temperature changed.

In Model #3, Sade and Gina proposed using a match to ignite the peanut and then using tongs to hold the peanut under the beaker of water to determine how much the temperature rose. They thought they would take the temperature of the water before and after heating to calculate the change in temperature.

During the final discussion of the three proposals, students agree that Model #3 is the most appropriate way to do the lab; however, Gina adds that not all the energy released from burning the peanut is absorbed by the water—some energy is lost to the air, and some is lost through the tongs.

Mrs. G. then asks, "Would the tongs absorb some of the heat?"

Gina answers, "Yes. We should use something thin like aluminum wire or a pin rather than those tong things."

As the students write up their lab procedures in their science journals, Teresa reminds them to identify safety concerns. Commercially produced labs usually address safety concerns, but because students are writing their own procedures, including safe practices reinforces safety and makes students more accountable for their own behavior in the lab.

A typical peanut lab looks like this:

Title/Question: How much energy is in a peanut?

Purpose: To measure the amount of heat energy released by a peanut as it burns.

Materials: Ring stand, ring clamp, wire mesh pad, graduated cylinder, 500-mL beaker, peanut, pin or wire, cork, water, matches, thermometer, electronic or triple-beam balance, and goggles.

Procedure:
1. Assemble a ring stand, ring clamp, and wire mesh pad.

2. Using a graduated cylinder, measure 100 mL of water and place it in a 500-mL beaker. Place the beaker of water on the ring clamp.

3. Using a thermometer, determine the temperature of the water in the beaker. Record the temperature in the science journal.

4. Assemble peanut holder by placing a pin, pointed side up, in a small cork stopper. Place a peanut on the pointed end of the pin. Position the peanut and holder under the beaker and ring clamp.

5. Using a match, light the peanut and allow it to burn completely.

6. After the peanut burns itself out, determine the temperature of the water after heating. Record the temperature in the science journal.

Safety procedures: Wear goggles, and be careful when using matches.

Data: Temperature of water before heating = _____

Temperature of water after heating = _____

Change in temperature = _____

When a group's write-up for the lab is complete, the teacher approves and signs off on the lab by placing a "smiley face" on the paper. While Mrs. G. circulates around the class placing approval smiley faces on papers, Rob and Dave ask, "Should we use a whole peanut or just a half?"

Teresa responds, "I don't know. Will it make a difference? We'll have to find out later." She purposely doesn't answer the students' question because she knows the class will answer that question at the end of the lab.

After the lab, students calculate the amount of joules of heat energy released by the peanut. Sade and Gina use the formula $q = mC\Delta T$ to determine the amount of energy; where q equals the heat in Joules, m equals the mass of water, C equals the specific heat capacity, and ΔT equals the change in temperature. Because the temperature of Sade's and Gina's water increased from 20 to 24 degrees and the specific heat of water equals 4.18 J/g K, their formula for the amount of heat is $100 \times 4.18 \times 4 = 1{,}672$ joules or 1.7 kilojoules. (In the investigation, students used 100 mL of water. Because the density of water equals 1 gm/mL, 1 mL of water weights 1 g. Following the formula, 100 mL of water weighs 100 g.)

As the students share their lab results with the class, Mrs. G. poses the question, "Was number of joules the same for each group? Why or why not?"

While some students report as few as 1,254 joules, others report as many as 2,926 joules. One student asks, "Why is there such a variation in the number of joules?"

Teresa responds, "Did different students use different-sized peanuts?"

"Yeah, I think so," answers Michael.

"Well, then," she continues, "do larger peanuts have more energy than smaller ones?" At that time, she uses the analogy comparing a regular-size and large-size Snickers candy bar for calorie content. She encourages several students to prove this statement by determining the number of joules per gram during the extension or "going further" stage of the lab.

A student then asks, "Should the amount of energy released equal the amount of heat absorbed by the water?"

Mrs. G. says, "That's a good question. What would you expect? Should it? Let's look at your data and see if we can find the answer." The lab closes with a discussion about how the amount of heat stored compares to the amount of heat released and measured by the change in temperature. Students then add the analysis section to the lab journal. After the analysis section, Teresa has students summarize their lab by suggesting ways, if any, to improve it.

Day 2

On Day 2, Teresa begins the period with a presentation in which students solidify their understanding of a joule. By providing examples and referring to the previous day's lab, students construct their knowledge of the heat concept and calculating joules. Among the question presented to students is "What is the equation for determining the amount of heat energy, in joules, that is involved in a reaction?" Several problems are presented, such as "How many joules are required to heat 150 grams of water from 30°C to 40°C?" Or "If 4 grams of water is vaporized at 100°C, how much heat energy is used?" Students are given problems in which they convert joules to kilojoules and integrate graphing skills by drawing a heating curve to show the changes that take place when you heat a 20 gram sample of ice at –5°C to a water vapor at 110°C. During the presentation, Teresa also reviews the formulas for the heat of vaporization and the heat of fusion.

Students use the data and evidence from their previous lab to design their own new investigation. In this student-initiated inquiry, individuals choose their own question to investigate, design and carry out the procedures, and collect and analyze the results. To initiate some ideas, Teresa places a can of mixed nuts on the front lab table. After a brief brainstorming session, students come up with the following questions to investigate:

- Which nuts contain the most joules? Hazelnuts, chestnuts, cashews, peanuts, pecans, walnuts, or Brazil nuts? (Anticipating this question and wanting to add a little humor to the class, Teresa shows a film clip from the movie *Best in Show* in which one dog owner describes his ability to name different types of nuts.)
- Do regular peanuts produce more heat than dry-roasted peanuts?
- What is the amount of joules given off by a mini marshmallow? A large marshmallow?
- Do potato chips or Doritos provide more energy?

Finally, Rob and Dave, who asked in the first lab whether they should use a whole or half peanut, decide to use different-size peanuts and determine the amount of joules per gram. Taking the mass of various sized peanuts will allow them to calculate the amount of joules per gram.

As the students design their extension or follow-up labs, Mrs. G. passes out the rubric for grading their investigations.

Day 3

The students are eager to get started on their investigations. As soon as the period begins, students move to the chemistry lab and start getting their materials together to carry out their investigations.

In a corner of the lab, one large group of students is determining the amount of heat given off by different kinds of nuts. The group divides into four subgroups, each taking a different type of nut to test.

In another section of the lab, Rick and Linda are testing regular peanuts versus dry-roasted peanuts, while Sandy and Sharon are measuring the amount of joules given off by a mini marshmallow versus a large marshmallow. Tim and Bernie's lab proves to be a bit troublesome as they try to test whether potato chips or Doritos corn chips provide more heat energy. They find that their samples burn up too soon to measure any substantial change in temperature.

Rob and Dave's interest from Day 1 focuses on whether size of the nut makes any difference. They test whole and half peanuts to determine the amount of joules per gram.

At the end of the first half of the period, each group has enough information to answer its question, so students begin to plan their presentations. Teresa informs the students that their investigations and presentations will be graded using the rubric handed out on the first day. Each group is required to make a 5-minute oral presentation using either a trifold poster board or a PowerPoint presentation to convey the results and conclusions of their peanut investigations. The class spends the rest of the period preparing their presentations.

Day 4

On this, the final day of the lab, each group comes up to the front of the class to communicate its investigation findings. At the end of each presentation, Teresa poses the question, "If you were to improve your investigation, what would you change?"

After all the groups make their presentations, students are given a test to assess their understanding of heat and calories.

AN INTERVIEW WITH TERESA GERCHMAN

How would you describe your approach to learning?

Teresa: I keep my students actively engaged. To do that, I lecture as little as possible and instead give them opportunities to come up with their own ideas that are practical and relevant to their daily lives. Very rarely do I give them 45 minutes of note taking. When I do lecture, I limit it to shorter periods to reinforce a topic that we are studying. When I started teaching, I used a typical lecture approach because that's the way I was taught. But as time went on, I saw more practical applications develop when students came up with the examples on their own. Students develop more meaning through their investigations than when I ramble on and on about some law. Now I get very few complaints when students have to take notes because they know it won't be all period long and that the information will apply to their questions and experiments.

In this class, you have both regular and special education students. To an outside observer, it would be difficult to tell which of the students are special education. Does learning through inquiry in a high school science classroom seem to blur the distinctions between students with learning disabilities and those without?

I believe so, because what I'm asking students to do is think. I'm not asking them to give back rote information. Having a learning disability often means that some students just learn in a different style. It does not mean that they cannot learn or are not smart. When you stop asking students to do something in a traditional way and instead use their abilities to raise questions and inquire, students with learning disabilities are placed on an equal footing with other students. I find that students with learning disabilities work better in an inquiry environment because special education students tend to think out of the box more easily. Experience tells me that kids who have the most trouble with inquiry are those at the top end of the spectrum. They are used to doing exactly what you tell them to do and are ready to give you back anything you tell them. So when you ask high-ability students to come up with their own ideas, it often "pushes" their comfort zone. There are always some students with learning disabilities who need special accommodations, but teaming students together in cooperative groups often compensates for any disability. In this class, I have a wonderful special education aide I work with. She is a firm believer in inquiry and is an active part of the learning process for both regular and special education students. So I think the students with special needs like inquiry because in inquiry classrooms, all students are engaged in the learning and are experiencing success. In this class, the special education aide interacts with all students, so it is difficult to identify students with special needs from those without. Working together is a true cooperative teaching model. The special education aide is especially helpful in thinking of ways to differentiate the instruction so we are certain to meet the needs of all students in the classroom.

How does inquiry help you differentiate instruction to meet the needs of all students in your class?

To begin with, it is truly an ideal individualized learning environment. What procedures students design and carry out in the lab varies based on their choices.

Some students develop labs with great minute, step-by-step details, whereas other students may keep their investigation simple and to the point. And that's fine, since inquiry-based instruction lends itself to self-selection and individualized learning.

In your classroom, you emphasize students designing their own investigations and labs. Do you think students like this approach?

At first, I sometimes think they hate it because it forces them to think, but later they come to understand that they are being encouraged to think in science and they come to enjoy the labs. They don't dread coming to class, so my average daily attendance rate is high. I also think students have a greater appreciation for what's going on in the lab and not just going through the steps. That's important to me.

In one lab, we did an identification of acids and bases. I told my students, "When you come in tomorrow, there will be five clear liquids on the desk. You need to identify which ones are acids and which ones are bases." And that was it. That was all the direction I gave them. I didn't even give them a lab sheet. So the night before the lab, they had to go through their chemistry reference tables and determine which chemical indicators to use to distinguish between acids and bases. They had to decide which indicator they were going to use, test each sample, and later classify the acids and bases according to strength. Oh, by the way, I told them they could use pH paper only to test their final results at the end of the lab. When they came in the lab the next day, I had vials of methyl orange, bromthymol blue, phenolphthalein, and thymol blue available. I also had some metals available to test for acids. The students then used the information they found to test each liquid and sequence them from the strongest acid to strongest base. Actually, they classified each liquid as a strong acid, a weak acid, being neutral, a weak base, or a strong base. The following day, we discussed what indicators were used in the investigation and how they are used in chemistry, along with the general properties of acids and bases. That led us to an understanding of pH. The students then brought in common household liquids from home, and we tested each one for pH and general strength. That, in turn, led to a bulletin board display of all the liquids we tested, along with their identification as either an acid or a base. It was an interesting display that students were proud of. On the final exam, there was a question for which students had to determine, given two liquids, which was an acid and which was a base. They remembered the lab and completed that question quite easily.

Do some students prefer to have the lab given to them?

They would at the beginning of the school year, but later they become accustomed to the inquiry style and really do enjoy learning this way. As I said earlier, it's the highest-ability students who I find have the most difficulty adjusting to inquiry. They prefer to memorize and give back the information. I think they have been conditioned to a recitation style most of their lives, and inquiry is a new and different type of learning. High-ability students are very good with a traditional model of teaching because that is what they are accustomed to. Later, as the transition occurs, they become quite comfortable with inquiry and realize how it encourages their thinking skills. But it takes nearly a year for the transition to occur.

In the beginning of the peanut lab, students were designing different models to test. There were two very unusual models presented. Does it surprise you to see what students are thinking about?

I don't think there is a specific process for modifying a lab; the process is different for different labs. I generally start with the question, "How can I get students to design this lab on their own?" For example, I have a traditional lab on the rate of chemical reactions. It's a standard lab, the iodine clock lab, I'm sure a lot of high school chemistry teachers use. But to make it more inquiry oriented, I pose the following task to my students: *Choose a factor you believe will affect the rate of reaction. Write a hypothesis statement regarding what factor you wish to test and what you believe the effect will be on the rate. Next, design and carry out an investigation to test your hypothesis.* This task is clear enough that I don't have to provide a list of the materials to use or the procedures to follow. I believe students can determine this information on their own. Some may need a bit of prompting, while others determine it on their own. Some groups choose heating the reaction, others choose varying the concentration or stirring, while some choose adding a catalyst. In this case, I can expect about four different experiments going on at the same time. Toward the end of the period, I'll get all of the heat groups together in one area to come up with some general conclusions about the effect heating has on the rate of reaction. The same goes for the other groups. This way, all the groups collaborate with each other and share their results.

None of my labs includes data tables. I want students to determine what data they have to collect and how they need to organize the information on a chart or table. This helps students take more responsibility for the lab and make decisions on their own. Also, I always have students write their own hypothesis. Then I ask, "How can you test your hypothesis?" By having students write their hypothesis, they are naturally led to the next step of writing the procedure to test their hypothesis.

What did your labs look like 10 years ago? What do they look like now?

Back then, I gave students the question to investigate, the materials that they will use, the steps to follow, an illustration of what the setup should look like, and so on. I even provided them with a table to organize their data and a grid to plot the results. Basically, the entire lab was laid out in front of them. Then, of course, there was a follow-up question to help them analyze their data and draw conclusions. The lab might have been three or four pages long. Now most of my inquiry chemistry labs are one sheet long. It certainly saves on paper!

Are you ever surprised by the ways high school students design their own chemistry labs?

If you remember, in the peanut lab there were two groups of students who had bizarre ideas for determining ways to calculate the amount of energy from the nut. One wanted to heat the peanut and put it in water and measure the temperature change; the other wanted to heat the peanut from the steam of boiling water. Those ideas stressed the need to walk about the classroom and interact with the groups. We have to know what they are thinking about. Sometimes, what the teacher is saying may be entirely different from what students are thinking about. I'm not always sure that the things they say will work actually do, but I often say, "Try it, and see what happens." We think students know what we are talking about, but sometimes they don't. That's the power of inquiry—students have to brainstorm their ideas and test them against the class and the teacher.

At the high school level, especially in chemistry, there seems to be an enormous amount of content you need to present throughout the school year. How do you manage to integrate an inquiry-based approach knowing inquiry takes more classroom time?

In the past, I would start a unit by presenting the topic through a lecture/discussion mode, then use inquiry as a way for students to design an experiment around the topic or concept. Back then, I would use a 40-minute period to teach the concept and then an 80-minute lab to apply the concept through an investigation. Now I prefer to use inquiry as a way to introduce concepts and then support the evidence we discovered from the investigation with formulas and background information. I make the introductory inquiry lesson part of a 40-minute period and then use the explanation portion in a follow-up 40-minute period. That saves me some time. I also find that with inquiry, the students "own" the knowledge, so I have to spend less time reviewing at the end of the unit.

Chemistry teachers who use inquiry have to be very efficient with their time. That means starting on time and using the entire class for instruction. I rarely provide time in class for students to do homework or write up their lab. That can be done at home. Classroom time is too precious to use for doing homework. Plus, a lot of the planning and design of the investigation can be done on their own time, not in class. I find that the more we use inquiry, the less often I have to use classroom time for the design phase of the investigation. After a few months, they know what to expect for labs, know how to write a hypothesis, and can design the procedures to test their hypothesis.

QUESTIONS FOR REFLECTION

1. How can inquiry help increase differentiation of instruction in a high school science classroom?

2. How can an inquiry-based classroom be a model for inclusion?

3. How can using inquiry help students gain a deeper understanding of the core concept?

12

Teaching Physics Through Inquiry

MEASURING CENTRIPETAL FORCE

In this case study, we will follow George Wolfe, a veteran teacher of 28 years, as he leads his 9th-grade students through a lesson on calculating centripetal force. George teaches Advanced Placement biology and a college preparatory physics course at Wilson Magnet High School, a large, urban high school in Rochester, New York. The class in this case study contains 18 students in the school's International Baccalaureate program. In this school, 9th-grade students begin their high school science sequence with physics.

George Wolfe is a nationally acclaimed teacher. In 1990, he received the Outstanding Biology Teacher Award from the National Association of Biology Teachers, and in 1999, he received the prestigious Presidential Award for Excellence in Math and Science. In 2002, George was recognized by the Radio Shack National Science Teacher Award, and he was recently nominated to the National Teacher Hall of Fame. George has also developed the Nasonia Project, an inquiry-based genetics program produced by Ward's Natural Science, to study heredity using parasitic wasps (*Nasonia vitripennis*) as an alternative to fruit flies (*Drosophila sp.*). (For more information on the Nasonia Project, see www.wardsci.com. Click on "biology," then go to "biology lab activities," "genetics," and "Nasonia Project.") Recently, George Wolfe has become a lab developer for the Cornell Institute for Physics Teachers. In this lesson, George uses the classic, well-known demonstration of measuring centripetal force by spinning a rubber stopper attached to a string threaded through a thin glass tube (Liem, 1987; Murphy, 1982). Rather than following a traditional laboratory procedure, students will design their own experiments in determining the relationship between centripetal force and one other variable identified by the student groups (mass of the stopper, velocity of the orbiting stopper, or radius of the orbit).

The centripetal force investigation aligns to the *National Science Education Content Standards* (NRC, 1996) for grades 9–12, as quoted below.

Science as Inquiry Standard

Students will

- Identify questions and concepts that guide a scientific investigation. (p. 175)
- Design and conduct a scientific investigation. (p. 175)
- Use technology and mathematics to improve investigations and communications. (p. 175)
- Formulate scientific explanations and models using logic and evidence. (p. 175)
- Communicate and defend a scientific argument. (p. 176)

Physical Science Content Standard

As a result of activities, all students should develop an understanding [that]

- Objects change their motion only when a net force is applied. Laws of motion are used to calculate precisely the effects of forces on the motion of objects. The magnitude of the change in motion can be calculated using the relationship $F = ma$, which is independent of the nature of science. (pp. 179–180)

The Prelab

"Think about this," Mr. Wolfe says to the class. "Where do you sit on a schoolyard merry-go-round if you want to move fastest? Do you sit near the center, in the middle, or out at the edge?"

"Oh, that's easy," Alberto shouts out. "Out by the edge."

"That's right!" the teacher responds. "Now, what if you went to an amusement park and went on the Tilt-a-Whirl?" he continues. "Why don't you fall off even when the ride tips vertically?" As the students look puzzled, George explains, "The answer is PHYSICS! In this lab, we want to take what we learned last week about Newton's three laws of motion and see if Isaac's ideas about linear motion apply to circular motion." At that point, George reaches behind the demonstration table and brings out a 2-gallon plastic pail with a long rope attached to the handle. He fills the pail one quarter of the way with water and begins to swing it over his head. "As I swing the pail in a circular motion, what would happen if I let go of the rope? Would it continue to travel in a circle, or would it fly directly outward?" Karen thinks it would continue to travel in a circular path, and Jennifer says it would continue to fly straight out.

"Try it and see what happens," Jason suggests.

"Well, actually," the teacher responds, "if I let go of the rope, the pail will move in a straight line tangent to the circular path. I'll draw a picture on the board to show what it would look like."

George continues, "When I whirl the pail of water around in a circle, I must keep pulling or exerting a force on the rope. Is a force being exerted? In what direction?"

"Inward," Yolanda says.

"That's right! This inward pull or force," George continues, "keeps the pail revolving over my head and in a circular path. This force is called *centripetal force.*

Centripetal force means 'toward the center' or 'center-seeking.' As I whirl the pail overhead, there is an inward pull from the rope. Now, I don't know if Newton ever tried this demonstration back in Lincolnshire, England, but he apparently wondered, like all good scientists do, if the sun exerts a force on the planets. Newton knew that when you exert a force on an object, it accelerates. So he tried to apply this idea to the planets. Newton realized that for an orbiting body, the force is directed inward toward the center of the orbit. Because acceleration is a change in velocity (positive or negative), the exerting force is causing a change in the direction of the orbiting object. That is what's called acceleration.

"I now want to demonstrate this in another way. To do this, I'll need a one-hole rubber stopper, a piece of glass tubing about 15 centimeter long with the ends rounded off, and a length of strong string. I'm first going to take a string and thread it through the glass tubing. Next, I'm going to tie a rubber stopper to one end of the string. As I hold on to the glass tubing in one hand and the string in the other, I'll twirl the rubber stopper above my head.

"Now, is there a force being exerted? Indeed there is. As the stopper rotates in an orbit, my hand holding the string represents the measurement of centripetal force. I can feel the centripetal force from the circular motion of the rubber stopper, but there is no way to quantitatively measure the amount of force. Can you think of any way we can measure the force?"

Judy responds, "Could you use a spring scale?"

"I sure can," George responds, "and I just happen to have one here!" George now attaches a spring scale to the string and has Judy come up and read the scale in Newtons as the rubber stopper whirls in a circle. The scale reads 1.5 Newtons.

George now poses a question to the class, "Knowing there is a force being exerted by the stopper, what is the relationship between a center-seeking force and the physical aspects of an orbiting stopper? Your task," he continues, "is to design an investigation to show the relationship between the centripetal force and the properties of the orbiting object. The challenge of this lab is to think like a scientist and design an experiment to fill in this statement." He then turns to the board and writes, *The amount of centripetal force needed to keep a body in orbit depends on the* _____. "By the end of the lab, you should fill in the blank and be able to prove it."

George knows he wants students to investigate three variables: the mass, the radius of the circle, and the velocity or speed of the stopper. To get the students thinking, he prompts the class by posing the following questions: What are some of the factors affecting centripetal force? Does the mass of the orbiting object affect the amount of centripetal force? In other words, if I have a bigger mass, would it take more force to keep the object in orbit? Does the distance the orbiting object is from the center affect the force? In other words, how does the radius affect the centripetal force? Does the velocity or speed of the orbiting object affect the force? Or, to say it another way, do I have to hold this harder if the object circulates at a faster rate?

Through a discussion, students conclude that three variables could affect centripetal force: mass, radius of the orbit, and velocity or speed. It is important to begin this portion of the lesson with a review of how to design an experiment. George now prompts the students toward choosing a question around one of the three variables and designing an investigation to answer their question. He asks, "What do you want to measure? What are the variables in the investigation?" Regardless of the variable the students choose, he knows that their data or answers imply a relationship.

That means each group should be prepared to produce a graph of the evidence it collects. From past experience, George knows he will have to provide a review on plotting data and determining the various relationships that students may get from their data.

Brainstorming and Planning the Investigation

At this point, there are six groups of students investigating the three questions. As it turns out, two groups choose to investigate the mass variable, two others choose the radius, and the last two choose the speed or velocity variable. As students design their investigations, they need sufficient time to exchange ideas about their models. Each group must decide which variable will affect the outcome of the experiment and which variables will be held constant. The teacher asks, "Out of the three variables, how many need to be controlled? How can they be controlled? Think about what are you looking for and how you will analyze the data. What is the relationship between the centripetal force and the variable you chose to investigate? Remember, your graph should show the relationship between the manipulated and the responding variables. You also need to determine which variable goes on the x-axis and the y-axis."

George uses this time to circulate among all six groups to review their designs and procedures. He has each group first identify the manipulated (or dependent) variable and the responding (or independent) variable, and then identify the controlled variables. As he rotates to each group, George checks and approves each group's draft of its investigation. He also tells students that as soon as their procedure is approved, they should determine the equipment they will need to carry out the experiment.

During its brainstorming session, one of the two mass groups finds the investigation relatively easy to design. The students in the group indicate to George that they want to find out how the mass affects the centripetal force. One student reminds the rest of the group that $F = ma$ but questions whether the formula holds true for circular motion as well as linear motion. The mass group then writes a hypothesis to test—"As the mass increases, the amount of force will also increase."

"What's the manipulated variable in your experiment?" George asks.

"The mass," a student answers. "We'll change the mass by adding stoppers to the end of the string. We'll put one stopper on and measure the force for three trials. Then we'll add a second stopper and measure the force again for three trials. Then we'll add a third stopper and measure the centripetal force again." The mass group explains to George that they will keep the radius and the speed constant throughout the investigation.

"But now how will you control the velocity?" George asks.

"Oh, that's easy," Michael explains. "We'll count how many times the stopper spins around in a certain amount of time, then duplicate that in each trial."

Another student adds, "I'll count how many spins the stopper makes in 10 seconds. Or we can make 10 spins and see how long 10 spins takes. Let's say we get 10 spins in 10 seconds; once we get that, we want to be sure we spin that with two masses. The speed won't be perfect, but it's close enough."

As expected, the radius experiment proves to be a bit more of a challenge. Subsequently, the brainstorming discussions for these groups are significantly different from what occurs in the other groups. One group's question is "Does the radius of the orbit affect the centripetal force?" This group knows the radius of the orbit will be the manipulated variable, while the mass and velocity of the orbiting stopper will remain the same.

"How are you going to change the radius?" George asks.

"We'll make the first radius equal to a half meter, the second radius 1 meter, and then the third radius 2 meters," Amy responds. "We'll also have the same person spin all three radii."

George then asks, "Will you change the number of stoppers?"

"No," Amy says. "We'll keep the same number of stoppers for all trials."

"Good! Now, how will you measure centripetal force as the responding variable?" George asks.

"We'll attach a spring scale to the string and read the amount of centripetal force in Newtons," Amy answers.

"That's great!" George replies. "Now for the tough part: How will you keep the velocity the same in each trial?"

Amy knows that determining the affect of the radius will be tricky because they have to find a way to control the velocity of the orbiting stopper as the radius becomes larger. The students in the radius group know the formula for velocity, $V = D/T$. They conclude that as the radius increases, so will the circumference or distance of the orbit. As they control for velocity, they must also control the time the stopper takes to make a full orbit. In other words, to control velocity, they must take into consideration the distance and time. As the distance or circumference increases, the time must also increase.

What seems like a simple experiment at first is now more difficult. The group now has to determine how to manipulate the radius while controlling mass and velocity. After some discussion with the teacher, the group remains puzzled on how to control the velocity. They know that radius #1 will result in velocity #1, and that radii #2 and #3 should also equal velocity #1. The dilemma they face, however, is how to increase the radius and keep the velocity the same. After considerable discussion, the group decides that a 1-meter circumference orbiting in 1 second will have the velocity of 1 meter per second. A circumference of 2 meters would have to take 2 seconds to equal the same velocity of 1 meter per second, and a circumference of 3 meters would have to take 3 seconds to equal the velocity of 1 meter per second. To maintain the velocity of 1 meter per second, the group decides to calculate the radii needed to make the three circumferences equal to 1, 2, and 3 meters (.15 m, .32 m, and .48 m, respectively).

The group also determines that each of the three radii will require three trials to find the mean. The three students in the radius group now face an interesting situation. Each student has a different hypothesis for the same question. Amy thinks that when the radius increases and the velocity remains the same, the centripetal force will increase, while Holly thinks it will decrease. Cathy, however, knows that the speed will affect the centripetal force, and because the speed in the experiment remains the same, the centripetal force should also remain the same. Rather than discourage their thinking, George tells them to record each of their hypotheses and see which one is correct after the evidence and data are collected and graphed.

As George gets around to the velocity group, he finds its plan is well underway. "What's your question?" he asks.

"What affect does speed of an orbiting body have on the centripetal force?" answers Alberto. The speed group also has a hypothesis. The members believe, using Newton's formula of $F = ma$, that if they increase the speed, the centripetal force will also increase.

George then says, "But remember, Newton derived the formula for linear motion. What are you determining?"

One student responds, "Circular motion. So we want to see if Newton's law of linear motion holds true for circular motion."

"Good!" George responds. "How are you going to investigate that? How are you going to control the speed, and how will you keep the radius constant?"

Calvin says, "We can either count the number of spins or orbits in 10 seconds or count how long it takes to make 10 spins. Because we know the radius, we can determine the circumference, which equals the distance. We'll keep the stopper constant and spin the stopper at slow, medium, and fast speeds. We'll count the number of spins in 10 seconds. Slow will be 5 spins in 10 seconds, medium is 10 spins in 10 seconds, and fast is 15 spins in 10 seconds. Then we can determine the speed in meters per second. And for each trial, we'll keep the radius the same at a half meter. We are going to tie a stopper to the string and put the string through the glass rod."

George tells the group, "It sounds like you have a good procedure."

Carrying Out the Investigation

In any good inquiry, students are constantly challenged by problems and discrepancies. They must learn to work and solve problems as a group. As the groups carry out investigations, some need help in where and how to hold the spring scale, and others need help in where and how to add more masses or stoppers. Some are learning to use timers to record time, and others are learning how to use an electronic balance to measure the mass of the stopper. All the students are encouraged to record results in their science journals. The notes from their science journals will be used later in a formal laboratory write-up.

During the investigations, George continues to rotate to all the groups and helps the groups work out their problems and ideas. He knows this part of the inquiry takes patience on the part of the teacher as well as from the students. George uses the metaphor of a circus performer trying to keep several plates spinning on a long stick at once to describe his role as a facilitator during inquiry lessons.

George now informs the groups that their oral presentations are due the next day. During that time, students, using a poster, a trifold display board, or a PowerPoint presentation, will communicate the evidence they collected during the investigation and share the data and conclusions with the class during a 5-minute presentation. "Be sure to include a graph with a best-fit line of the results," he tells them. "Remember, a final write-up of your lab report is due next week," he adds.

Communicating the Results

The next day's class begins with the question "What are the physical factors of an orbiting body that affect centripetal force?"

Mr. Wolfe starts the class lesson by saying, "You will share your data with the class, and we'll see what you young Newtonians have discovered. Each group will identify its question and hypothesis, then tell us the manipulated, responding, and controlled variables, along with the procedure, data, and conclusions."

The mass groups both report a direct proportional relationship when comparing the effect of the mass (*m*) and the amount of centripetal (*Fc*) force exerted, and they propose the formula that centripetal force is proportional to the mass (*Fc:m*).

The two radius groups also had results similar to each other's. Both groups discuss the challenge of keeping the speed of the orbiting stopper constant and say there is an inverse relationship between the centripetal force (*Fc*) and the radius (*r*). They conclude that as the radius increases, the centripetal force decreases, and that centripetal force is inversely proportional to the radius. The radius group summarizes its findings with the formula *Fc:1/r*.

After analyzing the data, the student in the radius group who offered the hypothesis about the centripetal force remaining constant as the velocity remains constant realizes that the data do not support her idea and changes her understanding of the relationship.

One of the speed groups shows that as they kept the number of stoppers (the mass) and radius constant, there was a squared relationship between the centripetal force and the velocity, and they propose the formula *Fc:v²*.

Summarizing the Results of the Lesson

George now summarizes and wraps up the lesson by combining the mass, radius, and speed data into one concept. "We now know," the teacher starts out, "that three physical properties or variables affect centripetal force. When you increase the mass, you increase the centripetal force. When you decrease the radius, you increase the centripetal force. When you increase the velocity squared, you increase the centripetal force. That is to say, the centripetal force is proportional to the mass and the velocity of the orbiting object. We also know that it is inversely proportional to the radius. We now can say these three proportions are represented by the formulas *Fc:m*, *Fc:1/r*, and therefore, *Fc:m/r*.

"Now take out your equation sheets. Do you see a formula that looks like this? $Fc = ma_c$ and $Ac = v^2/r$. From Newton's laws, we know that $F = ma$, so if we combine $F = mv^2/r$ from the lab and $F = ma$ from Newton, we determine that $Fc = ma_c$. Thus, $v^2/r = Ac = v^2/r$. When we combine the results from all the groups, we come up with the formula $Fc = mv^2/r$. You just figured out something that took Newton years to determine." George then applies the lab to common experiences such as the clothes dryer and the centrifuge.

The lesson ends as George shows students how the lab applies to the following problems:

Question #1: A 2-kg cart moves in a circular path with a 10-meter radius, and at a constant speed of 20 m/sec. What is the centripetal acceleration (*Ac*)?

Answer: $Ac = v^2/r = 20^2/10 = 400/10 = 40$ m/sec.

Question #2: What if the mass of the cart doubles? Using the formula $Fc = M \times Ac$, what force is needed in each case?

Answer: 2 kg (40 m/sec) = 80 Newtons; 4 kg (40 m/sec) = 160 Newtons.

AN INTERVIEW WITH GEORGE WOLFE

How would you describe your approach to teaching?

George: I think it depends on what I am teaching at the time. You have to be very flexible in your approach. Although inquiry is my preferred way of teaching, there are instances when there is a lot of information I have to get across and I cannot do that by inquiry. Sometimes I have to present a lesson in a didactic approach. I have to teach them the words and the interrelationship between the concepts I want them to understand. I prefer to have the student learn the science through doing rather than by hearing it. A big point in my teaching is the warm-up. I throw out leading questions with a historical background, then lead them to the point where they are asking the question.

The centripetal force lab started out with an introduction about Newton and moved into investigating forces. So we move from the historical perspective into the lab and the inquiry part. During the inquiry, they are in the planning stage of the lab where I help facilitate their planning. Later, we move into the implementation of the lab and the summary. For me, that's an ideal inquiry. Then, after the inquiry lab, we return to a more traditional approach to add meaning and mathematize to understand $Fc = mv^2/r$. I try to do about 8 to 10 of this type of lab in a school year. The rest of the labs are more directed because of safety or procedure requirements.

Here's what I do on the first day of each school year. I start with a very sophisticated physics question. A hunter is aiming a blow gun at a monkey. I ask them, "If the hunter shoots his gun at the same time as the monkey lets go of the branch, will he hit the monkey?" We spend two days, with no real physics background, arguing and discussing the concept. On the second day, we test their ideas, and before they know it, they are doing inquiry. Although they do not design the investigation on their own, from Day 1 students see that this physics class is about asking questions and investigating our ideas. I let them tell me what to do. I make that point on Day 1, and it sets the tone for the rest of the year. I'll set up the investigation based on their ideas because they are not ready to do three or four individual inquiries at once. We get to that in a month or so. Plus, it gets them excited about science from the start. They do get the importance of doing science in a meaningful logical method.

How did you learn science as a high school or college student?

I don't remember doing one exciting thing in science during high school. In fact, when I was a senior in high school, I said to my mother, "I don't know what I want to do, but I'm sure I don't want to go into science, and I certainly don't want to teach." Well, here I am, 20-something years later, a science teacher. How ironic! I made the transition to an interest in teaching through my love of camping and the outdoors. Although I started college as a Spanish major, in 1970 I became interested in the Peace Corps, and they needed teachers in Africa. I think I began as a traditional teacher but had a creative streak that made me an actor.

In this class, 9th-grade students were studying physics. Many schools, however, reserve physics courses to the 12th grade. What are the advantages of teaching physics first?

Consider the way most high school and college science departments are organized. There is a biology department, a chemistry department, plus earth science and physics. Today, you can't be a biologist without being a biochemist. Today, science takes a more integrated approach and physics seems to be the foundation for all the disciplines. Actually, to know biology means to know chemistry, earth science, and physics, so in some aspect, as a biologist, I think biology should be the last subject in the sequence. Now, many say you cannot do physics without higher-level math, but a conceptual-based physics approach like Hewitt's can be taught with an algebra background. Make physics for everyone, not save it for just 12th-graders. To use a biology metaphor, physics should be a pump, not a filter. It should act like the heart rather than the kidneys. To me, it's physics first and for everyone. Very few of our best science students are electing to be physicists. We need to excite kids about physics, not reserve physics for the elite.

How difficult is it to fit inquiry-based learning into a standards-based physics curriculum?

That's an important issue. First, you need to convince the school administration that we need block scheduling. In physics class, students met for a double period several times a week. It's difficult to do inquiry in 45-minute periods. Second, cut the fat out of the curriculum and reduce the number of concepts to a minimum. The trouble with most school curricula is that we are teaching too many topics. We need more depth and less coverage. Decide what concepts students can learn on their own, and structure your lesson accordingly. In the centripetal force inquiry, I took three double periods. I could have led them through the lab in two periods, but they would not have the opportunity to make decisions about their learning or do the problem-solving aspect of science. That's the decision a teacher makes in science. What do you value: more content, or an appreciation for the process? Plus, inquiry has to be very effective and efficient with instructional time. Give students time limits on planning. Some need additional help after school or at lunch. I always open my room for students who want to bring in their lunches and continue working on their labs or get extra help. I know this may not apply to every science teacher, but it's something that works for me. You have to find what works for you. Educators need good classroom management skills that many first-year teachers may not have. As I've heard you say, inquiry takes time.

You mentioned curricular limitations and time constraints that you experience in an inquiry-based classroom. Do you experience any physical limitations?

When kids are planning their investigations, there are no physical constraints. When we move into the implementation stage, students need space to spread out. In my class, I have a combined classroom/lab setting. You are going to have kids at different stages in their lab; you need space to spread out. There were six different groups doing three different labs, and that takes an enormous amount of energy to keep an eye on all groups at once. It's a technique you develop that comes only from years of experience.

How do you design an inquiry-based physics lab?

You start backwards, from what you want kids to know and understand. In the centripetal force lab, I want them to understand that $Fc = mv^2/r$. Next, I think what equipment and resources I have to teach the concept. In this case, I started with the standard centripetal force demonstration, then decided how I could get students to come up with that lab on their own. I tell them, "Suppose I have this equipment; what procedures can you design to prove the question?" I ask them how they will collect their data and how they will represent it on a graph or a chart. It's all up to them, but you have to believe that they can do it. I also think about the introduction—how to introduce the lab and provide the content background and historical perspective to make the lab relevant.

In this class, you introduced the inquiry lab with a prelab introduction. What is the importance of the prelab?

It introduces the question and places an emphasis on scientific history. There is a significant emphasis placed on historical development in the national science standards. I think students need an appreciation of the developments that led us to what we know today.

In the centripetal force inquiry lab, you knew that each variable (the mass, the radius, and the speed) had to be investigated so that in the end, the data from all three investigations contribute to the formula $Fc = mv^2/r$. What would you do if a group did not choose to test all three variables?

If that was the case, I would have two choices: either add the third variable at the end of the inquiry, when we analyzed the data, or prompt one group into selecting the variable. I would prefer to prompt a group into selecting the variable so that the data from all three variables comes from the class. One of the roles of an inquiry-based teacher is to know when and how to lead students in a direction that serves the objective of the lab.

In inquiry classrooms, teachers interact with small groups of students and question their understanding of a particular concept. Often, one student in the group seems to answer all the teacher's questions for the group. I noticed that when you interacted with each group, you paid special attention to be sure everyone in the group understands what is going on. What strategies do you use to assess students' understanding in an informal, small group setting?

You have to make good eye contact and read body language. I often say the eyes are the "mirror of the brain." You watch a kid's eyes, and you can tell whether he or she gets it or not. The eyes tell you when they get it, and when they don't. The eyes tell you who's bored to tears. It's all about reading body language. I often try to direct questions to individual students, not the entire group. That helps me to decide whether the individual understands the concept. I am always looking for visual and auditory clues to support them through the inquiry process.

QUESTIONS FOR REFLECTION

1. What are the advantages and disadvantages of offering physics as the first course in a high school science sequence?

2. How did George Wolfe prompt students into investigating the three variables identified in the case study? What would you do if students did not select all three variables?

3. In the experiment, the student in the radius group underwent a conceptual change in relation to her understanding of the relationship between radius and centripetal force. Would this have happened if the lesson was purely lecture-based?

4. What, if any, prior knowledge, skills, and experiences do students need to complete this inquiry investigation?

Reflecting on
a Teaching Career

According to the *National Science Education Standards* (NRC, 1996, p. 28), the standards for science are grounded in five assumptions:

1. The vision of science education described in the *Standards* requires changes throughout the entire system.

2. What students learn is greatly influenced by how they are taught.

3. The actions of teachers are deeply influenced by their perception of science as an enterprise and as a subject to be taught and learned.

4. Student understanding is actively constructed through individual and social processes.

5. Actions of teachers are deeply influenced by their understanding of and relationship with students.

Although the stories and case studies in this book focused on the *how to* or *mechanics* of an inquiry lesson and addressed assumptions 1–4, it is equally important to consider the *affective side* or *meaning* of inquiry and address the reason why most of us decided to enter the teaching profession—to influence young minds and instill a desire and love to study science. In our last case, we will read how one teacher reflects on his 30-year career and discovers that his professional life has been fulfilled through inquiry-based teaching.

The National Research Council (1996) suggests that teachers of science plan inquiry-based science programs for their students. In doing this, they

- Select science content and adapt and design curricula to meet the interests, knowledge, understanding, abilities, and experience of students. (p. 30)
- Recognize and respond to student diversity and encourage all students to participate fully in science learning. (p. 32)
- Display and demand respect for diverse ideas, skills, and experiences of all students. (p. 46)

Thus, it seems fitting that this last case study addresses the emotional and humanistic side of inquiry teaching.

THE STORY OF MR. BAKER

It was a rainy Friday afternoon when Ronald Baker got a call from a woman he did not even know. The students had all gone home for the weekend, and Ron gazed out over a sea of empty desks, enjoying one of those few quiet moments when all the noise and aggravations from teaching seemed to fade into the thought of a 3-day weekend lying ahead.

"Hello, Mr. Baker," the woman said. "This is Dr. Carol Bailey from Suffolk College. I'm the supervisor for student teaching placement, and I have a request from one of our science education majors to do a student teaching experience with you. I know," she continued, "Suffolk is quite a ways from your school, and we usually don't place student teachers that far from campus, but this is a special request. A young man, if I can find his name here—yes, Miguel Sanchez—requested a placement specifically with you."

Ron thought to himself—the name sounded familiar. Could it be the same Miguel Sanchez I had in my third period science class almost 8 years ago? In an instant, Ron recalled his first year teaching at West Hill High School as if it was just yesterday.

Having graduated from college in December, his teacher certification in hand, Ron quickly discovered that all the good teaching jobs were filled in September. He was offered, however, a substitute teaching position that would last the rest of the school year. Eager to start his science teaching career and naive enough to think he was going to make a difference in the lives of high schoolers, Ron accepted the position and found himself, a week later, in West Hill High School, Room 313.

In looking back, he thought, pure hell is the only way to describe that first year of teaching. Ron was assigned five classes and four preps: one 11th-grade general chemistry class for non-college-bound students, two 9th-grade general science classes, one environmental science elective for seniors (an easy course for those needing an additional science credit), and one infamous class of "Consumer Science" for students who had accumulated no science credit toward high school graduation. He soon discovered that he was the third teacher these students had had since September. The previous two were driven out of town, and in the eyes of the students, he was soon to become number three.

The first week, bound and determined to succeed, Ron started out with the "don't smile until Christmas" attitude. Unfortunately, Christmas had passed during the previous month, and this was the beginning of the second semester. He thought to himself, "Could I not smile until Easter?" For each of the classes, Ron followed the same approach: Be stern, and maintain classroom discipline. "Be fair and firm," my college methods professors had told him. He decided that his class lectures would keep instruction simple and to the point. After all, he had a lot of catching up to do because the students had not learned very much from their previous teachers.

Despite his noble intentions, Ron almost gave up by the February midwinter break. He felt he had failed miserably. And though the chemistry, general science, and environmental classes were starting to show some improvement, Consumer Science was a disaster. One student started each day's class by shouting out from the back of the room, "Hey, Mr. Baker, Why do we have to learn this stuff? This is 'bambino science.'" That student was Miguel Sanchez. Mr. Sanchez, as Ron referred to him, was constantly in trouble. By February, Miguel had been suspended for 3 days for insubordination to Mr. Riley, his English teacher, 1 day for smoking in the boys' lavatory, and 1 day for skipping Mr. Collins's seventh period social studies class. In short, school was a struggle for Miguel, but he still managed to pass from grade to grade, making low C's.

Miguel's teachers labeled him as a troubled student. His classmates often referred to him as "loco." Despite these words, Ron knew Miguel was not dumb; he was just another high school kid trying to struggle through the awkward years of being a teenager. In fact, it was because of Miguel that Ron decided he had to do something different to get through to these kids. "It is my responsibility," he thought, "to find ways to make their classes meaningful and assure them that I am in it for the long haul." That meant coming back next Monday, the Monday after that, and all the rest of the Mondays until the end of the school year. Ron became determined not to abandon them like the other teachers had.

Ron immediately got rid of the book he was using for Consumer Science and decided to make class relevant to the students' daily lives. After all, there were no age-appropriate textbooks for high school students like Miguel who were one to two grade levels below in reading. "Why not," he thought, "just make the course a practical, problem-solving approach?" Having shared his concerns with Miss Moore, another West Hill science teacher, Ron began to find out about inquiry-based teaching. She gave him a book, *Inquiry Techniques for Teaching Science*, by William Romey (1968). It was then that Ron decided that his classes would no longer be solely lectures. He started having students do their own investigations and guided them through discovery-based experiences. To do this, Ron realized that he needed additional coursework, so he enrolled in the first of many graduate-level courses on inquiry-based learning.

The second change centered on Miguel. Ron asked Dr. Austin, the school psychologist, to administer a screening test for Miguel's reading skills. They later found out that Miguel was not slow at all; in fact, he was quite smart. Unfortunately, Miguel had dyslexia—he wasn't able to see words as they are. To Miguel, some letters looked backwards, and some looked reversed. "He's a smart, curious kid with a phenomenal desire to see how things work," Dr. Austin wrote in her report. Upon further examination, they discovered that in 3rd grade, Miguel was assigned to a special-education class for learning disabled children. A year later, despite extra help, he still couldn't decipher a sentence. The school psychologist explained to Miguel that his brain wasn't impaired, just different.

Several months later, Miguel made it through Consumer Science with a B, and Ron Baker made it through his first year at West Hill. Ron was determined more than ever that inquiry-based teaching would become his passion. On graduation day, Miguel came up to Ron and handed him a note. Ron put it in his pocket, and they said their good-byes. As Ron drove home from the graduation ceremony, he remembered the note and pulled it from his sports jacket. Ron steered his dented 1965 green Ford Falcon to the side of the road and read the letter. *Dear Mr. Baker,* the letter began. *Thank you for being my teacher and having patience with me. Because of you, I was able to pass science and graduate from high school. I'm learning to live with my dyslexia. I know that I have to fight it for the rest of my life. I am sorry I was so much trouble in your class. You made learning fun and taught me how to inquire and think for myself. Maybe someday I'll be a teacher just like you. Your friend, Miguel.*

After graduation, some of the teachers at West Hill High School heard he joined the Army. Ron didn't hear about him again; until that rainy Friday afternoon, the day the woman from the college called.

Miguel had finally grown up. It was true—he had joined the Army, and upon an honorable discharge, enrolled in a local 2-year college, where he majored in sociology and received an associate degree. After his first 2 years, Miguel transferred to Suffolk College and enrolled in a science education program. In his senior year at Suffolk, thanks to the unusual, long-distance placement, he returned to West Hill, renewed his friendship with his former science teacher, Mr. Baker, and successfully completed his student teaching. This time, however, it was not from a seat in the back of the room. This time, it was Miguel up in front of the entire class, and now it was Ron's turn to shape this energetic young teacher into the inquiry-based teacher Miguel had inspired Ron to become 8 years earlier.

It has been 30 years now since Miguel returned to West Hill High School as a student teacher. The September following his student teaching experience, he was offered a teaching position at West Hill and became a member of our science department. For the first 2 years of his probationary status, Ron acted as Miguel's mentor. He helped Miguel to refine and sharpen his skills in becoming an inquiry-based teacher and has become an excellent teacher in his own right. While Miguel works as an inclusion science resource teacher and continues to struggle each day to compensate for his dyslexia, their friendship continues to grow.

This past June, after 33 years of teaching and 15 years as science department chairperson, Mr. Baker decided to retire. It gave Ron great pleasure when Miguel made the introductory greeting at his retirement party. What a wonderful irony and honor it was, Ron thought, that no finer gift could a teacher be given than to have the opportunity to see that the things we, as teachers, value result in a legacy of something important to us. Surrounded by family, friends, and devoted and talented teachers, Ron reflected on the pleasure of spending his career with Miguel Sanchez, his dearest student, his colleague, and his friend. Later in the introduction, Miguel presented Ron with a plaque. On it were inscribed the following words:

The average teacher tells us. The good teacher tells us and explains why. The better teacher shows us and explains why. But the greatest teacher inspires us to inquire for ourselves. You were always a great inspiration to us.

As Ron walked up to the podium to accept his plaque, he was overcome with a humbling pride. He and Miguel smiled at each other and embraced in a hug. Neither of them could hold back the tears any longer. During his retirement speech, Ron reminisced about the great joy he received being a high school science teacher and how that fateful first year inspired him to transform his teaching style and pursue questions that engage students in learning.

The important thing is not to stop questioning. Curiosity has its own reason for existing.

—Albert Einstein

Resource A

Inquiry Resources for High School Science Teachers

I f you make a commitment to become an inquiry-based teacher, you make a commitment to continue your intellectual and professional development. Professional growth often comes in the form of reading; participating in workshops, summer institutes, and seminars; taking graduate-level courses; and collaborating and exchanging ideas through support groups and online forums.

For some, this book may be the beginning of your exploration into inquiry. For others, it may be one of many resources that help you construct an understanding of inquiry. Whichever case applies, your reading and discussion into inquiry-based teaching should be ongoing.

The purpose of this section is to familiarize science teachers with some of the many resources that are available on constructivism and inquiry teaching.

PRINT RESOURCES ON INQUIRY

Adams, D., & Hamm, M. (1998). *Collaborative inquiry in science, math, and technology.* Portsmouth, NH: Heinemann.

This book provides a general overview for cooperative learning and critical and creative thinking skills as well as inquiry opportunities in science, mathematics, and technology. The science sections outline specific science process skills and offer several student activities that invite inquiry learning.

Bruno, M., & Chase, J. (1998). *School/college partnerships: Inquiry-based science and technology for all students and teachers.* Amherst, MA: Hampshire College.

This free guide provides suggestions for establishing partnerships on inquiry between schools and universities. Examples are offered for day and residential camps for children. The guide can be requested through the Science and Technology Education Partnership (STEP), Hampshire College, Amherst, Massachusetts. The guide also can be accessed on the STEP Web page at http://demeter.hampshire .edu/~manual.

Eisenhower National Clearinghouse for Mathematics and Science Education. (1999). *Inquiry and problem solving. ENC Focus, 6*(2).
   Features articles on teachers using inquiry and problem solving in their classrooms. Available online at www.enc.org. For a free subscription to *ENC Focus*, call 800-621-5785 or go to its Web site at www.enc.org/order/.

Kielborn, T., & Gilmer, P. (Eds.). (1999). *Meaningful science: Teachers doing inquiry + teaching science.* Tallahassee, FL: SERVE.
   This booklet traces the experiences of seven teachers who participated in inquiry-based research projects as part of their doctoral program. The seven teachers describe their research projects and how they applied their research and skills to their science classrooms. Available from SERVE, 1203 Governor's Square Blvd., Suite 400, Tallahassee, FL 32301.

Layman, J., with Ochoa, G., & Heikkinen, H. (1996). *Inquiry and learning: Realizing science standards in the classroom.* New York: The College Board.
   An introduction to inquiry with several classroom examples.

Llewellyn, D. (2002). *Inquire within: Implementing inquiry-based science standards.* Thousand Oaks, CA: Corwin Press.
   An introduction to inquiry-based learning for elementary and secondary school science teachers. Includes rubrics for assessing inquiry and a self-assessment.

Minstrell, J., & Van Zee, E. (Eds.). (2000). *Inquiring into inquiry learning and teaching in science.* Washington, DC: American Association for the Advancement of Science.
   An excellent collection of articles that will apply to both the novice and the experienced inquiry science teacher. Divided into three parts: (1) Why inquiry? (2) What does inquiry look like? and (3) What issues arise with inquiry learning and teaching?

National Research Council. (2002). *Inquiry and the National Science Education Standards: A guide for teaching and learning.* Washington, DC: National Academy Press.
   A new and comprehensive guide for implementing inquiry in the science classroom. Excellent reading to accompany the National Science Education Standards (see "Print Resources on Science Standards and Science Literacy"). Contains useful strategies for teachers and numerous vignettes as examples.

Thier, H. (2001). *Developing inquiry-based science materials: A guide for educators.* New York: Teachers College Press.
   Although the premise of the book is in developing guided inquiry-based programs and instructional materials, readers will find this book useful for issues related to defining inquiry, assessment and evaluation, and implementing an inquiry-based curriculum.

PRINT RESOURCES ON INQUIRY INVESTIGATIONS

Krasny, M., & the Environmental Inquiry Team. (2002). *Invasion ecology: Cornell scientific inquiry series*. Arlington, VA: NSTA Press.

Leads students into conducting investigations in plant ecology. Students learn how to do research with simple and inexpensive bioassays by studying real-life invaders like purple loosestrife. Includes a teacher guide and a student edition. Companion to *Assessing Toxic Risk*, by Trautmann and the Environmental Inquiry Team, listed below. An excellent biology and environmental science resource for grades 9–12.

Lechtanski, V. (2000). *Inquiry-based experiments in chemistry*. Washington, DC: American Chemical Society.

Contains 35 high school chemistry experiments. Each experiment identifies the "Experiment," the "Teacher's Notes," and a "Sample Lab Report." The Teacher's Notes are exceptionally useful in helping the teacher to introduce the lab and providing both common misconceptions students have about the topic and procedural and calculation errors to expect. Although the book is very useful, it may be difficult to find. Try several online book companies like Amazon.com.

Lonergan, T. (2001). *The basics of inquiry, measurement and science math*. New Orleans: Health-Science Education.

A brief but useful manual on the scientific method and the use of measuring skills in science. Offers several activities integrating math and science.

McDermott, L. (1996). *Physics by inquiry* (Vols. 1 & 2). New York: Wiley.

Includes laboratory-based modules that provide a step-by-step introduction to the physical sciences. Applicable for preservice and practicing elementary and secondary school teachers. The modules are designed to develop scientific reasoning in physics and the process of inquiry.

Trautmann, N., & the Environmental Inquiry Team. (2001). *Assessing toxic risk: Cornell scientific inquiry series*. Arlington, VA: NSTA Press.

Leads students into conducting investigations in toxicology. Students learn how to do research with simple and inexpensive bioassays. Includes a teacher guide and a student edition. Excellent biology and environmental science resource for grades 9–12.

Trautmann, N., & the Environmental Inquiry Team. (2003). *Decay and renewal: Cornell scientific inquiry series*. Arlington, VA: NSTA Press.

Leads students into conducting investigations in natural recycling, composting, and wastewater treatment. Students learn how to do research with simple and inexpensive bioassays. Includes a teacher guide and a student edition. Excellent biology and environmental science resource for grades 9–12.

Trautmann, N., & Krasny, M. (1997). *Composting in the classroom: Scientific inquiry for high school students*. Dubuque, IA: Kendall/Hunt.

A guide for grade 9–12 teachers and students interested in using composting for science and multidisciplinary projects. Includes additional information on composting and waste management.

PRINT RESOURCES ON CONSTRUCTIVISM

Abraham, M., Lawson, A., & Renner, J. (1989). *A theory of instruction: Using the learning cycle to teach science concepts and thinking skills* (NARST Monograph #1). Washington, DC: National Association for Research in Science Teaching.
Provides a theoretical and historical background on the learning cycle. Contains empirical studies and implications for the classroom.

Bransford, J., Brown, A., & Cocking, R. (Eds.). (2000). *How people learn: Brain, mind, experience, and school–expanded edition.* Washington, DC: National Academy Press.
Provides recent research findings on how learning occurs and offers recommendations about what teachers can do to facilitate student learning. Chapter 4, "How Children Learn," provides a constructivist approach to teaching and learning.

Brooks, J., & Brooks, M. (2001). *In search of understanding: The case for constructivist classrooms.* Upper Saddle River, NJ: Prentice Hall.
This book is an excellent starting point to read about constructivism and its application to teaching strategies. Although the book applies to all content areas, science teachers in particular will find this book helpful in gaining a baseline understanding of constructivism. The book is easy to read and is filled with practical suggestions for classroom practice. Combined with a set of accompanying videos by the Association for Supervision and Curriculum Development (see "Multimedia Resources on Inquiry"), it makes an excellent resource for professional development sessions.

Bybee, R. (Ed.). (2002). *Learning science and the science of learning.* Arlington, VA: NSTA Press.
A comprehensive look at teaching and learning through a constructivist perspective. Includes articles on curriculum design, assessment, and professional development.

Fosnot, C. (1989). *Enquiring teachers, enquiring learners: A constructivist approach for teaching.* New York: Teachers College Press.
Using an analogy of a plant starting from seed, Fosnot takes the reader through a generation of research that grows into an alternative to the traditional approach of staff development. She proposes that teachers engage as learners and researchers in education. In the foreword, Eleanor Duckworth says, "Fosnot makes it clear in this volume, we teach as we have been taught." This book, although not specific to science, provides applications to language development and mathematics.

Fosnot, C. (Ed.). (1996). *Constructivism: Theory, perspectives and practice.* New York: Teachers College Press.
The articles in this book provide the reader with applications of constructivism to mathematics, science, art, and language arts. For science teachers, the three introductory chapters by von Glasersfeld, Fosnot, and Cobb offer an introduction into constructivism's theoretical foundation.

Gagnon, G., & Collay, M. (2001). *Designing for learning: Six elements in constructivist classrooms.* Thousand Oaks, CA: Corwin Press.

The authors present a six-step Constructivist Learning Design with a constructivist perspective on how to structure student learning environments. Although not written specifically for high school science teachers, educators at all levels and areas will benefit from this book.

Marek, E., & Cavallo, A. (1997). *The learning cycle—Elementary school science and beyond*. Portsmouth, NH: Heinemann.

One of the best ways to start off in inquiry is to use the learning cycle approach to lesson development, and one of the best ways to learn about the learning cycle is with this book. The authors provide a theoretical framework that includes references to the work of Piaget, Ausubel, and Vygotsky. Whether you use the 3E or 5E format, the learning cycle includes strategies for integrating constructivism and inquiry into your science lessons. The book also includes sample science lessons for elementary classrooms that could easily be extended in the middle and high school grades.

Marlow, B., & Page, M. (1998). *Creating and sustaining the constructivist classroom*. Thousand Oaks, CA: Corwin Press.

Brings together constructivist theory and step-by-step guidance to make constructivism work in classrooms across subject areas. Provides a simple and easy-to-use self-assessment on constructivist teaching strategies.

Mintzes, J., Wandersee, J., & Novak, J. (Eds.). (1998). *Teaching science for understanding: A human constructivist view*. San Diego, CA: Academic Press.

The authors present a new aspect of constructivism, a human constructivist view. *Teaching Science for Understanding* begins with an overview of the changes in science education. It then presents a review of each major instructional strategy, information about how it is best used, and the effectiveness of the strategy for understanding and retention of information. Provides specific references to concept maps and graphic organizers.

National Research Council. (2000). *How people learn: Brain, mind, experience, and school* (Exp. ed.). Washington, DC: National Academy Press.

Comprehensive text on the research of how learning occurs and the implications for classroom practice. Provides an excellent connection from theory to practice.

Shapiro, A. (2000). *Leadership for constructivist schools*. Lanham, MD: Scarecrow Press.

A down-to-earth guide with practical suggestions for how administrators and teachers can work together to develop constructivist school climates.

Stavy, R., & Tirosh, D. (2000). *How students (mis-)understand science and mathematics*. New York: Teachers College Press.

Sophisticated reading for teachers interested in students' misconceptions. According to the Web site NSTA Recommends, this book "gives you a detailed framework to explain and predict cognitive behaviors. Then [the book] offers practical teaching suggestions for using the framework in your own classroom."

Steffe, L., & Gale, J. (Eds.). (1995). *Constructivism in education*. Hillsdale, NJ: Lawrence Erlbaum Associates.

This book is recommended for those with an established understanding of constructivism. The chapters provide an extensive background into the research and philosophy of constructivist principles. The introductory chapter by von Glasersfeld is interesting reading.

Stepans, J. (1994). *Targeting students' science misconceptions: Physical science activities using the conceptual change model.* Riverview, FL: Idea Factory.

The book begins with a brief discussion on misconceptions and conceptual change, followed by sample lessons on 15 physical science topics ranging from matter to light and color. This book may be helpful for those teaching a lower-level 9th-grade physical science course.

Tobin, T. (Ed.). (1993). *The practice of constructivism in science education.* Hillsdale, NJ: Lawrence Erlbaum Associates.

This is one of the most quoted sources on the topic. In Part 1, authors Tobin and von Glasersfeld describe the nature of constructivism. Part 2 explains constructivist teaching and learning practices in science and mathematics, and Part 3 provides a perspective for teachers on the conceptual change process. The book is recommended for those who already have a basic understanding of constructivism. It is an excellent resource but probably should not be the first book you read on constructivism.

Treagust, D., Duit, R., & Fraser, B. (Eds.). (1996). *Improving teaching and learning in science and mathematics.* New York: Teachers College Press.

From a series by internationally renowned authors, *Improving Teaching and Learning in Science and Mathematics* offers a theoretical background for understanding constructivist principles in science and mathematics. Of particular interest for science teachers is the introductory chapter, which provides an overview of students' preconceptions—an initial starting point for planning science instruction. The chapter on concept mapping by Novak deals with organizing student understanding into hierarchical schematic structures. The chapter by Duit and Confrey offers a rethinking of the aim of science and math instruction and suggests ways to implement a new course of action.

PRINT RESOURCES ON SCIENCE STANDARDS AND SCIENCE LITERACY

American Association for the Advancement of Science. (1990). *Science for all Americans.* New York: Oxford University Press.

A compelling vision for science reform and achieving scientific literacy. A companion report to *Benchmarks for Science Literacy*, below.

American Association for the Advancement of Science. (1993). *Benchmarks for science literacy.* New York: Oxford University Press.

Provides science educators with guidelines for improving science literacy. Recommends what students should know and be able to do by the time they reach certain grade levels.

Audet, R., & Jordan, L. (2003). *Standards in the classroom: An implementation guide for teachers of science and mathematics*. Thousand Oaks, CA: Corwin Press.

A program for understanding and implementing standards using a 5E Learning Cycle format.

Bybee, R. (1997). *Achieving scientific literacy: From purposes to practices*. Portsmouth, NH: Heinemann.

Teachers becoming proficient in inquiry should also establish themselves as knowledgeable agents in the area of scientific literacy and educational reform. One way to become more knowledgeable on these issues is to start with this book. Bybee offers a vision for improving science instruction, with the focus on achieving scientific literacy utilizing a standards-based approach. Topics include defining scientific literacy, establishing national standards, and creating a vision for the future.

National Research Council. (1996). *National science education standards*. Washington, DC: National Academy Press.

This book should be on every science educator's shelf. Outlines standards for educational reform. Includes standards for science teaching, assessment, content, and program development.

Texley, J., & Wild, A. (Eds.). (1998). *NSTA pathways to the science standards: High school edition*. Arlington, VA: National Science Teachers Association.

Provides guidelines for the vision of the *National Science Education Standards* (see above) in practice. Contains many examples and vignettes about teaching high school science.

PRINT RESOURCES ON
DEMONSTRATIONS AND DISCREPANT EVENTS

Borgford, C., & Sumerlein, L. (1988). *Chemical activities*. Washington, DC: American Chemical Society.

Provides high school science teachers with exciting chemical demonstrations.

Liem, T. (1987). *Invitations to science inquiry* (2nd ed.). Chino Hills, CA: Science Inquiry Enterprises.

If you like to perform dynamic demonstrations and discrepant events as ways to stimulate inquiry, this book contains more than 400 quick-and-easy means to get your students "fired up" with science. All of the discrepant events include a list of materials necessary to complete the demonstrations, the procedures to follow, questions to pose after the demonstrations that stimulate inquiry, and an explanation of the scientific concepts involved. Most demonstrations can be completed with common science materials. Demonstrations are provided for life, earth, and physical science. Although the book is aimed at upper elementary and middle school teachers, many high school teachers will find this book invaluable.

Shakhashiri, B. (1983). *Chemical demonstrations: A handbook for teachers of chemistry.* Available through Carolina Biological Supply or The University of Wisconsin Press at http://www.wisc.edu/wisconsinpress/books/1740.htm

The four-volume series provides teachers with detailed instructions and background information for using chemical demonstrations. Each volume contains general information on presenting demonstrations and safety concerns. Volume 1 contains 45 demonstrations on thermochemistry, 11 on chemiluminescence, 14 on polymers, and 11 on metal ion precipitates. Volume 2 contains 26 demonstrations on the physical behavior of gases, 29 on the chemical behavior of gases, and 14 on oscillating chemical reactions. Volume 3 has 32 demonstrations on acids and bases along with 52 on liquids, solutions, and colloids. Volume 4 contains 15 demonstrations on clock reactions and 33 on batteries, electrolytic cells, and plating. You should also visit Dr. Shakhashiri's interesting Web site at http://scifun.chem.wisc.edu. The four-volume series of chemistry demonstration books can be ordered through the Web site.

Sumerlein, L., & Ealy, J. (1988). *Chemical demonstrations: A sourcebook for teachers* (2nd ed.). Washington, DC: American Chemical Society.

Two volumes provide high school science teachers with a wealth of exciting chemical demonstrations.

PRINT RESOURCES ON ASSESSMENT

Atkin, J., & Coffey, J. (Eds.). (2003). *Everyday assessment in the science classroom.* Arlington, VA: NSTA Press.

A collection of 10 articles and essays on assessment techniques. Includes "how-to" strategies for conducting assessments in science.

Doran, R., Chan, F., Tamir, P., & Lenhardt, C. (2002). *Science educator's guide to laboratory assessment.* Arlington, VA: NSTA Press.

Provides extensive background information connecting assessment and inquiry. Includes sections on high-stakes assessment, alternative assessment formats, and sample assessments for grades 9–12 in biology, chemistry, earth science, and physics.

Enger, S., & Yager, R. (2001). *Assessing student understanding in science.* Thousand Oaks, CA: Corwin Press.

Presents assessment of six domains of science, rubrics, and assessment examples for grades 9–12.

Kulm, G., & Malcom, S. (Eds.). (1991). *Science assessment in the service of reform.* Washington, DC: American Association for the Advancement of Science.

Discusses current policy issues regarding science assessment and provides examples from classrooms.

Lantz, H. (2004). *Rubrics for assessing student achievement in science grades K-12.* Thousand Oaks, CA: Corwin Press.

Offers more than 100 ready-to-use analytic and holistic rubrics to assess and evaluate student performance.

Mintzes, J., Wandersee, J., & Novak, J. (Eds.). (2000). *Assessing science understanding: A human constructivist approach.* San Diego, CA: Academic Press.
Provides a look at science assessment through the eyes of constructivist authors. Chapter topics include assessing science through concept maps, Vee diagrams, and graphic organizers, and using assessment instruments like rubrics and portfolios.

National Research Council. (2001). *Classroom assessment and the national science education standards.* Washington, DC: National Academy Press.
Excellent resource to accompany the National Science Education Standards (see "Print Resources on Science Standards and Science Literacy").

Pellegrino, J., Chudowsky, N., & Glaser, R. (Ed.). (2001). *Knowing what students know: The science and design of educational assessment.* Washington, DC: National Academy Press.
Presents several recommendations for rethinking the implications of assessment. Excellent resource to accompany *How Children Learn* (see Bransford, Brown, & Cocking in "Print Resources on Constructivism").

PRINT RESOURCES ON GENERAL SCIENCE AREAS

Hartman, H., & Glasgow, N. (2002). *Tips for the science teacher: Research-based strategies to help students learn.* Thousand Oaks, CA: Corwin Press.
Provides instructional "tips" for teachers to consider. Many of the tips refer to inquiry-based and constructivist strategies. Very appropriate for the beginning high school science teacher.

Rhoton, J., & Bowers, P. (Eds.). (1996). *Issues in science education.* Arlington, VA: National Science Education Leadership Association/National Science Teachers Association.
Although not specifically about inquiry, *Issues in Science Education* offers the reader useful background material regarding the changing tide of educational reform. Chapter topics include issues in science research and reform, technology integration, assessment procedures, leadership, effecting change, and professional development. A chapter on "The Constructivist Leader" provides an application of constructivism to all science leaders, administrators, and supervisors.

Youngson, R. (1998). *Science blunders: A brief history of how wrong scientists can sometimes be.* New York: Carroll & Graf.
An interesting history of many of the many scientific theories and models that have been disproved. Includes "blunders" for earth, life, and physical sciences. Applies to the conceptual change theory.

MULTIMEDIA RESOURCES ON INQUIRY

Association for Supervision and Curriculum Development. (1995). *Constructivism* [video-tape]. (Available from ASCD, 1703 N. Beauregard Street, Alexandria, VA 22311)

A two-part video program complements Brooks and Brooks's *In Search of Understanding: The Case for Constructivist Classrooms* (see above, in "Print Resources on Constructivism"). Part 1 highlights the book's five guiding principles of constructivism: (1) posing problems of emerging relevance to students, (2) structuring learning about primary concepts, (3) seeking and valuing students' points of view, (4) adapting curriculum to address students' suppositions, and (5) assessing student learning in the context of teaching. Part 2 includes case studies for various constructivist classrooms. A facilitator's guide includes a suggested workshop format, overheads, and handout materials.

Decision Development Corporation. (1994). *Just in time teaching series: Creating the active classroom* [videodisc]. (Available from DDC, 2680 Bishop Drive, Suite 122, San Ramon, CA 94583)

Whether you are looking for professional development or college course resources, this interactive videodisc program will certainly meet your teaching needs. Following a constructivist approach to staff development, this program follows the lessons of five science teachers. Includes effective strategies for ESL/LEP instruction. Individual segments are bar coded for easy access. Includes workshop guide.

National Science Teachers Association. (2003). *Search for solutions.* [DVD]. (Available through NSTA or at www.nsta.org/sfs)

This new 10-part series developed by ConocoPhillips takes the high school science student on an "engaging, thought-provoking journey through the process of scientific inquiry and discovery." More than 60 different scientists tell their stories about science, their work, and scientific philosophies. A teaching guide accompanies the series. The series and teaching guide can be downloaded from www.teaching-tools.com

Northwest Regional Educational Laboratory. (Producer). (1998). *Why won't you tell me the answer? Inquiry in the high school classroom* [videotape]. (Available from IOX Assessment Associates, 28170 SW Boberg Road #1, Wilsonville, OR 97070; www.ioxassessment.com)

Explains what inquiry is, the continuum of inquiry (from structured inquiry to guided inquiry, to student-directed inquiry), and the importance of using questioning skills in the classroom. Specific to high school science teachers. Excellent for workshops and seminars on inquiry.

Schneps, M. (Producer), & the Science Media Group of the Harvard-Smithsonian Center for Astrophysics. (1987). *The private universe* [videotape]. (Available from The Astronomical Society of the Pacific, 390 Ashton Avenue, San Francisco, CA 94122)

According to Annenberg, "from its famous opening scene at a Harvard graduation, this classic of educational research brings into sharp focus the dilemma facing all educators: Why don't even the brightest students truly grasp basic science concepts? This award-winning program traces the problem with interviews with eloquent Harvard graduates, professors, and Heather, a bright middle-school student who has some strange ideas about the orbits of the planets. Equally fitting for education methods classes, teacher workshops, and presentations to the public, it is an essential resource for any educational video collection." Order online at www.learner.org/catalog/catalog.html

ONLINE RESOURCES ON INQUIRY

Annenberg/CPB at www.learner.org

Annenberg/CPB (Corporation for Public Broadcasting) is a premiere Web site for professional development resources and videos on inquiry-based science and mathematics. The Web site lists the schedule of the upcoming distance learning video series. Programs include Teaching High School Science (grades 9–12), Science First Hand (grades 7–9), and The Private Universe Teacher Workshops (grades K–12). According to Annenberg, "The Teaching High School Science library will help new and veteran science teachers integrate national science standards and inquiry learning into their curricula. Showing science classrooms around the country, the modules cover topics in life science, physical science, earth and space science, and integrated science. They also show a range of teaching techniques and student/teacher interaction." Programs include *Thinking Like Scientists,* where scientists in the field explain the concept of inquiry. In *Chemical Reactions,* students in a 9th-grade science class formulate and explore their own questions about a chemical reaction. In *Investigating Crickets,* 9th-grade biology students design and conduct experiments about crickets. In *Exploring Mars,* students in an 11th-grade integrated science class explore how the Mars landscape may have formed, and in *The Physics of Optics,* an 11th- and 12th-grade physics class looks at light, lenses, and the human eye. For more information, see www.learner.org/resources/series126.html

Chemistry Coach at www.chemistrycoach.com/home.htm

A comprehensive site for high school chemistry teachers. Includes tutorials, references to pedagogy, and extensive links.

Eisenhower National Clearinghouse at www.enc.org

The Eisenhower National Clearinghouse is a first-rate resource for educational reform in math and science. ENC's Web site includes K–12 curriculum resources, Web links, and professional develop resources. *ENC Focus* is a monthly magazine for classroom innovation available to teachers. Online versions also are available. To request a free subscription, visit ENC online at www.enc.org/order

The Eisenhower Consortia and ENC Demonstration Sites also offer regional support and online services to school districts across the country. Contact the Eisenhower Consortium or ENC Demonstration Site that serves your state by visiting the ENC Web site at www.enc.org

For links to outstanding inquiry-based high school biology, chemistry, and physics programs, go to www.enc.org and then select "topics," "innovative curriculum materials," "selected resources," and "high school science."

The Exploratorium Institute for Inquiry at www.exploratorium.com/IFI/index.html
    According to the site, the Institute for Inquiry was "created in response to widespread interest in inquiry-based science instruction. The Exploratorium Institute for Inquiry provides workshops, programs, online support, and an intellectual community of practice which affords science reform educators a deep and rich experience of how inquiry learning looks and feels."

"Has Inquiry Made a Difference? A Synthesis of Research on the Impact of Inquiry Science on Student Outcomes" at http://cse.edc.org/work/research/inquirysynth/default.asp
    This project, "Has Inquiry Made a Difference? A Synthesis of Research on the Impact of Inquiry Science on Student Outcomes," focuses on synthesizing research since 1984 that answers the question: What is the impact of inquiry science on student outcomes compared with the impact of other instructional strategies and approaches? The Center for Science Education at Education Development Center, Inc. has undertaken this 3-year research project funded by the National Science Foundation. Although still in working progress, this is a worthwhile project to follow.

Inquiry Learning Forum through Indiana University at http://ilf.crlt.indiana.edu
    The Inquiry Learning Forum (ILF) through Indiana University is a premiere resource for new and seasoned inquiry science teachers. You will need to register and provide a password. After that, this Web site will keep you engaged for months. Take time to visit several ILF classrooms where you can engage in discussions and scan for classroom resources and lessons.

Miami University (Ohio) Center for Chemical Education at www.terrificscience.org
    The Web site for Miami University's Center for Chemical Education. Excellent resources for chemistry teachers. Includes many inquiry-based lessons at the "lesson exchange" site.

The Northwest Regional Educational Laboratory at www.nwrel.org/msec/resources/index.html
    According to the Northwest Regional Educational Laboratory (NWREL), *Inquiry Strategies for Science and Mathematics Learning: It's Just Good Teaching* (a free publication offered online) "provides rationale for using inquiry-based teaching and offers specific strategies that teachers can use in the classroom to facilitate their students' learning of concepts and skills. Based on research and including interviews with Northwest teachers, the publication addresses such issues as new roles for students and teachers; choosing and presenting an inquiry topic; classroom discourse and questioning; and ensuring attention to content as well as process. A list of resources, including print materials, online sources, and organizations, enables teachers to explore additional tools to support their efforts in creating an inquiry-based classroom." Geared toward the upper elementary and middle school level, but new high school teachers will also find this resource very useful.

The Northwest Regional Educational Laboratory Science Inquiry Model at www.nwrel.org/msec/science_inq/index.html
    The Northwest Regional Educational Laboratory Science Inquiry Model Web site helps K–12 teachers infuse inquiry into their science instruction and curriculum.

High school teachers should pay special interest to the secondary school level inquiry rubric found at www.nwrel.org/msec/images/science/pdf/secondaryteachers.pdf (teachers' version) and www.nwrel.org/msec/images/science/pdf/secondarystudents .pdf (students' version).

Science Inquiry for the Classroom at www.nwrel.org/msec/images/science/pdf/ litreview.pdf

This program report is a literature review by the Northwest Regional Educational Laboratory (NWREL). *Science Inquiry for the Classroom* summarizes the inquiry model as proposed by NWREL and offers a definition of inquiry and the four essential traits of inquiry. An excellent complement to the NWREL Science Inquiry Model™ Web site previously cited.

"Visiting a High School Inquiry Classroom: How to Prepare and Observe" at http://cse.edc.org/pdfs/products/observerguide.pdf

This document, "Visiting a High School Inquiry Classroom: How to Prepare and Observe," is published by the Center for Science Education of the Educational Development Center (Newton, Massachusetts). The guide, according to the EDC, is intended "to help observers of high school classrooms recognize the dimensions of inquiry teaching underway in the classroom. It is designed for administrators, professional development specialists, or mentors in a position to support the efforts of teachers changing their practice." If you are a high school inquiry-based science teacher, a science department chair, or a teacher/leader, place this on your "must read" list.

Wisconsin Fast Plants Program at www.fastplants.org/home_flash.asp

To speed along your botany investigations, consider using the Wisconsin Fast Plants Program. Students can observe a plant life cycle, from seed to adult, in about 40 days. Site includes instructions, suggested activities, and ordering information. For inquiry-based high school biology activities, go to the Fast Plants Web site (see above). Click on "Teacher Resources," then "Activity by Grade," then "High School."

PROFESSIONAL ORGANIZATIONS

The American Association of Physics Teachers at www.aapt.org

The American Association of Physics Teachers (AAPT) was established in 1930 with the fundamental goal of ensuring the "dissemination of knowledge of physics, particularly by way of teaching." The association currently has more than 11,000 members in 30 countries around the world. *The Physics Teacher*, AAPT's magazine, publishes articles on physics research, the history and philosophy of physics, applied physics, curriculum development, pedagogy, and instructional lab equipment as well as book reviews. Recommended membership for high school physics teachers.

The Catalyst at www.thecatalyst.org

This site has been developed specifically for the secondary education/high school level teacher as a resource for finding relevant information for use in the teaching of chemistry.

The National Association of Biology Teachers at www.nabt.org

The National Association of Biology Teachers (NABT) is a professional organization for high school biology teachers. If you are a high school biology teacher, you should strongly consider joining NABT.

The National Earth Science Teachers Association at www.nestanet.org

The National Earth Science Teachers Association (NESTA) is an educational organization whose purpose is the advancement, stimulation, extension, improvement, and coordination of earth science education at all educational levels. Recommended membership for high school earth science teachers.

The National Science Teachers Association at http://nsta.org

The National Science Teachers Association (NSTA) is a professional organization for K–16 science teachers. Click on "High School" and find resources and articles on inquiry-based science. The high school journal, *The Science Teacher*, contains many useful articles on standards, instruction, and assessment. Several recent issues of *The Science Teacher* have been devoted specifically to inquiry-based instruction and assessment:

February 2002 (Vol. 69, No. 2)—What Is Inquiry?

December 2002 (Vol. 69, No. 9)—Inquiry Dot Com

April 2003 (Vol. 70, No. 4)—Inquiry-Based Activities

September 2003 (Vol. 70, No. 6)—Engage Your Students

December 2003 (Vol. 70, No. 9)—Authentic Investigations

January 2004 (Vol. 71, No. 1)—Designing Inquiry Pathways

If you are not a member of NSTA, you should strongly consider joining.

References

Abraham, M. (1997). *The learning cycle approach to science instruction* (Monograph #9701). Norman, OK: National Association for Research in Science Teaching.

Adams, D., & Hamm, M. (1998). *Collaborative inquiry in science, math, and technology.* Portsmouth, NH: Heinemann.

American Association for the Advancement of Science. (1990). *Science for all Americans.* Washington, DC: Author.

American Association for the Advancement of Science. (1993). *Benchmarks for science literacy.* Washington, DC: Author.

Arlin, P. (1987). *Teaching for thinking: The Arlin Test of Formal Reasoning applied.* East Aurora, NY: Slosson Educational Publications.

Atkin, J., & Karplus, R. (1962). Discovery or invention? *The Science Teacher, 29*(2), 121–143.

Audet, R., & Jordan, L. (2003). *Standards in the classroom: An implementation guide for teachers of science and mathematics.* Thousand Oaks, CA: Corwin.

Ausubel, D. (1968). *Educational psychology: A cognitive view.* New York: Holt, Rinehart and Winston.

Baird, J., Fensham, P., Gunstone, R., & White, R. (1989, March). *A study of the importance of reflection for improving science teaching and learning.* Paper presented at the National Association for Research in Science Teaching annual conference, San Francisco, CA.

Beisenherz, P., & Dantonio, M. (1996). *Using the learning cycle to teach physical science.* Portsmouth, NH: Heinemann.

Bell, B., & Gilbert, J. (1996). *Teacher development: A model from science education.* London: Falmer.

Bernstein, J. (2003). A recipe for inquiry. *The science teacher, 70*(6), 60–63.

Biological Sciences Curriculum Study. (1970). *Biology teacher's handbook.* New York: Wiley.

Biological Sciences Curriculum Study. (1997). *Biology: A human approach.* Dubuque, IA: Kendall/Hunt.

Bodrova, E., & Leong, D. (1996). *Tools of the mind: The Vygotskian approach to early childhood education.* Englewood Cliffs, NJ: Prentice Hall.

Brooks, J., & Brooks, M. (1999). *In search of understanding: The case for the constructivist classrooms.* Upper Saddle River, NJ: Merrill-Prentice Hall.

Bybee, R. (1997). *Achieving scientific literacy.* Portsmouth, NH: Heinemann.

Chiappetta, E. (1997). Inquiry-based science. *The Science Teacher, 65*(7), 22–26.

Clark, R., Clough, M., & Berg, C. (2000). Modifying cookbook labs. *The Science Teacher, 67*(7), 40–43.

Clough, M., & Clark, R. (1994). Cookbooks and constructivism. *The Science Teacher, 61*(2), 34–37.

Clough, M., Smasal, J., & Clough, D. (1994). Managing each minute. *The Science Teacher, 61*(6), 30–34.

Colburn, A. (1996). Invited paper. *The Science Teacher, 63*(1), 10.

Colburn, A., & Clough, M. (1997). Implementing the learning cycle. *The Science Teacher, 64*(5), 30–33.

Costa, A., & Kallick, B. (2001). *Describing 16 habits of mind.* Retrieved May 7, 2004, from www.habits-of-mind.net

Costenson, K., & Lawson, A. (1986). Why isn't inquiry used in more classrooms? *The American Biology Teacher, 48*(3), 150–158.

Dana, T., Lorsbach, A., Hook, K., & Briscoe, C. (1991). Students showing what they know: A look at alternative assessments. In G. Kulm & S. Malcom (Eds.), *Science assessment in the service of reform* (pp. 331–337). Washington, DC: AAAS.

DeBoer, G. (1991). *A history of ideas in science education.* New York: Teachers College Press.

Dewey, J. (1900). *The school and society.* Chicago: University of Chicago Press.

Dewey, J. (1902). *The child and the curriculum.* Chicago: University of Chicago Press.

Dewey, J. (1916). *Democracy and education.* New York: Macmillan.

Dewey, J. (1938). *Experience and education.* New York: Macmillan.

Doran, R., Chan, F., Tamir, P., & Lenhardt, C. (2002). *Science educator's guide to laboratory assessment.* Arlington, VA: NSTA Press.

Driscoll, M. (1994). *Psychology of learning for instruction.* Boston: Allyn & Bacon.

Duit, R., & Treagust, D. (1995). Students' conceptions and constructivist teaching approaches. In B. J. Fraser & H. J. Walberg (Eds.), *Improving science education.* Chicago: National Society for the Study of Education.

Dyrli, O. (1999, November). Gil Dyril's "Sweet sixteen." *Curriculum Administrator,* 60–67.

Edmondson, K. (2000). Assessing science understanding through concept maps. In J. Mintzes, J. Wandersee, & J. Novak (Eds.), *Assessing science understanding: A human constructivist view* (pp. 15–40). San Diego, CA: Academic Press.

Edwards, C. (1997). Promoting student inquiry. *The Science Teacher, 64*(7), 18, 20–21.

Gallagher, J. (1993). Secondary science teachers and constructivist practice. In K. Tobin (Ed.), *The practice of constructivism in science education* (pp. 181–191). Hillsdale, NJ: Lawrence Erlbaum Associates.

Galus, P. (2000). Seeds for thought. *The Science Teacher, 67*(5), 28–31.

Gibran, K. (1923). *The prophet.* New York: Alfred Knopf.

Gunstone, R., & Mitchell, I. (1998). Metacognition and conceptual change. In J. Mintzes, J. Wandersee, & J. Novak (Eds.), *Teaching science for understanding: A human constructivist view* (pp. 133–163). San Diego, CA: Academic Press.

Hackett, J. (1998). Inquiry: Both means and ends. *The Science Teacher, 65*(6), 35–37.

Hart, D. (1994). *Authentic assessment.* Reading, MA: Addison-Wesley.

Haury, D. (1993). Teaching science through inquiry (ERIC/CSMEE Digest). (ERIC Document Reproduction Service No. ED359048). Retrieved May 7, 2004, from www.ed.gov/databases/ERIC_Digests/ed359048.html

Hebrank, M. (2000). Why inquiry-based teaching and learning in the middle school science classroom? Retrieved May 9, 2004, from www.biology.duke.edu/cibl/inquiry/why_inquiry_in_ms.htm

Hester, J. (1994). *Teaching for thinking.* Durham, NC: Carolina Academic Press.

Hinman, R. (1998). Content and science inquiry. *The Science Teacher, 65*(7), 25–27.

Hinrichsen, J., & Jarrett, D. (1999). *Science inquiry for the classroom: A literature review.* Retrieved May 7, 2004, from www.nwrel.org/msec/images/science/pdf/litreview.pdf

Huxley, T. (1899). *Science and education.* New York: Appleton.

Ingram, M. (1996). *Bottle biology.* Dubuque, IA: Kendall/Hunt.

Inhelder, B., & Piaget, J. (1958). *The growth of logical thinking.* New York: Basic Books.

Jorgenson, O., & Vanosdall, R. (2002). The death of science? What we risk in our rush toward standardized testing and the three R's. *Phi Delta Kappan, 83*(8), 601-605. Retrieved May 9, 2004, from http://www.pdkintl.org/kappan/k0204jor.htm

Kowalski, T., Weaver, R., & Henson, K. (1990). *Case studies on teaching.* White Plains, NY: Longman.

Lawson, A. (2000). Managing the inquiry classroom: Problems and solutions. *The American Biology Teacher, 62*(9), 641–647.

Lawson, A., Abraham, M., & Renner, J. (1989). *A theory of instruction: Using the learning cycle to teach science concepts and thinking skills* (Monograph #1). Manhattan: Kansas State University, National Association for Research in Science Teaching.

Liem, T. (1987). *Invitations to science inquiry* (2nd ed.). Chino Hills, CA: Science Inquiry Enterprises.

Llewellyn, D. (2002). *Inquire within: Implementing inquiry-based science standards.* Thousand Oaks, CA: Corwin Press.

Marek, E., & Cavallo, A. (1997). *The learning cycle.* Portsmouth, NH: Heinemann.

Martinello, M., & Cook, G. (1999). *Interdisciplinary inquiry in teaching and learning* (2nd ed.). Englewood Cliffs, NJ: Prentice Hall.

Marzano, R. (1992). *A different kind of classroom.* Alexandria, VA: Association for Supervision and Curriculum Development.

McTighe, J., & Wiggins, G. (1999). *The understanding by design handbook.* Alexandria, VA: Association for Supervision and Curriculum Development.

Murphy, J. (1982). *Laboratory physics.* Columbus, OH: Merrill.

Nagel, G. (1994). *The Tao of teaching.* New York: Plume.

National Commission on Excellence in Education. (1983). *A nation at risk: The imperative for educational reform.* Washington, DC: Government Printing Office.

National Commission on Mathematics and Science Teaching for the 21st Century. (2000). *Before it's too late.* Washington, DC: Department of Education.

National Research Council. (1996). *National science education standards.* Washington, DC: National Academy Press.

National Research Council. (1997). *Science teaching reconsidered: A handbook.* Washington, DC: National Academy Press.

National Research Council. (2000a). *Inquiry and the national science education standards: A guide for teaching and learning.* Washington, DC: National Academy Press.

National Research Council. (2000b). *How people learn: Brain, mind, experience, and school* (Exp. ed.). Washington, DC: National Academy Press.

National Research Council. (2001). *Educating teachers of science, mathematics, and technology: New practices for a new millennium.* Washington, DC: National Academy Press.

National Science Teachers Association. (1998). NSTA position statement: The national science education standards: A vision for the improvement of science teaching and learning. *Science Scope, 65*(5), 32–34.

Nolan, T. (1991). Self-questioning and prediction: Combining metacognitive strategies. *Journal of Reading, 35*(2), 132–137.

Norton, M., & Lester, P. (1998). *K-12 case studies for school administrators: Problems, issues, and resources.* New York: Garland.

Novak, J. (1990). Concept maps and Vee diagrams: Two metacognitive tools to facilitate meaningful learning. *Instructional Science, 19,* 29–52.

Novak, J. (1998). *Learning, creating, and using knowledge: Concept maps as facilitative tools in schools and corporations.* Mahwah, NJ: Lawrence Erlbaum Associates.

Novak, J., & Gowin, D. (1989). *Learning how to learn.* New York: Cambridge University Press.

O'Brien, T. (2000). A toilet paper timeline of evolution. *The American Biology Teacher, 62*(8), 578–582.

Palmer, P. (1998). *The courage to teach: Exploring the inner landscape of a teacher's life.* San Francisco: Jossey-Bass.

Piaget, J. (1970). *The science of education and the psychology of the child.* New York: Orion.

Posner, G. J., Strike, K. A., Hewson, P. W., & Gertzog, W. A. (1982). Accommodation of a scientific conception: Toward a theory of conceptual change. *Science Education, 66,* 211–227.

Postman, N., & Weingartner, C. (1969). *Teaching as a subversive activity.* New York: Dell Publishing.

Reagan, T., Case, C., & Brubacher, J. (2000). *Becoming a reflective educator: How to build a culture of inquiry in the schools* (2nd ed.). Thousand Oaks, CA: Corwin.

Romey, W. (1968). *Inquiry techniques for teaching science.* Englewood Cliffs, NJ: Prentice Hall.

Roschelle, J. (1997). Learning in interactive environments: Prior knowledge and new experience. Retrieved August 25, 1999, from www.exploratorium.edu/IFI/resources/museumeducation/priorknowledge.html

Rowe, M. B. (1974). Wait-time and rewards as instructional variables. *Journal of Research in Science Teaching, 11,* 263–279.

Rowe, M. B. (1987). Using wait time to stimulate inquiry. In W. Wilen (Ed.), *Questions, questioning techniques, and effective teaching* (pp. 95–106). Washington, DC: National Education Association.

Rowe, M. B. (1996, September). Science, silence, and sanctions. *Science and Children,* 35–37.

Sergiovanni, T. (1996). *Leadership in the schoolhouse.* San Francisco: Jossey-Bass.

Shiland, T. (1999). Constructivism: The implications for laboratory work. *Journal of Chemical Education, 76*(1), 107–109.

Southerland, S., Smith, M., & Cummins, C. (2002). "What do you mean by that?" Using structured interviews to assess science understanding. In J. Mintzes, J. Wandersee, & J. Novak (Eds.), *Assessing science understanding: A human constructivist view* (pp. 71–93). San Diego, CA: Academic Press.

Stevens, D. (1991). Earth science final exam: A new approach. In G. Kulm & S. Malcom (Eds.), *Science assessment in the service of reform* (pp. 359–361). Washington, DC: American Association for the Advancement of Science.

Stigler, J., & Hiebert, J. (1999). *The teaching gap.* New York: The Free Press.

Texley, J., & Wild, A. (Eds.). (1998). *NSTA pathways to the science standards: High school edition.* Alexandria, VA. National Science Teachers Association.

Tretter, T., & Jones, G. (2003). A sense of scale. *The Science Teacher, 70*(1), 22–25.

The University of the State of New York. (2002). *Reference tables for the physical setting/chemistry.* Albany, NY: Author.

Volkmann, M., & Abell, S. (2003). Rethinking laboratories: Tools for converting cookbook labs into inquiry. *The Science Teacher, 70*(6), 38–41.

Vygotsky, L. (1978). *Mind in society: The development of higher psychological processes.* Boston: Harvard University Press.

Vygotsky, L. (1979). Consciousness as a problem in the psychology of behavior. *Soviet Psychology, 18*(1), 67–115. (Original work published 1924)

Vygotsky, L. S. (1962). *Thought and language* (E. Hanfmann and G. Voker, Trans.). Cambridge: MIT Press. (Original work published 1934)

Wilks, S. (1995). *Critical and creative thinking: Strategies for classroom inquiry.* Portsmouth, NH: Heinemann.

Windschitl, M. (1999). The challenges of sustaining a constructivist classroom culture. *Phi Delta Kappan, 70*(10), 751–755.

Wood, D., Bruner, J., & Ross, G. (1976). The role of tutoring in problem-solving. *Journal of Child Psychology and Psychiatry, 17,* 89–100.

Yager, R. (1991). The constructivist learning model. *The Science Teacher, 58*(6), 52–57.

Youngson, R. (1998). *Scientific blunders: A brief history of how wrong scientists can sometimes be.* New York: Carroll & Graf.

Index

Abell, S., 92
Abraham, M., 46
Activities. *See* laboratory activities
Adams, D., 59
Adolescents, learning process of, 40–46
Alternative assessments. *See* authentic assessments
American Association for Physics Teachers, 62
American Association for the Advancement of Science (AAAS), ix, 3, 6–7, 58, 146
American Biology Teacher, The (journal), 46, 62
Arlin, P., 34, 35
Assessment issues, 9, 86, 111–127
    authentic assessment, 115–127, 176
        application questions, 117–118
        body language, 176
        capstone projects, 120
        concept maps, 122, 123
        eye contact, 176
        monitoring charts, 119–120, 121
        performance tasks, 115–116
        rubrics, 116–117, 126
        self-evaluations, 124–126
        structured interviews, 122, 124
    and constructivism, 51–52
    and curriculum alignment, 112–113
    designing assessment, 113–115
    print resources, 192–193
    and transition to authentic assessments, 127
Atkin, J., 46
Audet, R., 113
Ausubel, D., 40
Authentic assessments, 115–127
    application questions, 117–118
    capstone projects, 120
    concept maps, 122, 123
    monitoring charts, 119–120, 121
    performance tasks, 115–116
    rubrics, 116–117, 126
    self-evaluations, 124–126
    structured interviews, 122, 124

Baird, J., 39
Baker, Ronald, 180–182
Before It's Too Late (NCMST), x

Beisenherz, P., 46
Bell, B., 8
Benchmarks for Science Literacy (AAAS), ix, 3, 6–7
Berg, C., 92
Bernstein, J., 92
Biological Sciences Curriculum Study (BSCS), xiv–xv, 9–10, 46, 48
Biology lessons, 129–144
    and Markowitz on inquiry-based instruction, 130, 140–144
    and Penders on inquiry-based instruction, 130, 140–144
    yeast laboratory activity, 129–140
Bodrova, E., 36
Bottle Biology (Ingram), 77
Brainstorming, 22–24, 170
Briscoe, C., 124
Brooks, J., 60, 92
Brooks, M., 60
Brubacher, J., 1–2
Bruner, J., 37
Bush, George W., x
Bybee, R., 46

Case, C., 1–2
Case studies. *See also* laboratory activities
    about, 13–14
    bottle ecosystem, 76–82, 87
    and brainstorming, 22–24, 170
    definition of, 13
    and definition of inquiry, 24
    and inquiry cycle, 13
    isopods case study, 14–21
    pendulum swing case study, 41–44
    and scientific inquiry, 13–25
Cavallo, A., 46
Center for Inquiry Based Learning (CIBL), 4
Centripetal force, measuring, 167–173, 176, 177
Chan, F., 116
Chemistry lessons, 155–165
    and Gerchman on inquiry-based instruction, 155, 162–165
    and peanut laboratory activity, 155–161, 165
Chiappetta, E., 4
Clark, R., 92

Classrooms. *See also* students; teachers
  and community learning, 85
  and constructivism, 28–32, 51–53
  culture of, 51–53
  and culture of inquiry, 1–3
  and individualized learning environment,
    162–163
  and inquiry-based instruction, 8, 56–57
  and inquiry-based instruction for students,
    57–60
  and investigations designed by students, 163,
    164–165
  and "just tell me the answer" issue, 104
  and learning disabilities, students with, 10, 162
  and lecturing by teachers, 162
  managing classrooms, 99–109
  and physical limitations for physics lessons,
    175–176
  and questioning techniques, 8, 101, 105–109
  and rotational station format, 83–84, 102–103
  and science education, 174
  and scientific inquiry, 56, 84–85
  teachers, and inquiry-based, 60–63
  and time management, 8–9, 86, 100–104,
    165, 175
  traditional, 28–32, 55–56, 163, 164
  and trust between teachers and students, 141
Clough, D., 100
Clough, M., 46, 92
Colburn, A., 46, 92
Colleges, and partnerships with secondary
  school teachers, 142
Combinational reasoning learning process, 34
Community learning, 85
Conceptual change theory, 44–45
Concrete level of learners, 34, 35
Confirmation activities, 68
Constructivism
  and assessment issues, 51–52
  in classrooms, 51
  and conceptual change theory, 44–45
  contemporary, 38–39
  and curriculum issues, 52
  and daily schedules of instruction, 52
  definition of, 28
  and Dewey, 32
  and 5E Learning Cycle, 35
  history of, 27, 32–38
  and language, making sense of, 45–46
  and learning process, 27, 40–46
  and metacognition, 39
  and misconceptions, 27, 40, 41–44
  and pedagogy for teaching science, 51
  philosophy of, 27
  and Piaget, 33–36
  print resources, 188–190
  and prior knowledge, 27, 40–41
  and professional development, 52

  and scaffolding instructional strategy, 37–38
  and science education, 27
  and standards, 52
  and textbooks, 52
  vs. traditional classrooms, 28–32
  and Vygotsky, 36–38
  and ZPD, 36–37
Content-related methods, 10
Cook, G., 1
Cookbook laboratory activities,
  7, 56, 68, 70, 86
Copper sulfate hydrate laboratory activity,
  96–98
Correlations learning process, 34
Costa, A., 2
Costanza, Jay, 76–86
Costenson, K., 99
Courage to Teach (Palmer), xi
Culture of classrooms, 51–53
Culture of inquiry, 1–3
Cummins, C., 122
Curriculum issues, 52

Daily schedules of instruction, 52
Dana, T., 124
Dantonio, M., 46
DeBoer, G., 4, 89
Demonstrations, 66, 67–68, 191–192
Dewey, J., 9, 13, 32
Didactic method, 174
Discrepant events, 67–68, 191–192
Doran, R., 116
Driscoll, M., 33–34, 45
Duit, R., 41
Dyrli, O., 108

Earth science lessons, 145–153
  and O'Brien on inquiry-based instruction,
    145, 151–153
  toilet paper timeline, 145–150, 153
*Educating Teachers of Science, Mathematics, and
  Technology: New Practices for a New
  Millennium* (NRC), xi
Edwards, C., 4
Einstein, Albert, 183
Evolution activity, 145–150, 153

Faddism, 9–10
Fensham, P., 39
5E Learning Cycle, 46–50
  and constructivism, 35
  and hydrate laboratory activity, 96–98
  and inquiry-based instruction, 151
  and teachers in inquiry-based classrooms, 61
  and toilet paper timeline, 145–150, 153
  yeast laboratory activity, 129–140
Formal level of learners, 34, 35
Franklin, Benjamin, 100

Gallagher, J., 53
Galus, P., 95
Gerchman, Teresa, 155, 162–165
Gertzog, W. A., 45
Gibran, K., xiv
Gilbert, J., 8
Glenn, John, x
Gowin, D., 39
Gunstone, R., 39, 45

Hackett, J., 4
Hamm, M., 59
Hart, D., 119
Haury, D., 10
Hebrank, M., 4
Henson, K., 13
Hester, J., 2–3, 35
Hewson, P. W., 45
Hiebert, J., xi
Higher education institutions, and
    partnerships with secondary
    school teachers, 142
Hinman, R., 8
Hinrichsen, J., 4
History of Ideas in Science Education, A (DeBoer), 4
Hook, K., 124
Huxley, T., 89
Hydrate laboratory activity, 96–98

Indirect and direct verification learning process,
    34–35
Ingram, M., 77
Inhelder, B., 33–34
*Inquire Within: Implementing Inquiry-Based Science
    Standards* (Llewellyn), x, xiv
Inquiry. *See* scientific inquiry
*Inquiry and the National Science Education
    Standards: A Guide for Teaching and Learning*
    (NRC), 5
Inquiry-based instruction, 4, 24–25
Inquiry cycle, 21–22
Inquiry Cycle (Llewellyn), 21
Inquiry Techniques for Teaching Science
    (Romey), 181
Integrating inquiry-based instruction, 65–87
    and bottle ecosystem case study, 76–82, 87
    Costanza on, 76–86
    and demonstrations, 66, 67–68
    and guiding students into inquiry, 72–76
    and invitation to inquiry, 66
    and laboratory activities, 66, 68–70
    and student-initiated inquiries, 66, 70–71
    and student inquiries, 65
    and teacher-initiated inquiries, 66, 70, 71
Interdisciplinary Inquiry in Teaching and Learning
    (Martinello & Cook), 1
Investigations, inquiry, 91, 141–142, 163,
    164–165, 187

Invitation to inquiry
    and activities, 66, 68–70
    and demonstrations, 66, 67–68
    grid, 66, 70, 72, 75–76
    and integrating inquiry-based instruction, 66
    and laboratory experiences, 68–70
    and structured inquiry, 68
    and student-initiated inquiries, 66, 70–71
    and teacher-initiated inquiries, 66, 70, 71
Isopods case study, 14–21

Jarrett, D., 4
Jones, G., 149
Jordan, L., 113
Jorgenson, O., 56
"Just tell me the answer" syndrome, 84–85,
    104–105

Kallick, B., 2
Karplus, R., 46
Kowalski, T., 13

Laboratory activities. *See also* case studies
    about, 66, 68–70
    cookbook laboratory activities, 7, 56, 68, 70, 86
    hydrate laboratory activity, 96–98
    and inquiry-based instruction, 7, 92–96
    and invitation to inquiry, 68–70
    and NRC, 90
    and peanut lab, 165
    for physics lessons, 168–170, 176
    prelab introductions, 176
    rubber band cannon laboratory activity,
        118–119
    sand and sugar laboratory activity, 93–96, 117
    science, and role of, 89–91
    and scientific inquiry, 68
    and structured inquiry, 68
    and traditional, 91–92
Language, and constructivism, 40, 45–46
Lawson, A., 46, 99, 100
Learning curve for students, and inquiry-based
    instruction, xiii
Learning cycle model. *See* 5E Learning Cycle
Learning disabilities, and inquiry-based
    instruction, 10, 162
Learning process
    of adolescents, 40–46
    combinational reasoning, 34
    concepts about, 34–35
    and constructivism, 40–46
    correlations learning process, 34
    indirect and direct verification, 34–35
    mechanical equilibrium, 35
    multiplicative compensations, 34
    and Piaget, 34–36
    probability, 34
    proportional reasoning, 34

Lenhart, C., 116
Leong, D., 36
Lester, P., 13
Liem, T., 67, 167
Life Sciences Learning Center (LSLC), 130
Llewellyn, D., x, 21, 32, 65, 70, 119
Lorsbach, A., 124

Marek, E., 46
Markowitz, Dina, 130, 140–144
Martinello, M., 1
Marzano, R., 2
McClane, Sara, 130
McTighe, J., 113–114
Mechanical equilibrium learning process, 35
Metacognition, 39
Minstrell, J., 7
Mitchell, I., 45
Mueller, Tom, 96
Multimedia resources, 194–195
Multiplicative compensations learning process, 34
Murphy, J., 167

Nagel, G., 100
Nasonia Project, 167
National Association of Biology Teachers, 62
National Board Certification (NBC), xi
National Commission on Excellence in
    Education, ix
National Commission on Mathematics and
    Science Teaching for the 21st Century
    (NCMST), x
National Earth Science Teachers Association, 62
National Institutes of Health (NIH), 142
National Research Council (NRC)
    and assessment issues, 112, 114–115, 124
    and authentic assessments, 115
    and bottle ecosystem case study, 77
    and centripetal force, measuring, 168
    *Educating Teachers of Science, Mathematics, and
        Technology: New Practices for a New
        Millennium*, xi
    and inquiry-based instruction, ix, 4–5
    and instructional reform, ix
    and isopods case study, 14
    and laboratory activities, 90
    and metacognition, 39
    National Science Education Standards, ix, xiv,
        77, 156, 168
    and peanut laboratory activity, 156
    and pedagogy for teaching science, ix
    and professional development, 52
    and science education, 179–180
    Science Teaching Reconsidered, xi
    and structured interviews, 124
    and students as researchers, 58
    and toilet paper timeline, 145, 146–147
    and yeast laboratory activity, 129

National Science Education Standards (NRC), ix,
    xiv, 77, 156, 168
    on beliefs and standards for teachers of
        science, xiv
    and inquiry-based instruction, 4–5
    and instructional reform, ix
    and isopods case study, 14
    and science education, 179
    and teachers in inquiry-based classrooms,
        60, 62
    and toilet paper timeline, 145
    and yeast laboratory activity, 129
National Science Foundation (NSF), 10, 142
National Science Teachers Association (NSTA),
    x, 10, 62
Nation at Risk, A (NCEE), ix
NIH. *See* National Institutes of Health
No Child Left Behind Act, x
Nolan, T., 39
Norton, M., 13
Novak, J., 39
NSF. *See* National Science Foundation

O'Brien, Tom, 145, 151–153
Online resources, 195–197
Open inquiry, 70–71

Palmer, P., xi
Peanut laboratory activity, 155–161, 165
Pedagogy for teaching science, ix, x, 51
Penders, Jana, 130, 140–144
Pendulum swing case study, 41–44
Philosophy for inquiry, 28–54
Physics lessons, 167–177
    and centripetal force, measuring, 167–173,
        176, 177
    and inquiry-based instruction, 175
    and Wolfe on inquiry method, 167, 174–177
Physics Teacher, The (journal), 62
Piaget, Jean, 33–36
Posner, G. J., 45
Postman, N., 10–11
Power of 10, The (film), 150
Prior knowledge, and inquiry-based instruction,
    27, 40–41, 142
Probability learning process, 34
Professional development, and constructivism, 52
Professional organizations, 197–198
Project 2061, 6
Proportional reasoning learning process, 34

Questioning techniques, 8, 84–85, 101, 104–109

Reagan, Ronald, ix
Reagan, T., 1–2
Renner, J., 46
Romey, W., 181
Roschelle, J., 40

Ross, G., 37
Rotational station format, 83–84, 102–103
Rowe, M. B., 61, 124
Rubber band cannon laboratory activity, 118–119

Scaffolding instructional strategy, 37–38
Scale, themes of, 152–153
Science education. *See also* biology lessons;
    chemistry lessons; earth science lessons;
    physics lessons
    and classrooms, 174
    and constructivism, 27
    and didactic method, 174
    and inquiry-based instruction, 8, 141, 151, 174
    and instructional reform, ix–x
    and *National Science Education Standards*, 179
    and NRC, 179–180
    print resources, 193
    and scale, themes of, 152–153
    and teaching careers in, 179–182
    and 9th-grade physics lessons, 175
    and timelines, 152
Science educators. *See* teachers
Science Educator's Guide to Laboratory Assessment
    (Doran et al.), 116
Science for All Americans (AAAS), 6
Science Inquiry for the Classroom (Hinrichsen &
    Jarrett), 4
Science literacy, and print resources, 190–191
Science Teacher, The (journal), 4, 62, 92
Science Teaching Reconsidered (NRC), xi
Scientific inquiry, 1–12
    and AAAS point of view, 6
    and Advancement of Science point of view, 6
    and brainstorming, 22–24, 170
    and case studies, 13–25
    and classrooms, 56
    culture of, 1–3
    definition of, 24–25
    and demonstrations, 66
    extended, case study for, 76
    and habits of mind, 2–3
    and inquiry cycle, 21
    inviting, 66
    and laboratory activities, 68
    and learning, 7
    and *National Science Education Standards* point
        of view, 4
    and science educators, 3–4, 140
    steps for scientific investigations, 91
    student initiated, 68
    teacher initiated, 68
Scientific investigations. *See* investigations, inquiry
Scientific method, 7, 143
Sergiovanni, T., 63
Shiland, T., 92
Smasal, J., 100
Smith, M., 122

Soft sciences, and inquiry-based instruction, 10
Southerland, S., 122
Standards, 52, 190–191
Stevens, D., 115, 116
Stigler, J., xi
Strike, K. A., 45
Structured inquiry, 68
Students
    and attitudes about inquiry-based
        instruction, 143
    and classroom using scientific inquiry, 84–85
    and 5E Learning Cycle, 49
    and guidance from teachers into inquiry, 72–76
    initiating inquiries, 70
    and inquiry-based classrooms, 57–60
    integrating inquiry-based instruction, 65
    and investigations designed by, 163, 164–165
    inviting inquiries, 66, 70–71, 71
    and "just tell me the answer" syndrome,
        84–85, 104–105
    and knowledge about inquiry-based
        instruction, 143–144
    and learning curve for inquiry-based
        instruction, xiii
    and learning disabilities, 10, 162
    and open inquiry, 70–71
    promoting inquiries from, 65
    as researchers, 58
    and science, showing interest in, 59
    and skills for inquiry-based instruction,
        143–144
    and skills for inquiry-based investigation,
        141–142
    and thinking skills, utilizing higher-level, 59
    trust between teachers and, 141
    working in groups, 58–59, 103
Sugar and sand laboratory task, 93–96, 117

Tamir, P., 116
Tao of Teaching, The (Nagel), 100
Teachers
    and attitudes about inquiry-based instruction,
        143–144
    and Baker story, 180–182
    and careers in science education, 179–182
    and classrooms, inquiry-based, 60–63
    and classroom using scientific inquiry, 60
    Costanza, 76–86
    and envisioning inquiry-based instruction,
        10–11, 53
    and 5E Learning Cycle, 50
    Gerchman, 155, 162–165
    guiding students into inquiry, 72–76
    initiating activities, 66, 70, 71
    and "just tell me the answer" syndrome,
        84–85, 104–105
    and knowledge about inquiry-based
        instruction, 143–144

and learning curve for students, xiii
and lecturing, 162
managing classrooms, 99–109
Markowitz, 130, 140–144
O'Brien, 145, 151–153
and partnerships with higher education
    institutions, 142
Penders, 130, 140–144
science educators view of scientific inquiry,
    3–4, 140
and scientific inquiry, 3–4, 140
and skills for inquiry-based instruction, 143–144
and stages for becoming an inquiry-based, 63
and tools for using scientific inquiry, 63
trust between students and, 141
Wolfe, 167, 174–177
Teaching Gap, The (Stigler & Hiebert), xi
Texley, J., 9
textbooks, and constructivism, 52
Third International Mathematics and Science
    Study (TIMSS), ix
Thought and Language (Vygotsky), 36
Timelines, and science education, 152. *See also*
    toilet paper timeline
Time management, 8–9, 86, 100–104, 165, 175
Toilet paper timeline, 145–150, 153
"Toilet Paper Timeline of Evolution, A"
    (O'Brien), 145

Traditional classrooms, 28–32, 55–56, 163, 164
Traditional laboratory activities, 91–92
Treagust, D., 41
Tretter, T., 149

Universities, and partnerships with secondary
    school teachers, 142

Vanosdall, R., 56
Van Zee, E., 7
Volkmann, M., 92
Vygotsky, L. S., 36–38

Weaver, R., 13
Weingartner, C., 10–11
White, R., 39
Wiggins, G., 113–114
Wild, A., 9
Wilks, S., 3
Windschitl, M., 51
Wolfe, George, 167, 174–177
Wood, D., 37

Yager, R., 32, 38
Yeast laboratory activity, 129–140
Youngson, R., 45

Zone of Proximal Development (ZPD), 36–37